Public and Private High Schools

PUBLIC AND PRIVATE HIGH SCHOOLS

The Impact of Communities

JAMES S. COLEMAN

THOMAS HOFFER

Basic Books, Inc., Publishers   *New York*

Library of Congress Cataloging-in-Publication Data

Coleman, James Samuel, 1926–
    Public and private high schools.

    Bibliography: p. 245
Includes index.
    1. Education, Secondary—United States.   2. Public
schools—United States.   3. Private schools—United
States.   4. Academic achievement. I. Hoffer, Thomas.
II. Title.
LA222.C544   1987   373.73   85–43105
ISBN   0–465–06767–0

CONTENTS

LIST OF FIGURES

List of Figures

LIST OF TABLES

List of Tables

List of Tables

List of Tables

List of Tables

List of Tables

ACKNOWLEDGMENTS

This research was carried out at the National Opinion Research Center at The University of Chicago. Consistent with its distinguished tradition, NORC provided us with ample resources for the execution of our work. We are particularly indebted to Calvin Jones and the staff of the High School and Beyond project, who at several points gave us the benefit of their extensive knowledge of the data files and data collection efforts. As the sponsor and original architect of the High School and Beyond project, the Center for Statistics of the U.S. Department of Education (formerly the National Center for Education Statistics) deserves credit for the creation of one of the most important and widely used data bases available to American social researchers. We owe a special note of gratitude to Martin Kessler at Basic Books, who encouraged us to undertake a further examination of public and private schools, and who supported our decision to elaborate that examination in the directions presented here.

As the analysis for this book progressed, two different goals began to emerge. One goal was to extend our earlier work on public and private schools. The second was to study the functioning of the school as a social unit in its social context. Work on the latter set of problems, which led us to an investigation of how social capital in school and communities affects school functioning, was suported by a grant from the Spencer Foundation.

Several colleagues provided us with comments and criticisms over the course of our work on this project. Bruce Carruthers was particularly helpful in this throughout the project, and also aided us with portions of the data analysis. Participants in the Mathematical Sociology Seminar at The University of Chicago also gave us valuable feedback on a number of conceptual and technical points on two occasions when we presented portions of our research. In this capacity, we would like to thank particularly Douglas Anderton, Anthony Bryk, Yong Hak Kim, Howard Margolis, Tina Morris, and Mindy Schimmel. Our colleague at NORC, Andrew Greeley, also provided us with several useful suggestions at early stages of this project, and we are grateful for his interest and insight.

While differing in a number of important ways from our earlier research on public and private school differences, the work presented here has its point of departure in the findings presented in *High School Achievement,* published by Basic Books in 1982. Although our co-author for that book, Sally Kilgore, had left The University of Chicago before work on the present book, we gratefully acknowledge her considerable efforts and expertise in the development of the larger project.

Last but not least, we would like to express our appreciation to the superintendents, the principals, the teachers, and particularly the students who generously gave their time and effort to the High School and Beyond study.

PROLOGUE

In 1980 the National Center for Education Statistics (NCES) of the U.S. Department of Education sponsored a large-scale study of high school seniors and sophomores throughout the United States, including students in various types of private schools. Although the study did not include a large number of private school students, as they are not a large percentage of American high school students, the inclusion of these students made possible the examination of two questions related to private schools. One question is how much the private sector contributes to social divisiveness or segregation: segregation of the rich from the poor, segregation among religious groups (since most private-sector schools are organized by a religious group), and segregation of blacks, Hispanics, and whites. A second question was the relative effects of the public and private sectors on achievement in basic skills, as measured by standardized tests in vocabulary, reading comprehension, and mathematics administered to sophomores and seniors.

These questions were particularly relevant in the context of policy questions raised with increasing frequency in the preceding decade. Some of these questions concerned potential policies that would have the effect of restricting enrollment in private schools (the possibility of using racial balance as a criterion for a private school's continued tax exemption), but most concerned policies that would have the effect of increasing private school enrollment. The two most important of these were the possible use of educational vouchers at the state level and the possible introduction of federal income tax credit for a portion of tuition paid by parents of the children attending private schools.

The authors (with Sally Kilgore) carried out a detailed examination of these two questions, first in a report to NCES in April 1981 (Coleman, Hoffer, and Kilgore 1981) and second in a book published in 1982 (Coleman, Hoffer, and Kilgore 1982a). The results were generally more favorable to the private sector than to the public sector on both counts, with some exceptions and some caveats. A major caveat was that the sample of non-Catholic private schools was insufficiently large (and possibly biased because of nonresponse) that any generalizations involving non-Catholic private schools could be made only tentatively. Another is that in any comparison where self-selection is as great as in public versus private schools, causal inferences about differential effectiveness must be done cautiously because of the possibility of selection bias. This second caveat, however, is reduced by the number and varieties of methods used to overcome selection bias, with the inference about effects surviving largely unscathed. (For discussion of these methods together with results, see Coleman, Hoffer, and Kilgore 1982b; Coleman and Hoffer 1983; and Hoffer, Greeley, and Coleman 1985.)

With these two caveats, it was found that with respect to the question of differential effectiveness, students in both Catholic and non-Catholic private schools (examined separately) showed higher performance on the standardized tests than did students from comparable backgrounds in public schools. The difference was roughly similar for vocabulary, reading, and mathematics, and of comparable magnitudes in Catholic schools and other private schools. The magnitude was about one grade level. For Catholic schools, but not in other private schools, this effectiveness was especially pronounced for students from disadvantaged backgrounds: those with less well-educated parents, blacks, and Hispanics.

The effects of the private sector on the degree of racial, economic, and religious segregation showed first that there was no net effect on racial segregation. The increment to segregation created by the smaller fraction of blacks in the private sector was exactly compensated by the decrement to segregation caused by the lesser segregation of black and white students within the private sector.

There was a slight effect of the private sector in increasing the degree of income segregation in education. This effect was much smaller than might be expected by an observer familiar with independent private schools catering to an upper-middle-class clientele. Only a minority of private school students attends such schools. Most attend Catholic schools; and of those who attend non-Catholic schools, most attend other religiously affiliated schools. The income distribution of families of students who attend schools in the private sector is not greatly different from that in the public sector. It is distinguished primarily by some differences at the high and low income extremes (see Coleman, Hoffer, and Kilgore 1982a, table 3.5 and figure 3.1).

The effect on religious segregation was more substantial. Most students in the private sector attend a school organized by their own religious group. This means that the private sector shows a considerable degree of religious segregation. If there were an expansion of the private sector, this would undoubtedly mean an increase in the degree of religious segregation in the schools. Just how great an increase would depend on the relative expansion of the religiously affiliated and non-religiously affiliated portions of the private sector.

These analyses, and the book containing them, provoked extensive controversy in the press and in the journals.* The controversy surrounded both questions: the segregative effect of the private sector on American education and the effect of the private sector on the achievement of those students who attend private schools. Behind the controversy lay practical questions of policy, for there was a delicate balance between political forces favoring an expanded role for private schools and forces favoring a more restricted role. A shift in that balance could lead to new policies, and evidence about the merits or faults of the private sector could make such a shift more likely.

The first analysis opened a pandora's box of questions, issues, and problems concerning public and private schooling. One set of questions is that remaining from the controversy, especially concerning our conclusion that private sector schools generally produced higher achievement than did public schools for comparable students. The major contention of critics of the research was that we failed to control adequately for background differences among public and private students, and that these uncontrolled differences could account for the apparent private school advantages. In particular, the cross-sectional control for background differences was inferior to comparison of public and private students who started high school at the same level of achievement.

As the data then available only allowed for comparison of students with comparable family backgrounds, we could not directly test this alternative explanation of the private school achievement advantages. These data limitations have now been reduced with the availability of information from the first followup of the High School and Beyond survey, collected in 1982. The followup administered the same achievement tests to the 1982 seniors that were completed two years earlier when these students were sophomores. These data thus allow us to compare public and private students' growth in achievement over the last two years of high school. The comparison of growth constitutes a much stronger test than was heretofore possible of the hypothesis that private schools are more effective in promoting achievement.

A second set of questions concerns other outcomes of secondary education. Students' high school experiences have an important impact on the formation of their plans for later life—whether to go on to college

*See *Harvard Educational Review* (1981), *Phi Delta Kappan* (1981), *Educational Researcher* (1981), and *Sociology of Education* (1982, 1983, and 1985).

and, indeed, whether to finish or drop out of high school, and what occupation to pursue once out of school. These other outcomes of schooling warrant examination. The 1982 followup data allow us to study the change in these outcomes over the last two years of high school.

A part of this second set of questions concerns what becomes of students once they finish high school. Looked at another way, a student's high school achievements and experiences are merely means to the ends of performing well in postsecondary educational and economic institutions. The question of how public and private students fare once they leave school is in this sense the critical test of the claim that private schools are more effective than public schools. The 1982 followup data are also well-suited to address this question, for the 1980 seniors were resurveyed two years later, when they were in college, in the labor force, in both, or in another activity.

An examination of these outcomes of education, not possible with the 1980 data but possible after the sophomores had been resurveyed and retested, and after the seniors were out of school for two years, constitutes a sequel to the earlier analysis. As with the results from the earlier analysis, these—particularly the longitudinal examination of achievement effects of private schools and the effects on dropping out and postsecondary education—are relevant to educational policy and to youth policy more generally.

But an extension of the earlier analysis to study additional outcomes is not the only aim of this book, nor even the principal one. For underlying the controversy surrounding private schools is a deeper issue involving both the goals of education and who will determine these goals. This issue was a sporadic and localized one so long as control of school policy was primarily at the local level, and battles over school policy were fought within local communities. But in the past two decades that has changed, as federal and state policies have been directed to the functioning of schools, and as the mass media have become increasingly important in transcending the boundaries of local communities.

The issue, stated in a strong form, can be described as an issue involving two quite different orientations to schooling, one represented by public schools and the other represented by private schools. Public schools represent an orientation that sees the school as an instrument of the society to free the child from constraints imposed by accident of birth. Private schools represent an orientation that sees the school as an agent not of the society but of the family, with authority vested *in loco parentis*, an extension of the parent's will, but with greater resources. Within this second orientation, there are two variations, represented in the present study by Catholic schools and other private schools. The first of these variations, the orientation on which religiously organized schools are based, sees the school not directly as an agent of the family but rather as an agent of the religious community of which the family is a part. The school is an institution of this community, the family is a part of the community, and the child attends the school as a part of this functional community. The second, the orientation on which independent private schools are based, sees the school as the direct agent of the family in a very individualistic sense: The parents search for that school which most closely accords with their values and send their child to this school. If the school does not meet expectations, they attempt to intervene, or more likely, move the child to another school. Thus, there are three distinguishable orientations to the school, not two: the school as agent of the larger society or the state; the school as agent of the (religious) community; and the school as an agent of the individual family. We have enclosed "religious" in parentheses because there are in principle other bases of community that could serve as basis for organization of a school—and the residential community, which is the most obvious of those, will be discussed in chapter 1. Thus, religion is not intrinsic to the orientation; what is intrinsic is the notion that the school is an outgrowth not of the individual family, but of a community of families that is both in direct interaction in everyday life and shares values.

These orientations, with their different goals, lead to schools that are designed somewhat differently. These different designs, in turn, attract different kinds of families and have different kinds of impacts on the children for whom they are designed—some intended and some unintended. This differential attraction and the differential impacts are among the questions raised by the first book and are among the questions to be examined in this one.

Because these different orientations have important implications for effects of schools on children and youth, we will begin with an examination of these two major orientations—not distinguishing at the outset between the two orientations represented by religiously based private schools and independent private schools. After examining these two orientations, one giving rise to public schools and the second giving rise to private schools, we will examine the differences between the two orientations that distinguish the two parts of private sector; the school as an outgrowth of the community, and the school as an agent of the individual family. In chapter 2, we turn to the empirical analysis to which the major portion of this book is devoted. Finally, in chapter 8, we draw together these results and discuss their implications for parents' decisions and for school policy.

As will become apparent, the questions we raise in this book have far deeper implications for schools as institutions in a changing social structure than did those examined in the first book. The family as an institution is undergoing extensive change, the geographically defined communities in which families reside are undergoing extensive change, and the structures of control under which public schools operate are undergoing extensive change. All these changes have implications for the way children and youth are brought into adulthood; and the sectors of education represented by public schools, religiously based private schools, and independent private schools interact differently with these broad social changes.

Public and Private High Schools

1

Two Orientations to Schooling

THROUGHOUT American history, there have been two different orientations toward schooling. These two orientations have created a dilemma for educational policy that has never been satisfactorily resolved, nor precisely stated. A direct confrontation of these orientations can be a step toward resolving the dilemma in a way that will benefit America and its children.

The first orientation sees schools as society's instrument for releasing a child from the blinders imposed by accident of birth into this family or that family. Schools have been designed to open broad horizons to the child, transcending the limitations of the parents, and have taken children from disparate cultural backgrounds into the mainstream of American culture. They have been a major element in social mobility, freeing children from the poverty of their parents and the low status of their social origins. They have been a means of stripping away identities of ethnicity and social origin and implanting a common American identity.

As the first orientation has been the basis for public schooling in America, a second orientation has been the basis for private schools. This second orientation to schooling sees a school as an extension of the family, reinforcing the family's values. The school is *in loco parentis,* vested with the authority of the parent to carry out the parent's will.

3

The school is, in this orientation, an efficient means for transmitting the culture of the community from the older generation to the younger. It helps create the next generation in the image of the preceding one.

These two orientations are not in fundamental conflict. When the community is an extension of the family, when the society is a homogeneous nation that is an extension of the communities within it, and when the state expresses the aims of the homogeneous nation, then these two orientations coincide for most families. But when one or more of these conditions does not hold, a conflict arises. Some illustrations of this follow.

• In early nineteenth-century United States, a homogeneous, Protestant, English-origin population had established schools that expressed its cultural, religious, and philosophical values, schools that served simultaneously the family's, community's, and nation's interests. For a new set of Irish Catholic immigrants these two orientations came into direct conflict: the religious values and customs transmitted in these schools directly conflicted with those of these families, and the result was an alienating environment for their children. In turn, the Irish Catholic schools they then established, outside the public school system, were seen as a threat by those in the community and the society transmitting the dominant Protestant English culture.

• The massive German immigration to the United States in the mid nineteenth century resulted in many rural communities in parts of the Midwest (Ohio, Illinois, Kansas, Nebraska, Wisconsin, and other states) that were culturally and linguistically German. In these communities, the cultural, linguistic, and religious conflicts were resolved in various ways. In some cases, children of the immigrants were taken into the public schools and imbued with a language, culture, and ideals foreign to those of their immigrant parents. In some cases, Lutheran schools were established outside the public school system, the school constituting for the family an alternative community, which would transmit at least the religious values of the parents and would keep the children from being wholly absorbed by the mainstream culture. In some cases, however, public schools reflected the family's and community's German background, with instruction in German, and the school transmitting a culture which at many points was alien to the dominant culture. Some of these public schools retained the German language until transformed by the nationalistic fervor that accompanied the First World War.

• In the South, the white-dominated, segregationist orientation of families and communities came into conflict with the egalitarian, color-

4

blind orientation of the nation as a whole. This conflict came to a head with the *Brown v. Board of Education* decision of the U.S. Supreme Court in 1954. Through a long and painful process extending into the 1970s, schools in the south underwent a transformation from being expressions of the local segregationist orientation to expressions of the color-blind orientation. Some southern white families created segregationist academies in the private sector, schools that were extensions of their own cultural values.

• The late 1960s was a period of great value conflict in the United States between the dominant traditional values of the generation in control and values extolling freedom for youth and release from the narrow views of the past. Some parents and teachers established "free schools" and "alternative schools" outside the public school system, in which children were participants in creating their curriculum, and in which the traditional classroom was abandoned in favor of more active, participative modes of learning. Some schools and some programs within schools in the public sector also took on the form of alternative schools.

• In the 1970s and 1980s, a number of conservative Christian schools and evangelical Christian schools have been established by parents concerned about the values transmitted by the public schools, secular and in opposition to Christian virtues as they perceive them. These schools represent attempts to recreate a cultural and value homogeneity for the children that insulates them from the values which permeate the larger society.

These examples of conflict between the functioning family and the schools as means of emancipation from the family show the diverse settings in which the conflict arises, as well as its fundamental character. What then is the current setting in which schools operate in the United States, and how does that setting affect this conflict between the two orientations?

Cultural Cleavages and Social Lacunae in America

A setting in which there is no conflict between the school as extension of the family and the school as emancipator of the child from the family is one in which there is perfect cultural consistency and social continuity between family and society. It is an ideal type, occurring only in the absence of social change and only in small homogeneous societies—perhaps best exemplified by communities prior to the industrial revolution. Those settings differ in two principal ways from the settings found in current Western society. First, there is social structural consistency. The adults whom children see and know outside the home—both in and out of school—are adults closely linked to the family. The other young people whom children see and know are children of these same adults. Second, and in part stemming from the social consistency, there is value consistency. The values to which children are exposed are the values of these same adults, not far removed socially from the family. There is value consistency between children and their friends, between parents and their friends, and between parents and their children.

Schools in such a setting of structural consistency and value consistency reinforce both. They provide a locus and occasion for transmission of the generally held values, and they provide a social context within which children whose parents know each other and hold similar values can interact.

Such a setting is not necessarily idyllic, of course. It is an "ideal type," representing a pure case of a certain form of social organization. But it has no mechanism for change, and it may be dull or oppressive to those embedded within it. It serves, however, as a useful comparison and contrast to American society in the 1980s.

The two elements of structural consistency and value consistency, although often found together, are nevertheless analytically distinct and are sometimes empirically separated as well.

Structural Consistency and Functional Communities

We may begin the examination of structural consistency and functional communities by recalling studies of schools in America in the recent past, exemplifying something close to the ideal type of structural consistency. Beginning in the 1920s, a number of community studies described what it was like to grow up in a town in middle America. The best known of these was *Middletown,* a study of Muncie, Indiana, in the early 1920s (Lynd and Lynd 1929). Another, in which attention was confined to youth and to the high school, was *Elmtown's Youth,* a study set in Morris, Illinois, in the early 1940s (Hollingshead 1949).

These studies and others made clear the way in which the social structure of the adult community was transmitted through the school to the next generation. In Middletown and in Elmtown, there was "closure" between the adult communities and the communities of youth in high school: Parents knew who their children's friends were and knew their parents. The norms that pervaded the school were in part those dictated by the needs of youth themselves (attractiveness to the opposite sex, for example), but in part those established by the adult community and enforced by the intergenerational contact that this closure brought about. This structural consistency between generations creates what can be described as a functional community, a community in which social norms and sanctions, including those that cross generations, arise out of the social structure itself, and both reinforce and perpetuate that structure.

This transmission of the social structure of one generation to the next in a close community, partly through inheritance of the parent's reputation by the child, was described by the Lynds and by Hollingshead, who documented this inheritance and showed its effects. One of the effects, especially deplored by these sociologists, was the stigma that a lower-class child carried as a result of the parents' social position. In the absence of a functional community of the sort described by the Lynds and by Hollingshead, this stigma would vanish, and the young generation would begin from a more egalitarian basis. In the absence of a functional community, the prostitute's daughter and the ne'er do well's son are no longer hampered by their parents' reputations and have an opportunity hampered only by the direct impact of their parents' activities on their own. Reputations will arise within the school, because every school is a functional community of the youth within it; but in the absence of a functional community embracing both parents' and child's generation, the child's reputation in school is not inherited from the parents.

There is, however, another effect of functional communities on the opportunity of children from different social backgrounds, one which remained unnoticed by the Lynds and Hollingshead. A functional community augments the resources available to parents in their interactions with school, in their supervision of their children's behavior, and in their supervision of their children's associations, both with others their own age and with adults. The feedback that a parent receives from friends and associates, either unsolicited or in response to questions, provides extensive additional resources that aid the parent in monitoring the school and the child, and the norms that parents, as part of their everyday activity, are able to establish act as important aids in socializing children.

Parents at all social and educational levels need these resources as an aid in raising their children and monitoring their schooling; but the parents in most desperate need of them are the parents with least personal resources: parents with little education, few organizational skills, little self-confidence, and little money. It is clear that those parents most seriously deprived by the absence of these community resources are those with least resources of their own, the most disadvantaged.

To describe functional communities with intergenerational closure as a resource for parents in raising their children is more than a figure of speech. The extraordinary social mobility that children from lower-class backgrounds, both rural and urban, have had in previous generations in America was accomplished by families with meager tangible resources. The parents had little money and little education. Yet their children showed the middle-class virtues of hard work, diligence, respect for the teacher, and good behavior in school: qualities that served them well in preparing them for further education and the mobility it brought. Where did the resources come from to develop and nurture this behavior?

These children were surrounded by functional communities, either in rural areas or in ethnic neighborhoods of urban areas. At this point it is only a conjecture (which we examine later in the book), but it may well be that the critical resource these parents had, which many modern parents do not, were those functional communities, with the norms, sanctions, and rewards that enabled them to shape the lives of the young. If this is so, it enabled lower-class parents to raise children in a middle-class manner. In contrast—if this conjecture is correct—the decline of such communities in the present leaves parents, whether middle class or lower class, without a strong set of social resources, able only to draw upon whatever individual resources they have.

Value Consistency and Value Communities

A functional community is neither a necessary nor a sufficient condition for value consistency, though the two have some affinity. Value consistency grows through the interactions found in a functional community, and when it exists it facilitates the norms that grow up in such a community. But there are value cleavages in functional communities, cleavages which may be intense. For example, in a highly stratified small town, some of the families at the lower end of the stratification ladder may actively reject the values dominant in the community.

At the same time, there are collections of people who exhibit value consistency, but who constitute no functional community at all. Parents of children attending certain schools of choice, whether in the public or the private sector, often constitute such a collection. In some cities there are elementary schools that exhibit a particular educational philosophy such as open classrooms or basic education, and attract parents from various residential areas who agree with that philosophy. Parents and children may even be required to sign a contract specifying the rules they will observe. These parents, and their children, exhibit a high degree of value consistency, but are strangers drawn from throughout the city.

At the secondary level, alternative schools and some public "magnet schools" attract students on the basis of their own and their parents' values concerning schooling; but they seldom constitute a functional community. Many private schools project certain educational philosophies and attract parents who agree with those philosophies. Quaker schools, for example, tend to have a character quite different from the typical preparatory school of the Northeast. They are more nurturant, less competitive, less academically exacting, and more environmentally and antinuclear activist, and they attract parents who concur with these values. Military academies express a value system almost directly opposite and attract parents with these values. The parents who send their children to these schools often have no contacts with one another, and they could never be described as a functional community. They do, however, share the same values and thus constitute a value community.

In contrast to these schools, many private schools organized along religious lines not only have value consistency, but constitute a functional community. Families attend the same religious services and know one another. This, however, is a functional community of a different kind from that which encompassed all adults and youth in Elmtown, and other geographic communities like it. It does not encompass all institutions and all areas of interaction, but only the religious one. When it is drawn from a larger society with members employed in different and widely spread economic institutions, as most religiously based schools do, then it is a functional community that lacks both some of the closure of the ideal-typical communities described earlier and some of the hierarchical structure of such communities. The consequences of this difference are not clear, but the difference itself is.

The example of nonreligious private schools on the one hand and religiously based schools like those in the Catholic sector on the other indicates that private schools differ considerably in the kinds of communities they constitute. Nearly all have a high degree of value consistency, but not all are part of a functional community. We will use the term "value community" to describe a collection of people who share similar values about education and childrearing but who are not a functional community. As the preceding examples indicate, some public schools of choice and some private schools in the independent sector have students whose parents are members of a value community, but not a functional community.

Residential Areas, Functional Communities, and Social Change

When residential areas served by a school were functional communities, it was not true that all members of the community shared the same values. The village drunkard who brought up his children in a shack along the road surrounded by brokendown automobiles did not share all the values of the farm family down the road whose children had their homework done every day and never missed a day of school nor of Sunday school. The difference in values may have been in part brought about by the former's rejection of a set of values that placed him low in the status hierarchy; or it may be that the value differences were what led him in the first place to adopt a style of life that put him low in the status hierarchy. Whatever the origin of the differences, it was always clear which values were dominant in the social system of the community.

In a functional community there is a clear and consistent set of norms that express these dominant values; and the degree of conformity to these norms determines, with few exceptions, the position of individuals and families in the status hierarchy. People conform differentially to these norms, in some cases because the status rewards, always in short supply, are not sufficient to balance the pleasures of deviant actions. This differential conformity brings differential status.

The end result is that whatever the diversity of values that exists in a functional community, one set of values is dominant, and others that differ from them are privately held or narrowly shared, but are clearly dominated in the school and community by those from which they deviate. In fact, in some such communities most people will be behaving according to a set of values—the dominant set—which they themselves do not hold privately. Or we may even say that many people accept a set of values that they did not choose and with which, privately, they do not agree.

Two major changes have occurred to alter this state of affairs. First, the daily activities of persons who live in proximity are much less often with one another and much more often with others outside, so persons in proximity are not required by the exigencies of life to come to terms with one another. This loss of inward-directed activities constitutes the decline of the residentially based functional community. Second, there has been a communications invasion from the outside in the form of mass media. Thus the communications and attention that were in the past directed toward others within the residential community have not merely been redirected to other persons outside that community; they have been redirected toward the mass media in various forms.

These new sources of communication, unconstrained by the norms that once dominated the community, now offer values that deviate sharply from those norms and provide a base of legitimation for these other values. No longer is there uncontested dominance of a set of values; different values can coexist simultaneously, unchallenged until some event creates a conflict.

It is this change that has made the task of a principal of a public school with attendance based on residence a difficult and sometimes intolerable one. In schools based on functional communities, the task of the principal in maintaining and exercising authority in a school could be readily accomplished, merely by first discovering the dominant set of values in the community and the norms supporting those values, and then exercising authority accordingly, imposing sanctions to enforce the norms.*

A principal of a school today in which attendance is based on residence has no set of dominant community values to uphold. Instead, there are a number of contending values, each claiming legitimacy, and

---

*Because the dominance of a set of values carried with it a status hierarchy, this meant that the principal would be under some inducement to observe the status hierarchy, behaving differently to persons according to their position in this hierarchy. Such differential treatment on the part of the principal and school staff was an important source of inequality of opportunity in those communities. Hollingshead (1949) describes the way this operates in the case of Elmtown. It was especially inequitous when inherited status did not correspond to actual behavior, and those high in the hierarchy failed to conform to norms but were not sanctioned. The country song "Harper Valley PTA," narrated by the town's divorcee mother of a junior high school daughter, illustrates this well. But the Harper Valleys of this country are largely a thing of the past.

at least some of them capable of being backed up by legal suits in court. It was once very unusual for a public school principal or superintendent to be engaged in legal battles. Now it is commonplace.

A principal with strong personal force can make a particular set of values dominant within the school. But the potential for challenge to such values is always there, whether from parents who support their son in his refusal to obey a dress code, or from a teacher's union which backs up a teacher's grievance about extracurricular burdens, or from a parent who takes a child out of school for a Caribbean vacation, or from a civil rights group which objects to a black student's suspension. The principal no longer has the strength of a tightly knit functional community to support authoritative actions and may easily be defeated by such a challenge, with authority undermined from that time forward.

The absence of a value consensus based on a functional community has led with increasing frequency to the creation of schools based on value communities that have no functional community base. In the public sector, this is exemplified by schools of the sort we described earlier, both at the elementary and secondary levels, in which attendance is based not on residence, but on choice of school by parent and child. These schools may differ in educational philosophy or in curricular emphasis, but their distinguishing property is that children attend them by their own and their parents' choice, and in so doing agree to accept the set of values around which the school is organized.

In the private sector, many schools are based on value communities that have little grounding in functional communities. Schools in the independent sector often have a small core of families who know each other well, share a set of values, and are perhaps a residue of one or another social elite in the city (or other area where the school is located). But around this is a much larger population of families who have little social connection to one another or to the core, and who enroll their children in the school either because of agreement with the values of this core group or because of agreement with the values of the school (which may, of course, coincide with the core group's values). These schools can hardly be said to constitute a functional community of adults, and the children in them may be drawn away from the functional communities of children who attend the neighborhood public school. Nevertheless, they constitute a value community.

Catholic schools attended primarily by non-Catholic black students, which is common in large central cities, can be described in much the same way as this. There is often a core of Catholic students (sometimes black, sometimes white), who attend the same parish church and know

12

each other, and a large periphery of non-Catholics, many of whose parents do not know each other. These schools appear to perform for innercity black families the same kind of function that the independent schools do for upper-middle-class families.

Religiously sponsored schools which have student bodies who share that religion (most Catholic schools, conservative and evangelical Christian schools, Lutheran schools, Jewish schools, and others) constitute first of all communities with strong values. They also are based, in most cases, on a functional community that shares the same place of worship. These schools are different from the geographically based functional communities of the past, because they are founded on interaction in only one arena of life—religion. For that reason they may escape some of the faults of schools of the largely closed geographically based functional communities described earlier (such as the transmission of the community's status system across generations), while retaining the capacity to maintain and reinforce a set of values. It is probably also true that the set of values they maintain are less easily manipulated to serve the interests of dominant families than were those of the geographically based functional communities.

As evident from the preceding description, the consequences of a value community in the school are great. Such a school is easy to manage and easy to teach in. The balance of power lies not with the children, but with the teachers and the principal. Such a school may be oppressive to some of its students because of the consistency of values. If its clientele are there by choice, it is less likely to be oppressive than a school serving a traditional value community based on a geographic functional community. It is not a school that suffers from disorder and absence of structure.

Policy Choices in Education

Historically, the policy choice of American education was that of the common school with attendance based on residence. It was a choice against those functional communities that were regarded as divisive of the social fabric. It was a choice against schools organized along social class lines.* It was a choice against schools organized along religious

---

*In contrast, the English school system was a two-tiered system even before the advent of public schooling, with the lower tier a set of "missionary" schools to the poor, financed by charitable institutions.

lines and against schools organized along ethnic lines. It was a choice against schools operated by the state government or by the federal government. It was a choice in favor of schools organized along residential lines and governed by the local community. The policy choice was not seen by the dominant majority as a choice between the two orientations of schooling—schooling as an extension of the family versus schooling as an instrument for bringing the child into the larger society— because for these families, the goals were not in conflict. The larger society was an extension of the local community which was an extension of these families. Society, community, and family were consistent in religious orientation, in ethnicity, and in culture. Thus the public schools of the late nineteenth and early twentieth centuries embodied these dominant religious (Protestant) and cultural orientations (English) and reinforced these as the dominant orientations of the community and of larger society.

For the ethnic, cultural, and religious minorities, however, this choice was a choice against schooling as an extension of the family and for schooling as an instrument for bringing the child into the larger society. The larger society was not an extension of the family for them, either religiously or culturally. The public schools were for them an instrument that alienated the child from the family, an instrument that benefited the child by bringing it into the mainstream of American society, but at a cost to the continuity and strength of the family. The cost was not great when a school served a local community that was ethnically and religiously homogeneous, for then the culture of the local community pervaded the school and made it consistent with the functional community of adults whose children it served. The cost was great, however, for cultural minorities in residential communities that were heterogeneous.

The organization of public schooling along residential lines in America (a choice that differed sharply from that in Europe, where schooling was organized along social class lines or religious lines, except where population density was so low as to force a common school) was an important integrating force for the larger society.* Functional communities and value communities along residential lines were strong, a consequence of many things: Technology had not yet facilitated the separation of work and residence, except where urban transit lines

---

*However, the question might be posed: Would the society now be less integrated if public schooling had been organized differently, with each immigrant group free to have its own public school? Conventional wisdom would respond that indeed the society would be far less integrated. But the evidence seems to us hardly conclusive.

existed. Technology, again, had not yet brought the mass media and electronically distributed culture. The ties of immigrant families were strong and ethnic cultural norms were strong. These strengths were reinforced by the tendency of members of an immigrant group to settle in close proximity. In addition, economic need forced families to depend on one another.

As a result of this strength of residential communities, the policy choice of the common school based on residence did not exact as a price the loss of resources which would attend lack of functional community. The strength of the functional community in its impact on school and children was reinforced by these various factors, together with the fact of local rather than state or federal control of the schools.

Value communities often did not exist in the school as a whole; but as described in the preceding section, there was generally a dominant set of values, which reinforced the status hierarchy in community and school.

Thus the policy choice of a common school defined by residential proximity generally preserved the benefits of functional communities and value communities. The homogeneity of some of these schools meant that the full benefits of emancipating a child from the narrowness of family were sometimes not realized, but the homogeneity also meant that neither were the full costs of this orientation paid. This policy choice in American education was a choice made in a specific social and political context. It imposed some costs on children, families, ethnic groups, and religious groups; but it also brought benefits, benefits to which these families and groups were able, in the conditions that existed then, to contribute. Since that time, basic policy in American education has followed the same pattern. However, the social context has changed extensively since that time, and some policy changes have occurred as well.

The major changes in social context have been twofold: the destruction of functional communities based on residence, and the realignment of value communities around some dimension other than residence. Functional communities have been destroyed by various social changes. Technological change, which has made it possible to separate residence from work and has brought women into the labor force, has effectively removed the adults from the local community, which remains a functional community only for the young. The replacement of independent towns by large urban agglomerates has facilitated a great expansion of sources from which adults choose friends and associates, and has led to the replacement of communities by networks built of pair relations. Immigrant groups (except for the most recent) have lost much of the strength and the physical contiguity of their ethnic communities. (It may not be accidental that children of some of the most recent immigrant groups, not yet swallowed up by the dominant culture, and embedded within an ethnic functional community spanning generations, do very well in school.) Growth in affluence has reduced families' need for one another.

Not all functional communities with a high degree of system closure have been replaced by open networks. There remain some groups with a common identity and definable boundaries. Most of these, unfortunately for the young, do not include children, but are only for adults. Work groups are probably the most important of these for most adults. A few such groups, most prominently religious groups, do include children as well as adults. And some, most prominently the school and the neighborhood group, consist of children, but include few adults, except for the paid staff in school.

Value communities were once largely developed and sustained by social interaction. Thus there was a high degree of correspondence between functional communities based on residence and value communities. But as functional communities have become weakened or have been replaced by open networks, the grounding of value communities in functional communities is much less strong. The value communities in modern society are often created not by social interaction but by a common response to mass media of communications. Regular readers of the *Reader's Digest,* for example, will have and will cultivate a different world view than readers of *The New Yorker.* Those values resulting from social interaction are much more the product of a social milieu based on the chains of an open network, or a sparsely connected collectivity, rather than the densely connected, relatively closed, functional communities of the past.

Because residential proximity is no longer the source of dense interaction and thus of value communities, residential areas tend to be heterogeneous in values—and without, as in the past, a dominant set of values to which all paid tribute. Values, when not held in place by dense interaction, diverge. The school is the principal locus in which those divergent values come into confrontation. In the same school, half the parents might wish the school required their children to wear uniforms, while another parent might sue the school for disallowing her daughter's miniskirt in school. Many parents might wish the school would require more homework, while others might demand that homework outside school hours be abolished.

Two Orientations to Schooling

Thus the public school with a geographically defined student body has become increasingly heterogeneous in values, increasingly contentious, increasingly unmanageable by principal and staff. It is in this context that schools based on value communities have come to be increasingly popular, both within and outside the public sector. Schools based on value communities, such as the schools of choice in the public sector and independent schools in the private sector, approximate voluntary associations, paralleling the shift of society generally from ascriptive organization to purposive organization. Like other voluntary associations, they are not based on a whole fabric of values which prescribe behavior in all areas of life, but upon a single value dimension which is relevant to the purpose of organization. Thus families who enroll their children in an elementary school that emphasizes basic skills education agree on what and how children should be taught in elementary school, but they may have little else in common. There is similar consensus in a Montessori school, but again on the single dimension. Or parents and children who choose a magnet school which has an emphasis on music instruction will be in agreement about the importance of studying things that facilitate a career in music, but not in agreement on a wide range of other matters.

Apart from the social changes that have led to the destruction of geographic functional communities and the dominant values they maintained, social policy as well has led away from the ideal-typical local school within which a dominant set of values held sway, overseen by a principal and staff whose task it was to act *in loco parentis*, to enforce those values as agents of the community of parents. Increasingly, state and federal policies have constituted challenges to the locally generated policies and the local authorities which administered them. School consolidation was an early such challenge, and continues to be so. School desegregation plans, often imposed by the court or a federal agency, constitute another. Various additional policies at the federal level have exerted forces in the same direction.

These policies have in part grown out of the broader social changes that destroy local functional communities, and in part, they extend and hasten these changes. All act in the same direction, to bring within the walls of the local public school a divergent and often incompatible collection of values and conflicting claims of authority.

It is within the context of these changes that the growth of interest in choice within the public sector, and the new entrants in the private sector, may be seen. These do not represent social policy so much as a kind of social evolution, brought about by actions on the part of the school's clients. (The earlier actions reflecting choice of school, beginning after World War II and continuing as suburbanization continued, were residential moves to a new suburb. But these suburbs have matured, diversified, and lost some of the value consensus they once had. Thus this avenue of choice is less attractive to parents.) This social evolution results from attempts by parents to create, in the new social context brought about by the extensive changes, either new functional communities in which there is intergenerational closure or new value communities, so that they can send their children to school with trust and confidence.

The Change in Families

One aspect of the social change which has brought a destruction of the functional community is the contraction of the family, the shrinking of the extended family down to the nuclear family, or, in many cases, down to the one-parent family. The extended family was a resource for parents, sometimes more tolerated than appreciated, but nevertheless a resource of great aid in raising children. Norms, carried over from generation to generation, gave strength to the parents' values in their competition with values picked up from the mass media and other children. Grandparents, aunts, and uncles constituted supplements to parents and even at times surrogate parents.

But the general contraction of families means that many parents have lost a set of resources that their parents had in raising them. The loss of resources began first outside the nuclear family and has progressively moved inside it as well. Thus it is not merely that "the parents" have lost resources that were once provided by extended family and cohesive neighborhoods. The resources of the parents themselves have been weakened. Increasingly children are raised by a single parent, and, increasingly, whatever parent or parents a child lives with are in full-time jobs away from home and neighborhood, with large amounts of their interests and energies devoted to activities in the workplace, and reduced amounts devoted to the activities of the child in school and neighborhood. Not only have residential communities and extended families become deficient as aids in raising children; many nuclear families have become deficient as well.

In this context of social change, the school, as one of the few remain-

ing institutional resources available to parents, increases in importance.
Kindergarten, nursery school, and day-care centers have allowed
schooling to begin anywhere from the first years of life up to the age
of five or six. Extended day programs for children of working parents
have been initiated in some schools, and some parents have begun to
look to summer school programs to solve the problem of what to do with
their children during the summer months. Parents in some high schools
have attempted to create a formal statement of rights and responsibili-
ties for students in the school, using the school as a setting within which
to construct an artificial replacement for the informal norms which
once grew naturally in the community.

This increased use of schools by parents indicates that the tasks of
school policy are not so simple as merely making the school function as
well as it did in the context of strong functional communities. If the aim
of social policy is not merely to make schools function well, but to make
it possible for parents, including those who constitute deficient families,
to raise their children well, then policy must address the broader question of what parents need if they are to raise their children well, and
how these needs may be met. To take this perspective is in the spirit
of the original aim which schools were designed to meet, at the time
public schooling came into being. That was the aim of supplementing
the activities of parents in raising their children, as the social context
changed from that of rural farm and village life to that of industrial
society. Today, with a similar aim, social policy must ask what additional
or different kinds of supplements are necessary, as the resources provided by functional communities have largely vanished and the family
itself has shrunk in size, function, and capability.

Parental Decisions, Governmental Decisions, and Public Goods

The destruction of the functional communities within which families
live and children grow up is a destruction in which the prime mover
is technological change, but in which intermediate actors have played
an important part as well. One of these actors is the family itself. Families make decisions which, taken individually, benefit the family, but at
a small cost to others. When enough families make such a decision, the
combined costs are harmful to all. For example, a family decides to

leave a community because of a better job offer elsewhere or because of a promotion and transfer. Each of the other members of the community experiences a small loss, because the cycles of intergenerational closure involving that family are broken and because the family's contribution to community activities and community norms are withdrawn. These ruptures will be repaired after the family is replaced by a new one, but the repairs take a period of time.

All this does not create a problem, up to a point. But when the *rate* of such mobility is high, both in the communities from which the movers came and the communities to which they go, then there comes a point when this high rate imposes costs on each member of the community that exceed the benefits of moving, even for the movers. The high rate means that the cycles of intergenerational closure are in a continual state of disrepair, and the norms and community activities remain in a continually weakened or disrupted state. Thus at the extreme, we may find each family with higher income, yet worse off than before, because of the loss of community resources resulting from the decisions of each. Yet it would be unwise for a family not to move as long as that move is beneficial to the family. Most of the costs it will experience from a weakened community come not from its own actions, but from the actions of others. So long as its own move provides a net benefit to it, it will move. Then taken in the aggregate, these moves, each beneficial to the mover, make everyone worse off.

There is a second point in the rate of movement, one in which each family's chance of imminent movement is sufficiently great that the investment in connections in the new community is unprofitable to the family. "Putting down roots is not worth it," is the common expression of this condition. When this point is reached, the new family that replaces the old will not establish the relations that re-create cycles of intergenerational closure, will not take part in community activities, will not accept, be governed by, and help enforce the norms of the community. When the community consists of such highly mobile families, then it is weakened on two counts: by its own high rate of turnover and by the high proportion of these mobile families whose prospective moves keep them detached from the community.

We have used this example of moving decisions as an illustration of the more general process. The decision need not be a moving decision. It may be a decision of the father to take a job outside the local neighborhood, or a decision by the mother to leave the household and her community activities and go to work. These are decisions driven by technological change and by the desire for economic gain, and the specific decision may be a correct one from the point of view of the individual or the family making the decision. But each individual and each family is a resource to the community, and decisions which withdraw these resources from the community are decisions which make the community a less valuable resource for its members. Taken together the decline in value of this resource may in the end mean that the quality of life for each is lower, rather than higher as was the intention of each.

It is in this way that family decisions often destroy the value of a community for socializing children. Government decisions do so in a different way. The policy of school consolidation provides an illustration of how this can occur. School consolidation is a policy of the county school district or state department of education that consists of bringing together two or more rural schools, each in its own small town or village, into one. It began on a large scale in the 1930s, and it continues even today. Consolidation is ordinarily justified on grounds of the benefit of better facilities, specialized courses, and specialized teachers for students in the school.* Because the small town's school is often its central institution, the towns involved in consolidation that will lose their school often object strenuously and sometimes have even brought suit against the county or state school system to block consolidation.

The benefits to the student of consolidation are direct benefits, provided by the greater resources of the consolidated school. The costs to the student are indirect, operating through the damage to the intergenerational closure, community norms, and other resources of the community, including the personal relation of the teacher to the child, that are damaged or destroyed by consolidation. But these costs are seldom taken into consideration in policy decisions.

Policies of this sort are ordinarily based on the direct benefits intentionally brought to the clients by the institution itself. The decision is seldom based on balancing against these benefits the indirect costs imposed on the clients by the destruction of or damage to informal social systems of which they are part. To be sure, these costs could be balanced against the benefits by studies of the outcomes for youth: In places where consolidation has occurred, how many drop out of school, before and after consolidation? How many go to college, and where?

---

*Sometimes greater efficiency is also used as justification of the policy, because of the smaller number pupils per teacher in some small schools. However, whether it is generally true that consolidated schools have lower per pupil costs than the small schools they replace is not clear, because of the greater administrative costs, greatly increased busing costs, and sometimes higher wages of the teachers employed in the consolidated school. (See Butler and Monk 1985.)

How are the trajectories of their lives after school affected? But such research is difficult and costly, it depends on some consolidation having been done, and as a consequence will not ordinarily be available to policy makers.

We of course do not intend to argue that all school consolidation has been harmful, nor even that it is generally harmful, for we have no conclusive evidence in either direction. The point, rather, is that policy decisions do not take into account the indirect costs of an action operating through resources that lie outside the institution through which the intended benefits are achieved. The asymmetry they introduce is similar to that produced by individual family decisions as described earlier, though the mechanism is different.

School consolidation is only an example of school policy decisions taken to achieve a particular objective without attention to other unintended and indirect effects. Busing to achieve school desegregation is another such policy. If a policy had been designed to break the cycles of intergenerational closure, it could hardly have been more effective. The objections to busing have very likely arisen in large part from this effect and the obstacles it creates for parental socialization.*

The general principles involved in the actions that families take and those that governments take which destroy the effectiveness of communities for raising children are similar. The principle in the case of family decisions is this: An action on the part of a family brings it large benefits, but imposes small costs to all others in the community (ordinarily through removing from the community the resources provided by that family or some of its members). These actions taken in the aggregate end up making each family worse off, through the loss of community, while each in taking its action had intended to be better off.

The principle in the case of government decisions is this: A policy is taken to achieve a particular effect on children through the school, as the instrument of social policy. This policy has small effects at many other points in the social system (ordinarily through breaking or reducing the strength of social relations that aided in the schooling or socialization of children) that act in a direction opposite to that of the in-

---

*It is no accident that both the policies of school consolidation and desegregation, which have created extensive protest, have involved busing children to a school away from their neighborhood or local community. Both have similar effects in weakening resources of a community that can aid schooling and socialization of children. Some objections to busing for desegregation are of course due to racial prejudice; but many studies have shown that white parents leave the school system in large numbers not when black children are bused into "their" school, but when their children are bused to another school. This would not be the case if racial prejudice were the principal motive responsible for families leaving.

tended policy. The resulting effect on children may then be opposite of that which was the policy aim.

Choice of School and the Schooling Dilemma

The two orientations to education—as an instrument of society and the common culture or as an extension of the family and its particular culture—come into particularly intense conflict around the issues of where control should be for a child's school attendance. If the larger society (in the United States, ultimately the federal government) has control over assignment to school, the dilemma is resolved in the "instrument of society" direction. If the parent has control over assignment to school, then the dilemma is resolved in the "extension of family" direction. Traditionally, the common-school residential-assignment policy has resolved the issue in the former direction, but always with two exceptions: Parents could send their children to private school, if they could afford to do so; and parents could choose a school by changing residence, if they could afford it. In some cities (especially in the older cities of the East and Midwest), there was an additional exception: Some schools, particularly at the secondary level, had a specialized curriculum, and could be attended by choice. A portion of these were examination schools, with admission contingent on passing an examination (for example, Stuyvesant High School in New York, Boston Latin, Central High School in Philadelphia, Walnut Hills in Cincinnati).

In recent years, all three of these exceptions to the common-school policy have come to be more widely used. As incomes have risen, a much larger fraction of persons is able to choose residence on the basis of school. Increases, though quite small, in the fraction of children attending private schools have taken place. And there has been a growth in the public sector of magnet schools, which draw their children on the basis of choices by parent and student.

Most of these movements away from the residentially based common-school policy have involved individual choice of parents and represent the individualistic, rather than communal, extension of the family. This is true for the residential moves toward a public school seen as more desirable; it is true for the magnet school choices; and it is true for the increased use of independent schools in the private sector. A much smaller part of the movement has been in the communal direction, primarily among fundamentalist Christian religious groups, but also among some other religious groups which have traditionally not made much use of private schools.

It is especially valuable, given these changes and given the social changes discussed earlier, to examine the functioning of public schools, religiously based private schools, and independent private schools, and to examine their effects on the students within them. Much of the analysis of this book is directed to that aim. However, to carry out this aim is not merely to compare public and private schools, nor is it merely to compare parental choice versus administrative assignment to school. It is to compare schools that are principally agents of the larger society, schools that are principally agents of the religious community, and schools that are principally agents of the individual family. As will become evident in the analysis, there are some ways in which the two parts of the private sector (which we have termed communal and individualistic, or schools based on a functional community versus those based on a value community) differ more than either does from public sector schools. This will lead to complex issues of social policy in education, issues on which persons of good will may strongly disagree.

Preliminary to examination of the central questions of the book is an examination of the design of the schools in each sector and of the kinds of students who attend them. How do public, Catholic, and other private schools differ in organization and in character? Answers to this question may give some hint of the differences in goals held for schools in each of these sectors by those who design them, but their primary value is simply descriptive. As it will turn out, many of the differences seem to be due more to different constraints under which the private sectors and the public sector operate than to different aims. Nevertheless, the differences in design are valuable, both to give an overview of the institutions under discussion and to give an idea of the kinds of schools that some parents choose in lieu of public school.

Accompanying the examination of school design is a characterization of the types of families from which students in each sector come. This, along with the descriptions of the schools themselves, is intended to give some sense of what the schools and student bodies in each sector are like.

The analysis following chapter 2 can be seen as consisting of two parts, one directed toward the effects of these three sets of schools on outcomes during the period of high school itself, and the other directed toward their effects in the early years beyond high school. Chapters 3, 4, and 5 focus on the outcomes that occur during the high school period,

24

and chapters 6 and 7 examine effects on education and occupation in the early years beyond high school.

The focus of chapter 3 is most closely related to one of the central questions of *High School Achievement* (Coleman, Hoffer, and Kilgore 1982a) which was expressed there as the relative effects of public, Catholic, and other private schools on achievement. Here the examination is broadened to include achievement in a larger number of areas, and it is an examination of achievement growth during the last two years of high school, not merely levels of achievement.

In addition, the examination of achievement is set in the context of the deeper differences underlying these schools, which have been discussed in this chapter. On some grounds, one would expect schools designed to liberate children from the constraints imposed by parents —that is, the public schools—to bring about greater achievement, for they are less constrained by the parochialism and cultural homogeneity one can expect to find in a private sector school.

On other grounds, however, one would expect higher achievement in both sets of private sector schools, merely because those parents who spend the extra money necessary for a private school may have stronger interests in their childrens' achievement, an interest that should provide a stronger environment to achieve, and thus higher achievement.

There may, however, be additional differences due to the functional communities underlying Catholic schools or the value communities underlying other private schools that produce differential achievement apart from these two factors. Chapter 3 will examine these differences and their effects.

The remaining analytical questions, examined in chapters 4 through 7, concern questions that were not addressed (or in the case of the topics of chapter 5, only cursorily) in the earlier book. One of the most important of these is high school dropouts.

About a quarter of American high school age children leave school before finishing. We would expect that proportion to be smaller in the private sector than in the public sector because of the different mix of backgrounds in the public and private sectors. But what about dropouts among children of comparable backgrounds? And what about children in each sector who by their behavior or poor schoolwork are at risk of dropping out part way through high school?

In addition to dropping out of school, another outcome is transferring to a different school. It is commonly believed that the private sector gets rid of its failures by sending them back to the public schools. To what extent is this true? It is also believed by some that private schools get from public school students who are "not doing well," who are unchallenged or overlooked by the public high school. To what extent is this true? Many transfers, of course, are due to families moving or other factors unrelated to the student's performance or the school's functioning. An examination of transfers, and their past histories, can give some understanding of this. These outcomes, dropping out of school and transferring, are examined in chapter 4.

Chapter 5 is devoted to an examination of the relative effectiveness of public, Catholic, and other private high schools for students from different kinds of backgrounds and for students from different kinds of settings. The role of a functional community like that of which a Catholic school is a part and the role of a value community as provided in an independent private school differ depending on the student and the family background of that student. The question we will examine here is just how that role differs in these different background conditions. An especially important aspect of this examination concerns students from families that are deficient in some fashion, since change in family structure and function is an important aspect of current social change.

There are other outcomes of high school, however, beyond high school. Among those students who remain in their current school until graduation, there are various destinations. One outcome is just which destination a boy or girl is headed toward at the point of graduation. As with the other outcomes, the postgraduation destination is in considerable part a consequence of aspects of a student's background, in particular the family. But it is in part also a consequence of the school and the way that school functions. What can be said about the different destinations of students from comparable backgrounds and with comparable achievement levels, in public, Catholic, and other private high schools? These outcomes are examined in chapter 6.

Beyond high school are further questions. How do the intended destinations of students at the end of high school fare after a period of time has elapsed? In the High School and Beyond study, a sample of seniors in 1980 was followed two years later, examining what happened over that two year period and where they were in 1982. They were then restudied again in the Spring of 1984, four years out of high school. The 1980 sophomores were also followed at these two times, as seniors (or dropouts) in 1982, and two years beyond high school, in 1984. These data allow examining the important question of just what the more extended post-high school outcomes are that can be attributed to having attended a public school, a Catholic school, or an other private school. All these questions, concerning success in whatever activity beyond high school is chosen, are examined in chapter 7.

Two Orientations to Schooling

Finally, in chapter 8, we come back, in view of the evidence examined in earlier chapters, to the relation between the school and the family, community, and society. Schools complement the family and the immediate community as agents of socialization, which means that as the role and functioning of the family changes in modern society, different problems are posed for the school. It means also that the role and functioning of the school must change if the school is to constitute an effective complement to the changing institutions of the family and the community.

2

The Design and
the Clientele of Public
and Private Schools

SCHOOLS are constructed institutions. They contrast to the natural institution of the family in much the same way that constructed buildings contrast to the natural environment. They exhibit, like a building, the intent of those who designed and constructed them. In this chapter, we will examine differences in the design of public and private schools, both to see how different goals and constraints shape these schools, and for the simple descriptive purpose of giving an idea of how they are similar and how they differ.

In chapter 1, we described three orientations of schooling: as an agent of the family, an agent of the community, and an agent of the society. Both private and public schools embody these three orientations, but the mixture is different. Further, in examining separately the private sector in two parts, the Catholic schools as exemplifying the religious sector, and the other private schools as exemplifying the independent sector, we are examining schools that are to differing degrees agents of the family and the community. This difference results in somewhat

The Design and the Clientele of Schools

different goals and constraints, and somewhat different designs. Separating the influence of these two general types of factors—goals and constraints—on public, Catholic, and other private school differences is a problem we will address in a variety of ways throughout this chapter. The problem is most pronounced with respect to differences in school organizational form and functioning, and these are differences that are most consequential for what students learn or fail to learn in high school. It is then useful to examine how public and private schools compare in terms of three constraining factors: the types of students they enroll, financial resources, and school size.*

Who Chooses Private Schools?

"Private schools are not for everyone" is a truism heard whenever the subject of public and private school differences is addressed. Many people assume that any differences that may be found can be ultimately traced to differences in the students that public and private schools recruit. They do recruit somewhat different student bodies, and the differences are consequential for both school design and student outcomes. Whether the differences are sufficient to account for public and private school difference in school design and outcomes is a problem we will address at several points throughout this study.

High School and Beyond data allow us to assess the extent of similarities and differences. We will examine background variables that research has repeatedly shown to have important consequences for the organization of schools and the experiences of students: family income, parental education, race and ethnicity, family structure, and parental and student educational aspirations.

FAMILY SOCIOECONOMIC BACKGROUND

Private schools in the United States charge tuition and set their own admission criteria. On these grounds alone, one would correctly expect that one difference in backgrounds of students enrolled in private and

*An additional set of schools was included in the High School and Beyond sample, to correspond to what many people think of when they think of "elite" private schools. These were eleven private schools which had, in 1979, the highest ratio of National Merit Scholarship semifinalists to the number of seniors. One of these is a Catholic school, the others are schools in the independent private sector. In chapter 2 these are included in the tabulations for descriptive comparisons; in a few places they are included in the analyses of chapters 3 through 7.

29

public schools would be family income. The median income of parents of public sector students is $18,700, that of parents of Catholic sector students is $22,700, and that of other private school parents is $24,300. What is perhaps surprising is that the difference is not greater. There is a widespread assumption that private schools serve a socioeconomically elite clientele. The assumption is incorrect in a number of respects. In the first place, the historically dominant form of private schooling in the United States has been the Catholic schools. These schools are concentrated in urban areas, charge relatively little tuition by middle-class standards, and were originally designed for anything but an elite, serving instead recent immigrants struggling to find a place in American society. In the second place, elitest tendencies have never found the nation's public schools to be an uncongenial stage for expression and cultivation, thanks to the joint effect of the policy of assignment to school by residence and the practice of parents to locate residence according to income.

An examination of the distributions of family income and parental education in public and private schools bears out these points. In table 2.1, we see a considerable overlap between public and private school enrollments at each level of income. Private schools as a whole are less likely to enroll students from the lowest level of family income and more likely to enroll students from the highest income families. The non-Catholic "other" private schools enroll a number of students from very high-income families, in contrast to the Catholic schools. However, most of private school enrollment is from the middle income range.

A second aspect of family background likely to influence school

TABLE 2.1

Percentage of Students in Public and Private Schools, by Family Income Level: 1980 Sophomores

Annual Family Income	Public (%)	Catholic (%)	Other Private (%)	High-Performance Private (%)
$6,999 or less	8	2	2	1
$7,000 to $11,999	13	7	7	1
$12,000 to $15,999	18	15	16	4
$16,000 to $19,999	20	18	16	7
$20,000 to $24,999	18	21	20	6
$25,000 to $37,999	13	18	12	13
$38,000 or more	10	19	27	69
	100	100	100	100
Sample Size	(19,569)	(2,102)	(419)	(273)

Percentages are calculated using the High School and Beyond sample weights.

choice is parental education. The more schooling that a parent has completed, the more that parent will understand about what different schools have to offer, and the more likely the parent will place a high value on education. The greater knowledge is a product of both the parents' own experiences with schools and greater access to the information needed to make an informed decision.

Table 2.2 shows that private school students do have parents with higher levels of educational attainment (measured here by the mother's level of education). Again, the sector differences are most pronounced at the extremes of the distributions: private schools enroll proportionally fewer students whose mothers did not complete high school and more whose mothers completed a four-year college degree or higher. Of the three major sectors, the other private schools clearly are the most selective with respect to parental education. The Catholic and public schools are virtually identical in the representation of students whose mother's education ended with high school graduation or some college, accounting for almost 70 percent of the student bodies in both sectors.

A third dimension of family background is race and ethnicity. The 1980 public school sophomore cohort was 13 percent black and 13 percent Hispanic. The remainder was almost entirely non-Hispanic white, and in all of the subsequent breakdowns, this remainder will be simply referred to as "non-Hispanic white." Catholic schools enroll a smaller proportion of blacks (6 percent) but a comparable proportion of Hispanics (10 percent). Blacks are very sparsely represented in the other private schools (2 percent) and Hispanics are also underrepresented, though to a lesser extent (8 percent).

Minorities thus constitute a sizable part of Catholic school enroll-

TABLE 2.2

Percentage Distribution of Public and Private School Enrollments by Mother's Education

	Public (%)	Catholic (%)	Other Private (%)	High-Performance Private (%)
Less than high school	20	9	7	1
High school graduate	45	44	27	6
Some college	22	23	30	18
Four-year college degree	8	16	24	47
Graduate or professional degree	4	8	12	28
	100	100	100	100

ments, though not of other private school enrollments. While blacks are the most underrepresented group in the Catholic schools, the 6 percent figure is striking when one considers that relatively few blacks are Catholic. When enrollment rates are compared separately among Catholic and non-Catholic religion students, the same percentage of Catholic blacks and Catholic whites (18.7 percent) are enrolled in Catholic schools, and Catholic schools enroll a *higher* percentage of non-Catholic blacks (1.5 percent compared to 1.0 percent). Hispanic Catholics in contrast are much less likely than other Catholics to enroll in Catholic schools. (Coleman, Hoffer, and Kilgore 1982a: table 3–13).

Certain of these background variables on which public and private sector schools differ are indicators not of orientations held by parents, but of the resources they have. Income, in particular, is a direct measure of ability to pay for school tuition. In contrast, education (except as it is correlated with income) is an indicator of a difference in orientation, perhaps most fully an indicator of the value placed on education by parents. Other background characteristics are not clearly a measure of one or the other, resources or orientation. Race and ethnicity exemplify this. The fact that when religion is statistically controlled, black children are just as likely as whites to be in a Catholic school, despite their lower average income, implies that the orientation of black Catholics and black Protestants toward Catholic school is stronger than that of whites. The lesser likelihood of Hispanic Catholics to be in a Catholic school may represent different resources (because Hispanic income is lower on average than that of non-Hispanic whites) or a different orientation from that of non-Hispanic Catholics.

STUDENTS' EDUCATIONAL ASPIRATIONS

The influence of income, education, race and ethnicity on school organization is mediated in a number of ways: the academic preparation with which students enter high school, the students' values and aspirations, and the day-to-day support that students receive or fail to receive from their parents. Examining the students' own educational aspirations, students in private schools enter high school with higher educational aspirations than public students. The sophomores were asked to recall whether or not they expected to go to college when they were in 6th, 7th, 8th, and 9th grades. Table 2.3 indicates that private school students were more likely to plan on college when they were younger. The public-Catholic difference increases as the students advanced in school, while the public-other private difference decreases

TABLE 2.3

Percentage of Students Indicating Plans for College in 6th, 7th, 8th, and 9th Grades, by Sector

Grade	Public (%)	Catholic (%)	Other Private (%)	High-Performance Private (%)
6	39.0	52.2	55.0	89.8
7	42.5	58.2	58.0	93.3
8	49.7	70.4	66.2	95.9
9	57.4	75.9	69.7	96.9

slightly. While some part of these sector differences is likely due to school effects, some part is due to differences in family background.

FAMILY STRUCTURE AND FUNCTION

Another important aspect of students' background is the structure and stability of their home lives. Table 2.4 shows that whatever the difficulties for students and schools that single parent households or households where both parents work outside the home may entail, they are somewhat less frequent among private school students. Twenty-two percent of public students come from single parent households, compared to 14 percent of Catholic students and 16 percent of other private students. The pattern for mothers' labor force participation indicates that Catholic and other private students are about 5 percent less likely to have working mothers at each age level. Thus public-private differences in these aspects of students' household exist, but they are not large.

The items asking about parent-child relationships show only slight advantages for the private school students. The one exception to this pattern of comparability is found in the extent to which fathers monitor their sons' and daughters' progress in school: 10 percent more of the Catholic and other private school students report that their fathers keep close track.

The sector similarities in family structure and relationships do not carry over into the educational expectations that parents communicate to their children. The last two rows of table 2.4 show that about 20 percent more private sector students than public school students have parents expecting them to go to college after high school.

To summarize the answer to the question of who chooses private

TABLE 2.4

Characteristics of Students' Households and Parental Relationships by School Sector

	Public (%)	Catholic (%)	Other Private (%)	High-Performance Private (%)
Single-Parent Household	22	14	16	14
Mother's full-time labor force participation when student was . . .				
in high school	46	41	41	33
in elementary school	36	31	31	20
pre-school	26	21	22	19
Talk with parents about personal experience (at least once a week)	41	43	41	57
Mother keeps close track of school progress (true)	86	91	90	92
Father keeps close track of school progress (true)	68	78	78	85
My parents always know where I am and what I'm doing (true)	80	82	77	84
Mother expects me to go to college (1980)	58	79	74	98
Father expects me to go to college (1980)	50	72	74	95

schools, Catholic and other private school students tend to come from families that have somewhat higher incomes and educational levels, somewhat greater structural integrity, and higher expectations for their children's educational attainments. This pattern of advantage is not surprising, given the cost of private schooling in the United States. But the differences between student averages should not obscure the fact that private schools do enroll substantial numbers of students who do not come from advantaged backgrounds, and that the average differences themselves are not especially large. The Catholic schools in particular tend to approximate the public schools most closely in these respects. Because there are differences in student backgrounds among the school sectors, and because these differences are likely to have consequences for school organization and student outcomes, we will frequently introduce adjustments to provide statistical controls for these effects.

Organizational Constraints

SCHOOL EXPENDITURES

The principals of the High School and Beyond schools were asked to indicate the per pupil expenditures in their schools in both the 1980 and 1982 surveys. Table 2.5 presents the distribution and average of their responses for each of the four sectors. In this and most of the subsequent tables in this chapter, the school-level data are presented in terms of the number of students they enroll. Thus we see that for the average public school student, the expenditure was $2,016. Expenditures in Catholic schools are substantially lower than the public levels, coming to only $1,353 per student. Expenditures are considerably higher than the public schools in the other private and high-performance private schools, where expenditures on the average student are $2,777 and $4,648, respectively. Because the Catholic sector is larger than the

TABLE 2.5

Annual Per Pupil Expenditures in Public and Private Schools in 1979–80

| | School Sector | | | |
	Public	Catholic	Other Private	High-Performance Private
Mean	$2016	$1353	$2777	$4648
Std. Deviation	(759)	(446)	(1,643)	(1,810)
< $1,000	5.9	24.3	0	0
$1,000–1,500	15.5	39.0	17.4	0
$1,500–2,000	31.0	26.8	21.2	4.6
$2,000–2,500	23.9	7.1	23.7	0
$2,500–3,000	14.2	2.6	6.6	10.0
$3,000–4,000	7.8	0.2	2.3	24.2
$4,000 +	1.7	0	28.8	61.2
	100.0	100.0	100.0	100.0
Sample Size (N of Schools)	800	73	17	10

Weighted by number of students.

other private sector, the average for the private sector as a whole is $1,837, about $200 less than the public school average.

The distributions of students by expenditure level show quite different patterns across the four sets of schools. The public and Catholic schools are distributed in a roughly normal fashion around their respective means, but the other private schools are distributed in a distinctly bimodel pattern, with about 60 percent of students attending schools below the sector average, and a fraction in schools with very high expenditures. This points to a marked heterogeneity among the other private schools, a diversity that is evident in a variety of ways through the course of this study.

The differential constraints due to the different means of financing education are apparent both in the Catholic schools and in the low-expenditure mode of the other private schools. In both of these sectors, the average income of parents is above the public school average. And for both of these sectors, the parents have exhibited their interest in their children's education, which must on average, be above the level of parental interest in the public sector. On two counts, then, we would expect more to be spent on the average private school student than on the average public school student.

Why, then, is expenditure less than the public school average in the Catholic sector and in a large proportion of the other private schools? The answer, of course, lies in the fact that public schools are financed through use of the government's power to tax, while private sector schools are financed directly by parents' payments (together with subsidies from the religious body in some religiously based schools). This does not in itself imply that everything else being equal, per pupil expenditure would be higher in public schools than in private ones. The fact that it is higher, even when parental income and interest are lower in the public sector, would, however, hold implications for a public finance theorist in economics. It would imply that there is both a private interest in a child's education and a public interest. The difference between what average parents would pay for their child's education and what is actually paid in public schools would be a measure of the degree of societal interest in the education of all children in the society. Along with that additional interest comes an interest in different things, leading the schools to spend the money in somewhat different ways, as indicated later in the chapter. At this point, however, we can think of the additional expenditure on public education beyond that which would obtain if education were entirely financed by parents as a measure of the public interest in education (in contrast to parents' private interests in their own child's education).

The Design and the Clientele of Schools

Little more need be said at this point concerning the levels of student expenditures in the different schools. It is clear from table 2.5 that much less is spent on students in the Catholic schools than in the other sectors, but that considerable variability within and overlap between sectors is also present.

SCHOOL SIZE

The financial resources available to a school represent one important constraint on school functioning, with strong implications for how the school is staffed and the programs the school is able to offer. From the perspective of the school principal, a second basic constraint is school size. School size is likely to have a number of consequences for the differences examined later in this chapter and the rest of the book. At the level of the school, one consequence of school size is the constraint it sets on curricular and extracurricular diversity. A larger school should be able to provide more in the way of program offerings and diverse professional expertise.

Additional program offerings and specialization are not the only consequences of larger school size. Larger size results in less intensive relations between students and teachers, for students spend a smaller proportion of their school experience with any single teacher. Larger schools also have smaller proportions of their students engaged in extracurricular activities.* Parental involvement in the school may also suffer with larger school size. Perhaps as a result of these processes, larger schools tend to have greater problems with student social integration and discipline.

These negative consequences of larger size are likely to be particularly distasteful to members of closely knit functional communities, such as that of a Catholic parish, for social cohesion is a crucial component of these communities' goals for these schools. On this account, we would expect private religiously based schools to be smaller on average than public schools, even if the limited potential clientele within easy access were not a constraint. It is likely also that the closer teacher-student relations inherent in small schools constitute a value for the individual parents of other private schools, so that we would expect them also to be smaller than public schools, even if there were no lack of clientele.

Table 2.6 shows the distributions of public and private schools and students by school enrollment size. This table indicates that public schools tend to be much larger than private schools. The average public

*(See Barker and Gump 1964, and Morgan and Alwin 1980).

TABLE 2.6

Size Distribution of Public and Private Schools

School Size	Public	Catholic	Other Private	High-Performance Private
Mean	1381	797	533	344
Std. Deviation	(810)	(421)	(636)	(98)
8–99	1.0	0.8	19.7	0
100–299	6.3	10.1	38.3	36.4
300–499	7.2	16.4	10.5	63.6
500–999	20.6	44.5	17.3	0
1,000–1,499	24.6	21.9	0	0
1,500–1,999	19.6	4.3	14.3	0
2,000–2,999	17.5	1.9	0	0
3,000 +	3.4	0	0	0
	100.0	100.0	100.0	100.0
Sample Size	816	82	26	10

Weighted by number of students.

student attends a school enrolling 1,381 students. In contrast, the average Catholic student attends a school with only 797 students, and the average other private student attends a school with only 533 students. Seventy percent of the public schools, enrolling 35 percent of public students, have enrollments of less than 1,000 students in grades 10 through 12. The comparable figures for the Catholic sector are 88 percent of schools and 72 percent of students in schools with less than 1,000. Virtually all of the other private schools fall into this lower end of the size range.

The movement toward consolidating small schools into large ones has been justified in part by the argument that larger schools are able to realize economies of scale. The existence of overall economies of scale, however, is in considerable doubt, because of offsetting increases in management costs. In order to assess whether such economies are present, one would need to compare different sized schools that provided comparable services. While such comparisons are beyond the scope of the present study, we can obtain an idea of the relationship of size to expenditures, and how these differ in the public and Catholic sectors by calculating the average per pupil expenditures for schools of different enrollment sizes in these two sectors.

Table 2.7 shows extensive differences between the public and Catholic sectors. In both the public schools and the Catholic schools, per pupil expenditures are highest in the smallest schools (schools with less than 100 students in the public sector; schools with less than 300 students in the Catholic sector). For public schools, expenditures are lower and

TABLE 2.7

Average Per Pupil Expenditures (in thousands of dollars) by School Size and Sector

	School Sector		
School Size	Public	Catholic	Other Private
< 100	$2.52	$0.80	$1.83
	*(13)	(1)	(5)
100–299	1.91	1.76	2.60
	(43)	(10)	(6)
300–499	1.87	1.34	5.87
	(46)	(12)	(2)
500–999	1.88	1.38	1.77
	(146)	(29)	(3)
1,000–1,499	2.06	1.30	NA
	(177)	(16)	
1,500–1,999	2.05	0.87	2.01
	(147)	(3)	(1)
2,000–2,999	2.13	0.96	NA
	(140)	(1)	
3,000 or more	2.36	NA	NA
	(18)		

*Sample sizes are in parentheses.

roughly stable for the broad middle range, but increase in the largest public schools to a level that is comparable to that of the smallest. In contrast, in the Catholic schools, larger school size bears a consistent, though modest, negative relationship with expenditures (ignoring the smallest and the largest school categories, where only one Catholic school is found in each). Quite clearly, the factors that lead to these apparent economies of scale in Catholic schools do not appear to be operative among the public schools.

School Functioning

The constraints of students' backgrounds, school size and expenditures, can be expected to exercise an important influence on the types of programs and variety of courses that a school offers. While on this account alone we should find differences in the courses and programs of public and private schools, it is also likely that the goals of the schools will differ, owing to different relations they have with students, their families, and the state. Differences in goals are particularly evident when the curriculum organization and course offerings of public and private schools are compared. As many observers have noted, public schools typically have a much more complex set of goals, seeking to do many different things for many different kinds of students. Vocational curricula, handicap programs, remedial and gifted programs, bilingual and bicultural programs, specialized art and music curricula, and a great variety of nontraditional academic courses are frequently found in public schools and can be seen as responses to demands not only from parents but also from interest groups acting through the state via legislation. This sort of complexity is generally not found in the private high schools. In this section, we will describe in some detail the nature of the public and private differences along these lines and, to a limited extent, address the question of why these differences are present.

PARTICIPATION IN FEDERAL PROGRAMS

One of the more striking consequences of the different orientations of public and private schools is the difference in the schools' federal program participation. As agents of the state, the public schools have incorporated a number of these programs into their curricula. Private schools, in contrast, generally maintain only minimal ties to the federal government.

Table 2.8 shows the participation rates by school sector in each of the programs that were asked about in the 1980 High School and Beyond administrator questionnaires. Substantial private school participation is limited to a few of the Elementary and Secondary Education Act programs, and most of this involvement is by Catholic schools. Virtually all Catholic schools use federal funds for library purposes, and Catholic schools are about as likely as public schools to participate in the supplemental centers program and ethnic heritage series. Catholic schools are much less likely to obtain Title I and VII funds for economic disadvantaged students and bilingual programs, respectively.

Private schools make only minimal use of federal vocational education dollars. About 14 percent of Catholic schools participate in the cooperative education program, where students are placed in outside jobs that complement their school program, but this is the only area of notable private sector participation.

This extreme of differential participation in federal programs mirrors only in part the obvious difference in orientation of the three sectors: public schools as agents of the state, Catholic schools as agents of the religious community, and other private schools as agents of the family. They reflect also the constraints instituted by some state education

TABLE 2.8

Participation Rates by School Sector in Selected Federal Programs:
Spring 1980[a]

| | | School Sector | | |
| | U.S. Total (%) | Public (%) | Catholic (%) | Other Private (%) |
Program				
Elementary and Secondary Education Act (ESEA)				
Title I Economic Disadvantaged	56	70	24	1
IVB Library	80	87	99	40
IVC Educational Innovation	31	38	22	0
IVD Supplementary Centers	22	24	31	12
VII Bilingual Education	11	13	0	3
IX Ethnic Heritage Series	7	8	13	0
Vocational Education Act 63 (VEA)				
Consumer and homemaking	59	76	8	1
Basic program	53	68	5	1
Persons with special needs	38	49	5	1
Cooperative education	45	56	14	6
High school work study	44	56	6	6
Comprehensive Employment and Training Act (CETA)	65	82	17	4
Upward Bound	17	21	8	2
Talent Search	13	16	4	1
Indian Education Act	7	9	0	0
Emergency School Aid Act—Desegregation	7	8	2	0
ROTC	7	9	1	0

[a]Weighted by number of students.

agencies which effectively limit to public schools participation in some federal programs that formally permit private sector participation.

PROGRAMS AND COURSES

The relationships of student background, school size, and school financial resources to student educational outcomes are not direct. Rather, they are mediated in numerous ways that often vary significantly between schools. The single most important aspect of school internal organization is the allocation of students to curriculum programs. Schools typically divide their student bodies into three more or less distinct programs: academic or college preparatory, general, and vocational. Both the kinds and quality of courses that students take in high school are largely determined by the program they are assigned to or choose. Not surprisingly, student outcomes bear a close relationship with their program placements, with academic program students consistently showing higher levels of achievement, lower rates of dropping out, and higher rates of college attendance.

Because of its importance for student outcomes, curriculum differentiation or "tracking" has generated considerable controversy. Defenders of the practice argue that grouping students into homogeneous ability groups within subject areas allows instruction to be paced according to the varied preparation of students, and thus enhances learning for all. And by allowing students to choose the subjects they want to study, program differentiation increases student interest in school and thereby reduces dropping out. In contrast, critics have charged that tracking generates greater inequalities in outcomes by instituting lower expectations, and by foreclosing academic paths for general and vocational students.

On the grounds of the student background differences among public and private schools alone, one would expect to find differences among the schools in the allocation of students to different programs. Nonetheless, we have also shown that private schools enroll substantial numbers of students from less advantaged backgrounds, and substantial numbers who, at least at the beginning of high school, did not plan to go to college. Yet there are also other grounds from which sector differences can be predicted as well. In chapter 1 we discussed two possible consequences of a functional community for schooling outcomes, possible egalitarian consequences from the greater responsiveness to parental preferences, and the possible inegalitarian consequences from intergenerational transmission of status within functional communities. On the basis of the egalitarian consequences, one would predict that Catholic and other private schools would be less likely to pursue extensive curriculum differentiation and would be more likely to place students in college-preparatory programs. On the basis of the inegalitarian consequences, the prediction is the opposite.

Student Curriculum Programs and School Organization. Table 2.9 shows the distribution of public and private school students across the different types of curriculum programs. Catholic and other private students are much more likely than public school students to be in academic or college-preparatory programs and much less likely to be in a vocational or general program.

Vocational program enrollments in the Catholic and other private schools are concentrated in business or office training and are practi-

The Design and the Clientele of Schools

TABLE 2.9

Percentages of Students Enrolled in Academic, General, and Vocational Programs, by Sector

	Public (%)	Catholic (%)	Other Private (%)	High-Performance Private (%)
Academic	35.7	72.1	71.1	97.5
General	34.9	17.8	18.6	1.7
Vocational—total	29.4	10.1	10.3	0.8
Agriculture	3.3	0.3	1.5	1.0
Business or Office	10.9	6.9	1.4	0
Trade or Industrial	7.2	1.1	2.3	0
Distributive Education	2.2	0.6	0.8	0
Health	1.3	0.2	0.6	0
Home Economics	1.8	0.2	1.2	0
Technical	2.6	0.9	2.5	0
	100.0	100.0	100.0	100.0
Sample Size	(20,758)	(2,339)	(439)	(321)

Percentages are based on student self-reported program participation, taken from the 1982 followup of the 1980 sophomore cohort.

cally nonexistent in the other areas. As the other areas are likely to be more expensive than business training, the lower rates of private schools having them probably reflect in part the lower budgets of private schools.

The manner in which programs are incorporated into schools can take either of two forms: the school can specialize around a particular type of program, or the school can provide a variety of programs under the same roof. Table 2.10 presents a classification of public and private schools based on their students' programs. A school is classified here as academic if the administrator indicated that 90 percent or more of the school's students are enrolled in a college-preparatory program; vocational schools are schools with 90 percent or more in vocational programs; general schools have 90 percent or more in a general program of studies. Comprehensive schools are schools with a mix of academic, vocational, and general program enrollments (this typology is drawn from Lewin-Epstein, 1982).

This table shows very large differences between public and private school organization. Two-thirds of the public schools, enrolling three-quarters of all public school students, are organized as comprehensive schools. The corresponding figures for the private schools are much

TABLE 2.10

Percentage Distribution of Students by School Curriculum Specialization and School Sector

School Program Organization	School Sector			
	Public (%)	Catholic (%)	Other Private (%)	High-Performance Private (%)
Comprehensive	76.6	48.1	33.4	0
Specialized:				
Academic	3.3	49.6	54.2	100.0
Vocational	9.7	2.1	0	0
General	9.9	0.2	12.4	0
Other	0.5	0	0	0
	100.0	100.0	100.0	100.0

Weighted by numbers of students.

lower: about one-half of the Catholic school students, one-third of the other private school school, and none of the high-performance school students are enrolled in comprehensive schools. The Catholic sector is about evenly split between the comprehensive form and specialized academic schools. The other private sector enrolls a majority of its students in academic schools, but also has a substantial number of general schools, enrolling about one-eighth of the students of this sector.

The comprehensive schools within the public and private sectors also exhibit different mixes of program enrollment. While public comprehensives are roughly balanced between the three program types, the Catholic and other private schools tend to have most students (two-thirds in each) enrolled in academic programs (from tabulations not presented here).

Curriculum programs are not the only way in which students are grouped. Instruction within schools is also commonly differentiated by ability groups, particularly in the areas of English, history, mathematics, and science. One of the items included in the principal's questionnaire asked whether the school employs ability-grouping for 10th grade English.* Table 2.11 shows the percentages of students enrolled in schools using ability-grouping. The first row of this table indicates that ability-grouping is used extensively by both public and private schools:

*The questionnaire also asked if ability-grouping is used for 12th grade English. We have chosen to use the 10th grade item, because 12th grade English is frequently not required by schools and is thus often self-selected, usually by higher ability students. This may well account for the fact that substantially fewer schools report using ability-grouping in 12th grade English.

The Design and the Clientele of Schools

TABLE 2.11

*Percentage of Student Enrollment in Schools Using Ability-Grouping,
by School Specialization and Sector*

	Public (%)	Catholic (%)	Other Private (%)	High-Performance Private (%)
All Schools	62.8	65.8	43.4	9.8
By School Specialization				
Comprehensive Schools	66.9	55.0	89.6	NA
Academic Schools	36.6	78.9	16.9	9.8
Vocational Schools	63.6	NA	NA	NA
General Schools	37.9	NA	42.5	NA

Over 60 percent of both public and Catholic school students and about 40 percent of other private school students are in ability-grouped schools.

The lower four rows of table 2.11 show the prevalence of ability-grouping within each of the four school types that we identified earlier. These figures indicate that grouping in the public sector tends to be highest in comprehensive and vocational schools, where about two-thirds of their students are grouped. Ability-grouping is somewhat less frequent in the Catholic comprehensives but is pervasive in the Catholic academic schools, where almost 80 percent of the students are ability grouped. In the other private sector, ability-grouping is used extensively in the (larger) comprehensive schools. Ability-grouping is used by only one of the high-performance private schools in our sample.

The data indicate, then, that the dominant mode of school organization in the public sector is the comprehensive form, with students about equally divided among the three programs. Most private school students, in contrast, either attend specialized academic schools or enroll in academic programs within comprehensive schools. Despite these differences in school organizational form, public and private students are about equally likely to attend schools that use ability-grouping, at least for sophomore English instruction. Catholic schools are distinguished from public and other private schools in that the former use extensive ability-grouping within specialized academic schools, while ability grouping in the public and other private sectors is used most extensively in comprehensive schools.

The most striking difference between public and private school curricula is the much greater likelihood of academic program placement in the private schools. How might these differences be accounted for? At least three alternative hypotheses are plausible. One explanation is that the differing constraints of size, material resources, and student backgrounds for public and private schools can account for the organizational differences. According to this explanation, schools differentiate their curriculum to meet the needs of different student backgrounds. However, if a school is small, it cannot afford to differentiate programs and must treat all students similarly even though students come from diverse backgrounds. Schools with homogeneous student bodies will specialize their curriculum accordingly: High socioeconomic status (SES), schools will be academic, low SES schools will be vocational (if resources are available) or general (if resources are low). By this argument, private schools are predominantly academic, because their constituencies are predominantly higher SES and because the schools are constrained by small enrollments.

A second possible explanation is that the different patterns of school organization follow from differences in the orientations of the communities that the schools serve. According to this explanation, the more diverse curriculum and standards found in the public schools reflect the diversity and lack of consensus found in the localities the schools serve. The narrower and more focused curriculum of the private schools reflects the consensus or dominant value orientations in these schools.

We can test the hypothesis that student body and resource constraints account for the public and private differences in curriculum organization by using data on the schools and the students they enroll. The question we address here is whether the average private school would exhibit a rate of academic program enrollment comparable to the average public school rate if the private schools recruited a student body of the same size and with a social background comparable to the average public school. To answer this question, we regressed the proportion of students enrolled in an academic program on school average socioeconomic status (SES), the school proportion black and Hispanic, the proportion of students in the school who indicated plans for college in the 8th grade, the proportion of students who indicated their mothers expect them to go to college, the standard deviation of student SES in the school, the natural logarithm of the school's 12th grade enrollment, and school sector (two 0–1 variables, one for Catholic school and one for other private school).

The regression results (not tabulated here) indicate that, controlling for the different constraints that public and private schools are subject to, Catholic schools are still predicted to enroll about 23 percent more students in an academic program than are public schools. The other private versus public gap is slightly less, about 19 percent, and both the Catholic and other private increments are statistically significant.

The Design and the Clientele of Schools

The evidence from this analysis then indicates that the first of the two hypotheses cannot account for all of the public-private differences in academic program assignments. This gives only indirect support, of course, for the other hypothesis, that higher academic program enrollments in the private schools reflect the stronger ties of these schools to the communities they serve. At this point we can say that the tendency of private schools to enroll more students in academic programs cannot be explained by the smaller school size and the more advantaged background of private school students.

Course Offerings and Coursework. The sector differences in programs just examined are likely to have a number of important consequences for students. One set of consequences is the courses that students are required to take or are directed toward.

Table 2.12 presents the average semesters of coursework completed by students from the beginning of the 10th grade through the end of the 12th grade, separately by the student's program of study and school sector. The first five subject areas listed in this table represent the traditional academic courses of high school. Comparing the sectors in these courses, we find that, with few exceptions, private school students in all three curriculum programs take more semesters than their public school counterparts. The exceptions to this pattern are found exclusively in the other private schools, largely for vocational program students (which are few in number in these schools). In the public-Catholic comparisons, the largest differences are between general program students. The general program in the other private schools appear to be quite comparable with the public schools' general program. The largest sector differences for academic program students are found in mathematics and foreign language, where both Catholic and other private school students take substantially more courses than public school students.

The last four subject areas listed in table 2.12 represent the vocational courses taken by students. Here we find that the pattern of sector differences previously observed is reversed: Public students take a greater number of vocational courses. An exception to this is that Catholic school students in general and vocational programs tend to take more courses in business, office, and sales. The vocational area that Catholic schools are most lacking in is trade and industry. This likely reflects at least in part the high cost of providing these courses.

In sum, table 2.12 shows that private students tend to take a more academically focused set of courses than public students, and that this greater focus is found even when students within the same programs are compared. The greatest sector differences in academic coursework

TABLE 2.12

Average Semesters of Coursework Completed, 10th to 12th Grades, by Curriculum Program and School Sector

Subject Area	Curriculum Program		Public	Catholic	Other Private	High-Performance Private
				School Sector		
1. Mathematics	Academic	(A)	5.01	5.38	5.38	5.69
	General	(G)	3.64	4.45	4.08	5.17
	Vocational	(V)	3.41	3.66	2.77	—
	Total		4.07	5.00	4.80	5.68
2. English or		A	6.01	6.12	5.99	6.13
Literature		G	5.69	6.03	5.94	6.44
		V	5.58	5.92	6.31	—
	Total		5.77	6.08	6.00	6.14
3. Foreign		A	2.85	3.84	4.28	5.70
Language		G	1.14	2.25	1.35	4.01
		V	0.83	1.78	0.69	—
	Total		1.66	3.28	3.19	5.70
4. History and		A	4.75	4.82	4.91	4.46
Social Studies		G	4.49	4.80	4.57	5.61
		V	4.33	4.54	4.09	—
	Total		4.54	4.79	4.75	4.50
5. Science		A	4.38	4.52	4.56	4.50
		G	2.96	3.52	3.13	4.44
		V	2.55	2.76	3.18	—
	Total		3.36	4.13	4.07	4.50
6. Business,		A	1.77	1.69	1.08	0.20
Office, Sales		G	1.98	2.30	2.06	0.44
		V	2.63	3.23	1.87	—
	Total		2.09	1.98	1.40	0.24
7. Trade and		A	0.53	0.13	0.31	0.09
Industry		G	1.14	0.52	0.69	0.33
		V	1.62	0.83	1.38	—
	Total		1.05	0.29	0.51	0.13
8. Technical		A	0.56	0.24	0.32	0.25
		G	0.66	0.44	0.51	1.03
		V	1.02	0.94	0.71	—
	Total		0.72	0.36	0.41	0.29
9. Other		A	0.82	0.73	0.73	0.16
Vocational		G	1.30	0.82	1.15	0.56
		V	1.71	0.95	2.13	—
	Total		1.24	0.77	0.98	0.19
Total Semesters of		A	23.0	24.7	25.1	26.5
Academic Coursework		G	17.9	21.1	19.1	25.7
Completed		V	16.7	18.7	17.0	—
	Total		19.4	23.3	22.8	26.5
Total Semesters of		A	3.7	2.8	2.4	0.7
Vocational Coursework		G	5.1	4.1	4.4	2.4
Completed		V	7.0	6.0	6.1	—
	Total		5.1	3.4	3.3	0.7
Total Semesters of		A	26.7	27.5	27.5	27.1
Coursework Completed		G	23.0	25.1	23.5	28.0
		V	23.7	24.6	23.1	—
	Total		24.5	26.7	26.1	27.2
Percentage of Students		A	35.5	67.4	65.6	95.8
in Each Program		G	36.6	22.0	24.7	3.5
		V	27.9	10.6	9.8	0.7
			100.0	100.0	100.0	100.0

are found in the areas that most students find most difficult—foreign language and mathematics.

Why do private school students take more academic coursework than public students, even when curriculum program is controlled? Again we are faced with a set of alternative hypotheses. One hypothesis is that the differences are a simple function of public and private students' family background differences: Private students tend to come from families that have higher academic expectations for their children and thus require their children to take a more academically focused set of courses.

An alternative explanation is that it is the schools that exercise this authority over students and not the parents, who lack the time and information to effectively monitor their children's school schedules. A school's power to exercise this authority is limited, however, if the school has a differentiated curriculum program, for differentiation implies that different standards are applicable to different students. A student who would rather not do the work involved in another semester of mathematics then has appeal to a set of standards that legitimate his wishes. A school that has less variability in the standards and expectations that it holds for students has less room for students to maneuver in a less demanding direction. The school program in this case functions to constrain students in a way that is consistent with parental preferences, which parents could not achieve on their own.

A straightforward test of the first hypothesis can be made by comparing the public and private differences in coursework completed after controlling for the effects of student background. Table 2.13 presents the predicted differences for students with two different types of family and academic background, that of the average public school student and that of the average Catholic school student. This table indicates that the Catholic school advantages in mathematics, English, and foreign language coursework cannot be wholly or even largely attributed to the more advantaged family and academic backgrounds of Catholic students. The Catholic school advantages in all areas shown in table 2.13 except foreign language are about the same size as the advantages shown in table 2.12. The Catholic foreign language advantage is reduced by one-half with the controls for background, but is still large and statistically significant.

However, comparison of other private schools with public schools shows that substantial advantages are present only in English and foreign language once the controls for background are introduced. In mathematics, social studies, and science, other private and public school

TABLE 2.13

Predicted Public-Private Differences in Semesters of Academic Coursework Completed, Controlling for Family and Academic Background

	Average Public Background		Average Catholic Background	
	Catholic Minus Public	Other Private Minus Public	Catholic Minus Public	Other Private Minus Public
1. Mathematics	0.27*	−0.15	0.33*	0.01
2. English or Literature	0.20*	0.23	0.13*	0.20
3. Foreign Language	0.50*	0.19	0.52*	0.57
4. History or Social Studies	0.08	−0.03	−0.06	−0.04
5. Science	0.06	−0.03	0.12	0.01

Semesters of coursework completed in 11th and 12th grades.
Based on weighted least squares regressions of the coursework variables on SES, siblings, rooms in household, both parents present, mother worked-elementary, mother worked-pre-elementary, talk with parents, father's and mother's college expectations, race, ethnicity, sex, 8th grade college plans, and sophomore achievement. Sophomore achievement controls varied with the type of coursework: math courses—math achievement; English and foreign language courses—vocabulary, reading, and writing achievement; history courses—vocabulary, reading, writing, and civics achievement; science courses—science and math achievement.
*Estimated sector effect statistically significant at $p < .05$ level.

students with the same backgrounds take about the same number of courses.

The background hypothesis thus is not sustained for the Catholic advantages in academic courses but does appear applicable to several of the other private school advantages. Stated differently, the results indicate that student background has relatively little effect on coursework in the Catholic schools and a relatively large effect in the other private schools. The larger effect in the latter may be either a between-schools or a within-schools phenomenon, and the alternatives have quite different substantive implications. As a within-school phenomenon, the greater effect of background would mean that students from less advantaged backgrounds are channeled into less demanding lines of study, with fewer academic course requirements. As a between-school phenomenon, the greater effect would imply that schools organized by less advantaged communities tend to maintain less demanding school-wide standards for coursework. We will return to these questions about the functioning of other private schools at a later point.

EXTRACURRICULAR ACTIVITIES

In addition to the program of academic courses, virtually all high schools offer a variety of extracurricular activities for their students.

The Design and the Clientele of Schools

Some activities are direct extensions of the graded curriculum, providing more highly motivated students with opportunities to deepen their interests in particular subjects and to associate with students and faculty who share their interests. Most activities, however, are relatively independent of the regular curriculum and represent an additional or alternative source of affiliation with the school.

The most obvious reason to expect differences among public and private schools in their rates of extracurricular participation is the smaller size of private schools, for earlier research has shown that smaller schools have greater participation (Barker and Gump, 1964). But to focus on size alone ignores the sources of demand for extracurricular activities, and the demand may well vary with the social context of school, independently of size. Most extracurricular activities are designed to enhance the social integration of students, and the need for such integration reflects the lack of alternative bases of attachment. In this light, one would expect the Catholic schools to show lower rates of extracurricular participation, for if our argument is correct, the Catholic schools, of the three types of schools, are most closely linked to the communities they serve.

Table 2.14 shows that public and private schools exhibit a number of differences in the levels of student participation in extracurricular activities. In general, participation rates are comparable for most activi-

TABLE 2.14

Percentage of Students Participating in Extracurricular Activities, by Sector

	Public (%)	Catholic (%)	Other Private (%)	High-Performance Private (%)
Varsity athletics	36.1	37.3	57.4	70.1
Other athletics	40.4	47.7	46.3	58.7
Cheerleading, prep club	14.8	15.8	11.5	18.7
Debating or drama	13.1	14.9	28.4	30.7
Band or orchestra	15.5	8.6	9.6	7.2
Chorus or dance	19.6	18.3	29.1	27.3
Hobby clubs	19.4	20.3	17.2	26.9
Honorary clubs	16.3	21.0	13.4	16.7
School newspaper, yearbook	17.5	28.5	43.0	55.3
School subject-matter clubs	21.1	20.6	15.5	17.3
Student Council	16.9	19.0	22.7	27.9
Vocational education clubs	26.4	4.1	9.6	1.2
Percentage of students participating in three or more activities	26.7	24.3	33.7	37.9
Percentage of students participating in no activities	10.5	14.3	8.0	3.6

ties between the public and Catholic schools but are higher in the other private and high-performance private schools. Public school students are more likely than private school students to participate in band or orchestra and, to a much greater extent, in vocational education clubs. The other private and high-performance private school advantages are greatest in athletics, debate or drama, chorus or dance, and newspaper or yearbook.

The comparability of the public and Catholic school participation rates suggest that these two types of schools rely to a similar extent on the extracurriculum to integrate students. Whether this translates into a comparable capacity to keep students in school is a question that will be examined in chapter 4.

PARENTAL INVOLVEMENT IN THE SCHOOL

As school officials are quick to point out, one of the most important factors in a child's success in school is the degree to which his or her parents are actively involved in the child's education. Parental involvement is of course in part a reflection of the parent's orientation toward education, but involvement is also affected by school design, the extent to which opportunities for satisfying involvement are made available.

Parental involvement takes a great variety of forms. At a minimum, it may entail simply talking to the child about his or her school experience. Parents may also talk to teachers and school administrators, help with school projects, participate in PTA or related organizations, and otherwise become directly involved in the life of the school. Indirect mechanisms of parental influence can be of considerable importance, depending on the structure of the school. Such mechanisms might involve parents of children in the same school talking together about the school and its personnel, and thereby forming opinions in favor of or against what they understand about aspects of school life. Indeed, such informal networks of parents are frequently the origins of "issues" that come before school boards and school administrators.

The information available to us about the kind and extent of parental involvement is limited. One source is the High School and Beyond 1982 senior questionnaire, which asked students to indicate how frequently their parents or guardians engaged in various school-related activities. The percentages of students in each sector indicating their parents had participated in each of these functions are shown in table 2.15. Some

The Design and the Clientele of Schools

TABLE 2.15

Parental Involvement in the School as Reported by Students, by School Sector

Since the beginning of this school year, how often have your parents (or guardians) . . .	School Sector			
	Public (%)	Catholic (%)	Other Private (%)	High-Performance Private (%)
Attended a parent-teacher conference	39.2	56.4	47.3	64.4
Attended a PTA meeting	19.9	35.1	33.3	23.8
Visited classes	21.0	25.2	22.9	26.8
Phoned or saw a teacher, counselor, or principal when you had a problem	45.5	43.1	49.8	51.6
Did volunteer work such as fund raising or assisting on a school project	27.2	45.8	43.6	47.2

Percentage of students responding "once in a while" or "often."

large differences are found between public and private schools in this respect. Parents of private school students are more likely to attend parent-teacher conferences, PTA meetings, and to do volunteer work for the schools. In contrast, public and private school parents are about equally likely to phone the school when their children have problems and to visit classes.

A second source of information on parental involvement in the school are the 1980 and 1982 High School and Beyond principal's questionnaires. The administrators were asked to indicate the extent to which parents' lack of interest in students' progress and school matters were generally problems in their schools. The first two rows of table 2.16 show that public school administrators are much more likely to consider these as problems than private school officials. Principals of almost 20 percent of the Catholic school students believe that parental lack of interest in school matters is a problem, but even this relatively high rate is still less than half of the corresponding public school rate.

Administrators were also asked to indicate the extent of parent-school hostile confrontations and contacts occasioned by student disciplinary or academic problems. Confrontations tend to be rarest in Catholic schools, but about equally common in the public and other private schools. Parent-school contacts over students' problems tend

TABLE 2.16

Parental Involvement in the School as Reported by Administrators, by School Sector

	Public (%)	Catholic (%)	Other Private (%)	High-Performance Private (%)
Parents lack interest in students progress[a]	52.9	6.7	7.6	0.0
Parents lack interest in school matters[a]	54.9	18.0	7.4	0.0
Verbal confrontations between parents and teachers[a]	21.7	8.3	19.2	13.5
Verbal confrontations between parents and administrators[b]	31.8	5.8	44.1	NA
Average percentage of parents contacted re: student discipline problems[b]	9.1	5.8	8.4	8.1
Average percentage of parents contacted re: student academic problems[b]	14.4	10.3	18.9	11.2

[a]"Serious" or "moderate" problem in the school (1980 items).
[b]"At least once a month" (1982 items).

to be infrequent in all schools and show little relation to school sector.

In summary, tables 2.15 and 2.16 show that parental involvement in the school tends to be greater in the private schools. Public school officials are less likely to feel that parents are interested in their childrens' educations and are more likely to have hostile confrontations with parents.

We can also pose the question of to what extent the sector differences in parental participation are a reflection of sector differences in family background and orientation as opposed to consequences of differences in school organization. Table 2.17 presents predicted levels of public-private participation differences, controlling for family background. The items used here are the same as those used for table 2.15, except that the variables have been coded as scales in order to facilitate the use of ordinary least squares regres-

TABLE 2.17

*Predicted Public-Private Differences in Parental Participation[a]
Standardizing to Family Background[b] of the Average Public School
Student[c]*

	Catholic Minus Public	Other Private Minus Public	High-Performance Private Minus Public
Attend PTA	0.18 (0.027)	0.17 (0.078)	0.30 (0.257)
Attend parent-teacher conferences	0.23 (0.028)	0.02 (0.073)	−0.05 (0.248)
Visit classes	0.07 (0.021)	−0.07 (0.049)	−0.12 (0.186)
Contact school officials re: student problems	−0.01 (0.025)	0 (0.069)	−0.04 (0.246)
Volunteer for school projects	0.22 (0.030)	0.13 (0.086)	0.13 (0.309)

[a]The participation variables are coded: 0 = never, 1 = once in a while, and 2 = often.
[b]Background controls include parental education, father's occupation, family size, both parents present, mother's labor force participation, parental college expectations, race, Hispanic ethnicity, student's sex, whether student is handicapped, frequency of talking with parents, rooms in home, and whether students planned to go to college in 9th grade.
[c]Standard errors of differences in parentheses are adjusted for assumed design affect of 1.5.

sion techniques. The results indicate that the higher rates of parental participation found in the Catholic schools are not explained by the more advantaged backgrounds of Catholic students and their parents: On the three items that table 2.15 showed large Catholic advantages (PTA, conferences, and volunteer work), the background-controlled differences remain large and statistically strong.

The greater participation of other private school parents in these areas does, however, appear to be largely explained by family background. These results are consistent with the functional versus value community differences discussed in chapter 1. In a value community, the involvement of families in the school is largely determined on an individualistic basis, while the scope of community involvement is greater in the functional community. Thus, parents who would otherwise avoid the school or be uninvolved in its activities are induced to participate through the social relationships that define the functional community.

Conclusion

This chapter has examined public and private differences in a number of aspects of school design: family background, school size, expenditures, curriculum programs and offerings, extracurricular activities, and parental involvement in the school. A common issue that surrounds these comparisons is the extent to which observed differences are due to differences in the social composition of the schools versus differences in school-community relations. We have shown that the sector differences are large and in most cases not reducible to differences in family background. Private schools tend to be smaller and enroll much larger proportions of their students in academic programs of study. Within curriculum programs, private, particularly Catholic, school students take more academic courses and fewer vocational courses. Parental involvement in private schools is greater. This cannot be attributed to the more advantaged backgrounds of Catholic students, but is largely explained by background in the other private schools.

While important in their own right, these differences in school design can also have important consequences for student schooling outcomes, and we will examine these in the chapters that follow.

3

Achievement Outcomes
of Schooling

Introduction

If the two orientations to a school—as an agent of the state or as an agent of the family, to describe the orientations in extreme form—have different consequences for children and youth, then the outcomes of public school and private school should differ. It is not true, of course, that public schools are a pure embodiment of the "agent of the state" orientation, for a small school in a small school district continues to emanate largely from the community it serves and the families that make up that community. Nor is it true that private schools are a pure embodiment of the "agent of the family" orientation, for in many ways they merely emulate the dominant public school practice.

Yet as the evidence in chapter 2 indicated, public schools are, on average, more nearly agents of the state than are private schools. And private schools are more likely to constitute a functional community (for the religious sector) or a value community. As a consequence, outcomes of education should differ between the two sectors. Those differences may vary from time to time, depending on the dominant goals held by parents who send their children to private schools and depending on the dominant goals held for the schools by the larger society. For example, when upper-class parents used private schools primarily to

57

maintain elite status in the face of an egalitarian orientation in the public schools, or when Irish immigrants hastily put together Catholic schools to maintain their religion in the face of the dominant Protestantism of the public schools, it seems unlikely that either would produce especially high achievement outcomes relative to the public schools. Or when the role of the public school as a "melting pot" was a major goal of the larger society, one would look for greater cultural cohesiveness and national identity in the public schools, rather than for greater academic achievement. Or schools operated by the Amish for their children in lieu of public high schools can be expected to produce children that have virtues prized by the community, rather than those prized by the larger society.

In addition, there can be differences between public and private schools that are unintended or at least arise less directly from the goal differences between the sectors. Perhaps the most important of these is the existence of a functional community in those private schools built around a religious group, or a value community for other private schools. In addition, there are differences in size of schools, differences in staff recruitments, differences in resources resulting from the public schools' access to tax revenues, differences in parents' ability and the state's ability to respond to feedback from children about school experiences, and other differences which can lead to outcomes that do not follow directly from differences in orientation.

The particular differences in outcomes of schooling, then, do not follow directly from the different mix of the two orientations of schooling found in public and private schools. The differences among American public and private schools in the 1980s were not always and everywhere present.

But this does not reduce in any way the importance of discovering what those current differences are. Those differences show how the two orientations differentially embodied in public and private schools affect the youth today. It is these current effects that are relevant to current educational policy.

Where Should We Look for Differences in Achievement?

As we indicated in the prologue, attention has been focused on one major educational outcome of private schools, in part by our own earlier work (Coleman, Hoffer, and Kilgore 1982a): achievement on standardized tests in verbal and mathematical skills. The controversy that subsequently surrounded those results was even more narrowly focused on this outcome of education. The focus on this outcome arises, very simply, from two facts: First, it is a measure of the central core of cognitive skills on which most other learning in school depends, and on which most career opportunities beyond high school depend. This dependence gives face validity to the measure. Second, unlike grades in school, it is a common measure across schools. A boy or girl who has left high school is no longer being compared only to classmates. The yardstick beyond high school is a common one, with the same standards used to measure the performance of the products of different high schools. Grades in school are not like this. An *A* in one school may be given for performance that would not even merit a *B* in a second school. Yet the student who received an *A* in the first high school and the student who received a *C* in the second will be measured by common standards of performance in their lives beyond high school. It is these common standards that are approximated by standardized tests.

In 1980, sophomores were given six standardized tests, in these areas:

1. reading comprehension
2. vocabulary
3. mathematics
4. science
5. civics
6. writing

Seniors in 1980 were given tests in the first three of these areas (reading comprehension, vocabulary, and mathematics) with some items identical to those in the sophomore tests. The principal analyses of achievement using the 1980 data were based on these common-item subsets of the first three tests, and the performances of both sophomores and seniors were compared in the public, Catholic, and other private schools. It is these analyses that formed the basis for our first comparison of the effects of public and private schools, and these analyses that have been at the center of the controversy that followed publication of these results.

This controversy, which was primarily methodological, is treated at some length in three issues of *Sociology of Education* (April/July 1982; October 1983; and July 1985) and can be examined there. At this point, it is sufficient to say that most critics have come to agree, on the basis of analyses already completed using the 1982 data (see *Sociology of*

Education, July 1985) that there is a positive Catholic sector effect on achievement in the areas of reading comprehension, vocabulary, mathematics, and writing, but not in science or civics. The remaining disagreement about the Catholic sector effect appears largely to focus on the size of the effect. With respect to the effect of other private schools, we agree with the critics' point that the High School and Beyond (HSB) sample was sufficiently flawed (because of small size, possible bias due to some school refusals to participate in the research, and heterogeneity of the population of non-Catholic private schools) that no strong inferences could be made about achievement effects of this sector.

Our analysis focuses on growth in achievement between sophomore and senior years in the areas covered by the six standardized tests. In this analysis, we will include the other private sector despite the aforementioned problems of the sample. We do recognize that the sample is flawed, but we also recognize that flaws in the sample are likely to have a less strong impact on growth in achievement than on levels of achievement. For if there is similarity of functioning among the other private schools, but wide differences in backgrounds of students in the different schools of this sector, then it is the level of achievement that should be more affected by variations in the sample, while the growth (particularly when measured by controlling on backgrounds of students in the sample) should be less affected. Nevertheless, it is important to keep in mind that because of the sample, inferences about the other private sector are less firm than are inferences about the public and Catholic sectors.

Predictions About Achievement in Each Sector: Economic Resources and Social Resources

Before examining achievement growth in the different sectors, it is useful to examine the basis for predictions about where achievement would be highest for students of comparable backgrounds.

In this book, we want principally to examine the consequences of the different orientations on which schools in the three sectors are based. One set of predictions arises from the differences in economic resources available to the schools. From this we would predict that the high performance private schools in our sample would show highest growth, because their per pupil expenditure, on average, is higher than in any of the other sectors. However, because these schools were selected on a measure of performance on standardized achievement tests (frequency of National Merit Scholarship Semifinalists among seniors), inferences based on comparison of their growth in achievement with that in other schools are not warranted. Only in the first tables of this chapter are scores in these schools presented.

Among the three sectors to be compared, the per pupil expenditure is highest in the other private schools, as shown in chapter 2, though only slightly greater than that of the public sector. Per pupil expenditure is by far lowest in schools of the Catholic sector. Thus their effectiveness, for children of comparable backgrounds, should be less than that in schools of the other sectors. Effectiveness of the other private sector schools should be slightly higher than that of the public schools, corresponding to their per pupil expenditure. All this, of course, assumes comparisons for students from comparable backgrounds, for it is the school's effectiveness that is in question, not that of the family background and school taken together.

A second basis for prediction is the functional community found in religiously based private schools and the value communities found in other private schools. The general prediction would be that both these kinds of communities lead to dominance of values in the school toward academic achievement. However, this would be predicted to arise in different ways in functional communities and value communities. For a strong functional community, there is a single dominant value in the community, which all observe, whether or not they agree. In a school based on a functional community, whether the community is that surrounding a one-room rural schoolhouse in nineteenth-century America or a Catholic school in the 1980s, that value is nearly always one which places importance upon learning. There may be many students in the school, with some parents of the students having quite different private values, but the existence of the functional community silences those private values, and the "official" values of the school maintain their dominance. This is especially important for those communities in which the families are uneducated and rural or working class, for there the lack of value dominance (that is, the lack of legitimate authority in the schools) can allow free reign to values and behavior quite opposed to learning. The schools described in books of the 1960s and 1970s in which there was no value dominance (for example, see Silberman 1970 and Kozol 1967) show the chaos that can arise in lower-class schools when it is absent.

In schools that are not based on a functional community, but attract families with similar values, the source of value dominance is quite different. The values are based on a value consensus by staff and school toward academic achievement, with values shared by students, parents, and teachers. Such a value consensus does not depend on suppression of opposed private values, nor on authority, other than the authority of the group itself. It does depend, however, on the prior existence of similar values. If these are to be directed toward learning, this ordinarily requires both that parents be strongly oriented to their childrens' learning in school and that the children themselves adopt these parental values, rather than those they pick up from the mass media or elsewhere. Thus, it would seem to depend on a high concentration in the school of students from families that both have middle-class values and are able to transmit these values to their children.

It would appear from these considerations that a value dominance based on value consensus rather than a functional community is a kind of value environment that is more conducive to learning than the value dominance based on authority buttressed by a functional community. Yet it appears to be an environment that is less robust to variations in backgrounds and orientations of students than is that generated by a functional community.

The absence of value dominance in a school, as exists in a value-heterogeneous residential area once the functional community has vanished, means that standards and demands can no longer be imposed by teachers, as is true where there is a functional community or where the teachers' values are shared by students. Rather, the demands, the efforts put forth, and the sets of standards must arise as a negotiated compromise between teacher and students, a compromise that in some settings may be very different from that which would be imposed by the same teacher if that teacher had the authority, legitimate in the students' eyes, to do so.

A distinguished colleague at University of Chicago reports that when he entered his Latin class in the 10th grade of a public school in 1941, his Latin teacher, recognizing his last name, thundered at him words to this effect: "I threw your father out of class, I threw your uncle out of class, and I threw your older brother out of class. I suggest you stand in the hall for a few minutes and ponder that before you enter this class."

A statement like this reflects a value dominance in the school that is seldom successfully broached. It is not the sort of statement a teacher could be expected to make in the 1980s, for that value dominance is no longer present.

On these grounds, then, we would predict, as far as effort and achievement are concerned in the schools, that the private sector schools would show considerably higher levels of effort than would the public schools, based on the authority of the functional community in the Catholic schools or the value community in the other private schools, and that this greater effort would lead to greater growth in achievement. The comparison between the Catholic schools and the other private schools, however, is less clear. We would predict that at best, an other private school would show higher levels of effort and achievement than would a Catholic school, but that this achievement would show greater variation, both within schools and between. What this will average out to is not clear.

Thus there are different predictions for a functional community and a value community about variation in achievement. Those will be addressed in chapter 5. In this chapter, we will examine only effects of the sectors on growth in overall level of achievement, that is, growth standardized to a particular student background.

The two bases for predictions about achievement, per pupil expenditure and the existence of functional or value communities, may be described as based on economic resources and social resources, respectively. The two predictions give quite different predictions about relative effectiveness of the three sectors. The economic-resources predictions place the effectiveness of the Catholic schools at the bottom, with the other private schools slightly higher than the public schools. The social-resources predictions place the effectiveness of the public schools at the bottom, leaving open the position of the two private sectors relative to each other. In the next section, we examine the evidence on achievement growth.

Evidence on Achievement Growth, Sophomore to Senior

Achievement growth in public and private schools over the two years from sophomore to senior was not large, as shown in table 3.1. In a 21-item vocabulary test on which the average sophomore answered correctly 11 items, the average gain was 1.8 items, only 18 percent of the number of remaining items on the test. In the 19-item reading comprehension test, on which the sophomore average was about 9.5 items correct, the average gain was 1 additional item, only 11 percent

TABLE 3.1

*Sophomore and Senior Achievement Test Means and Standard
Deviations for All Students: 1980 Sophomore Cohort*

Test and Number of Items	Grade		Gain	Percentage Learned of What Remains %
	10	12		
Reading 19	9.42	10.47	1.05	11
	(3.88)	(4.14)		
Vocabulary 21	11.25	13.05	1.80	18
	(4.30)	(4.50)		
Mathematics 38	19.47	21.00	1.53	08
	(7.38)	(8.12)		
Science 20	11.29	12.09	0.80	09
	(3.70)	(3.74)		
Civics 10	5.99	6.83	0.85	21
	(2.01)	(2.09)		
Writing 17	10.65	11.97	1.33	21
	(3.86)	(3.84)		

of the number of remaining items. As table 3.1 shows, on none of the tests was the gain a large one. Thus, the very first point that can be made is that not much of what these tests measure was learned over the two-year period.

Table 3.2 shows what the gains were for each of these tests in each of the sectors. The gain in number of items correct is generally larger in the Catholic and other private sectors than in the public, though in the high-performance private sector, the gains are uniformly smaller.

The differential growth in the different sectors is not, however, a measure of the relative effectiveness of the different sets of schools. There are some factors that lead the absolute gains to be understatements of differential effectiveness of the private sector schools, and some that lead them to be overstatements. The principal source of understatement is the fact that the 10th grade scores in the private sector schools are higher, making the same level of gain harder to achieve. At the extreme, for example, a number of students in the high-performance private schools (and some students in every sector) answered all items correctly as sophomores, so that no gain was possible for them. A measure of effectiveness that eliminates this source of bias (a "ceiling effect") is one based on the recognition that the number correct divided by the total number of items is the proportion of items correctly answered or the probability of answering an item correctly. For such proportions, a logit, $\log [p/(1-p)]$, where p is the proportion

TABLE 3.2

Sophomore and Senior Achievement Test Means and Standard Deviations by Grade Level and Sector: 1980 Sophomore Cohort

Test	Public			Catholic			Other Private			High-Performance Private		
	10	12	Gain	10	12	Gain	10	12	Gain	10	12	Gain
Vocabulary (21)	11.05 (4.27)	12.80 (4.50)	1.75	13.08 (3.91)	15.18 (3.72)	2.10	13.33 (4.49)	15.68 (4.00)	2.35	17.57 (2.54)	18.92 (2.54)	1.35
Reading (19)	9.28 (3.87)	10.29 (4.13)	1.01	10.69 (3.59)	12.03 (3.75)	1.34	10.81 (4.06)	12.35 (3.75)	1.54	14.62 (2.82)	14.71 (3.29)	0.09
Mathematics (38)	19.14 (7.36)	20.60 (8.09)	1.46	22.10 (6.50)	24.49 (7.15)	2.39	23.20 (7.59)	24.84 (8.27)	1.64	30.28 (4.57)	31.65 (4.91)	1.37
Science (20)	11.19 (3.73)	11.98 (3.77)	0.79	12.09 (3.23)	12.95 (3.23)	.93	12.68 (3.29)	13.29 (3.44)	0.61	15.14 (2.29)	15.55 (2.76)	0.41
Writing (17)	10.49 (3.87)	11.80 (3.87)	1.31	12.12 (3.39)	13.58 (3.02)	1.46	11.89 (3.69)	13.42 (3.50)	1.53	14.81 (1.81)	15.07 (2.60)	0.28
Civics (10)	5.92 (2.02)	6.76 (2.10)	0.84	6.61 (1.85)	7.44 (1.81)	0.83	6.57 (1.74)	7.73 (1.93)	0.96	7.78 (1.38)	8.28 (1.79)	0.50

correct, is an appropriate measure.* Despite the fact that the use of logits eliminates the bias due to initial level of achievement, for technical reasons, we will not use it in analysis of sector differences in achievement.† Instead, we will continue to use number of items correct as a measure of performance, recognizing that the ceiling effect leads to an understatement of growth which is greater when initial achievement is higher.

We will examine growth through the use of an analysis which partly, but not wholly, eliminates this source of bias. This involves expressing the senior score of a student as a function of the sophomore score and an unexplained component.

A first estimate then, of the effects of the private sectors, as well as the effect of sophomore achievement, can be obtained by regressing senior score on sophomore score in each sector.‡ There are four equations, one for each sector. The expected growth in each of the sectors for students with a given initial score y_1* can be obtained by substituting y_1* into each of the four equations. For example, the predicted value of y_2 in each sector for a student who scored at the public school average as a sophomore is obtained by substituting the public school sophomore average into each of the four equations. This gives a preliminary measure of sector effect on achievement growth. The effects of public, Catholic, other private, and high-performance private schools for the six tests that were given are expressed in table 3.3, which shows the predicted growth for each test in each sector for a student with achievement as a sophomore of the average student in the public schools. This table shows estimates of substantial private sector effects. These effects can be expressed in terms of grade equivalents (where the size of grade equivalent is calculated as half the two-year growth in the public sector). On average, achievement growth by students in Catholic schools was, during the two-year period, an additional 0.9 to 1.8 grade-

*See Fienberg (1977) for a discussion of the logit transformation. For its use in a context like the present, see Coleman (1981).

†For those students who got zero correct or all correct, the logit takes the value of − or + ∞. Thus a linear regression in which the senior score is expressed in logits in the dependent variable cannot include these observations unless arbitrary values are inserted when there is zero or all correct. Either alternative, however, constitutes a bias. It is possible to overcome this difficulty through maximum likelihood estimation involving iterative methods, as used in chapter 4 for dropouts. However, those methods require elimination of cases for which observations are missing, which is undesirable when the equation is a large one.

In addition, the interpretation of parameters from a logit analysis is less straightforward.

‡The regression of senior score on sophomore score can be rewritten in a way that expresses sophomore-to-senior growth as a function of sophomore score:

$$y_{2i} - y_{1i} = a + (b-1)y_{1i} + e_i.$$

TABLE 3.3

Estimates of Effect of Sector on Growth in Achievement in Six Tests[a] for a Student Achieving at Average Public School Level as Sophomore[b]

	1	2	3	4 Private Sector Increment Beyond Public Sector Growth in growth			5 Private Sector Increment Beyond Public Sector Growth as grade equivalent		
Test	Number of items	Average number correct in public school as sophomore	Average growth in public school	Catholic	Other Private	High-Performance Private	Catholic	Other Private	High-Performance Private
Reading	19	9.3	1.00	0.71 (.10)	0.98 (.26)	1.09	1.4	2.0	2.2
Vocabulary	21	11.0	1.75	0.94 (.10)	1.28 (.24)	3.24	1.1	1.5	3.7
Mathematics	38	19.1	1.46	1.29 (.16)	0.56 (.44)	1.66	1.8	0.8	2.3
Science	20	11.2	0.79	0.44 (.09)	0.25 (.24)	1.36	1.1	0.6	3.4
Civics	10	5.9	0.84	0.38 (.06)	0.46 (.16)	0.96	0.9	1.1	2.3
Writing	17	10.5	1.31	0.80 (.09)	0.69 (.23)	1.43	1.2	1.1	2.2

[a]The test scores reported here and in the remaining tables of Section 2 are the numbers of items correctly answered. All analyses use the sample weights (codebook variable PNLTSTWT).
[b]Standard errors in parentheses are adjusted for an assumed design effect of 1.5. This adjustment is carried out throughout the chapter.

equivalents beyond the two-grade-equivalents gained in the public schools. Achievement growth by other private school students was 0.6 to 2.0 grade equivalents greater. In the high-performance private schools, achievement growth was 2.2 to 3.7 grade equivalents greater.

However, the high-performance private schools can hardly be reliably compared to the other sectors, because their distributions of sophomore achievement have little overlap with the distributions of achievement in the other three sectors. Thus although they are included in table 3.3, they will be excluded from subsequent analyses of achievement.

A better understanding of achievement growth for low- and high-achieving students in each sector can be obtained by examining the average achievement levels as seniors, for students at each achievement level as sophomores. Figures 3.1 to 3.6 show the average number correct on each test as seniors, for students classified according to the number correct as sophomores. For example, public school students who got 12 vocabulary items correct as sophomores got an average of 13.8 correct as seniors, and Catholic school students who got 12 correct as sophomores got an average of 14.6 correct as seniors. Above the 45-degree line in the figures, the senior average is higher than the sophomore score, below the line, the senior average is lower.

These figures show that Catholic school students and other private students at almost all levels of sophomore achievement outperformed public school students when they were seniors. The greatest difference between Catholic and public schools, relative to the sophomore-senior gain, was in mathematics and was about the same magnitude as the sophomore-senior gain for public school students (that is, about the same as the vertical distance from the solid (public) line to the 45-degree diagonal). The greatest difference between other private and public schools was in reading comprehension and was about equal to the sophomore-senior gain in the public schools.

This first examination, then, suggests that the second set of predictions is valid, that the differences in economic resources of the schools are less important than the difference in social resources—the functional or value communities that reinforce the demands made by the schools.

But despite the fact that this analysis controls on initial achievement and thus controls for the effect of selection on achievement at grade 10, there is a potential source of upward bias in the private sector effects, because there is no control for an effect of selection on *growth* in achievement. Put another way, the different environments ex-

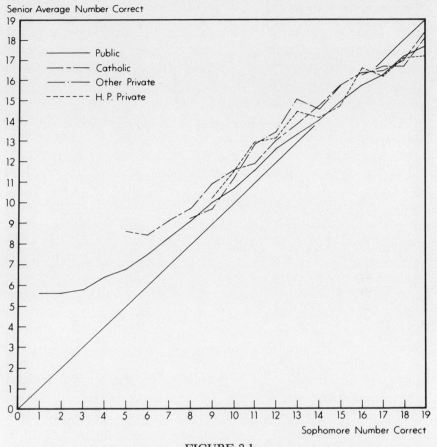

FIGURE 3.1

Average Senior Score by Sophomore Number Correct: Reading

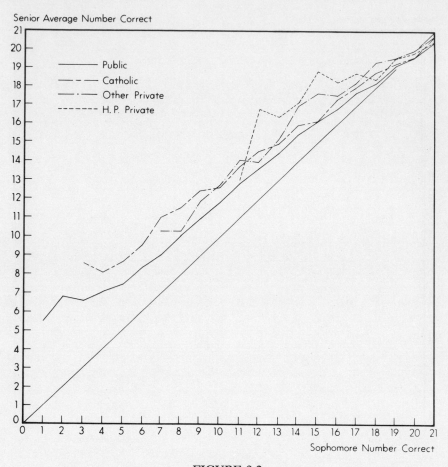

FIGURE 3.2

Average Senior Score by Sophomore Number Correct: Vocabulary

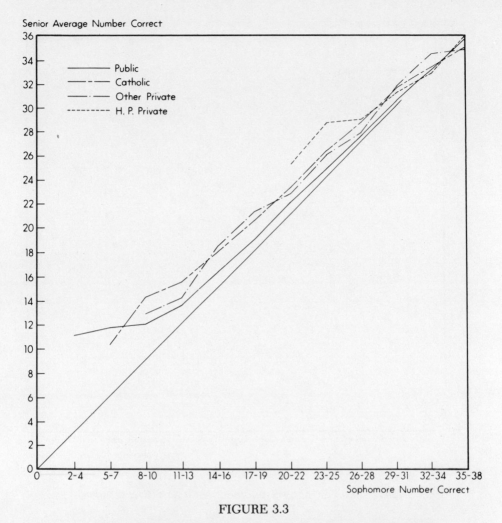

FIGURE 3.3

Average Senior Score by Sophomore Number Correct: Mathematics

The classification categories are collapsed to improve the resolution of the curves.

Senior Average Number Correct

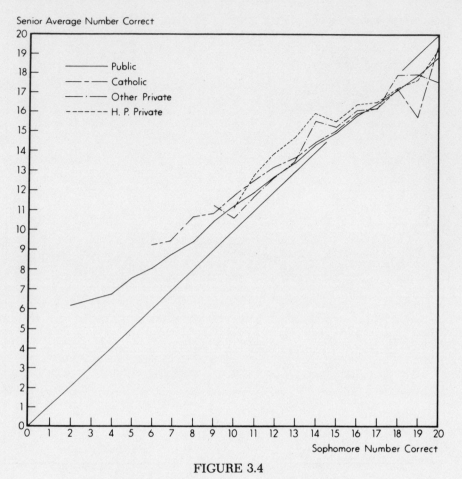

FIGURE 3.4

Average Senior Score by Sophomore Number Correct: Science

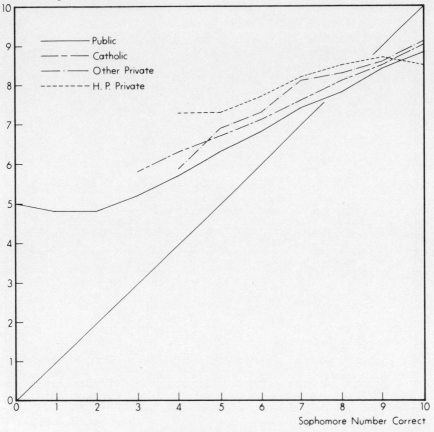

Senior Average Number Correct

Public
Catholic
Other Private
H. P. Private

Sophomore Number Correct

FIGURE 3.5

Average Senior Score by Sophomore Number Correct: Civics

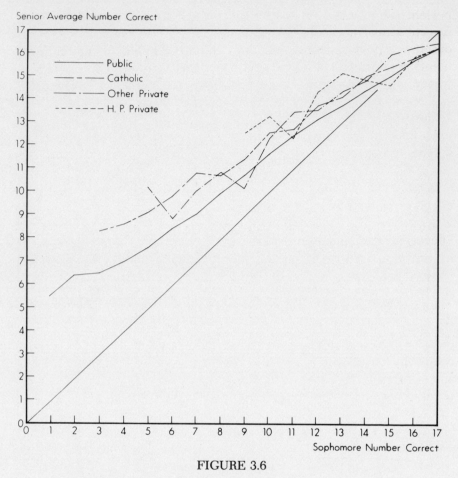

FIGURE 3.6

Average Senior Score by Sophomore Number Correct: Writing

perienced by students in the public schools, Catholic schools, and other private schools over this two-year period consisted of not only their different school environments, but also their different home environments. Two students who have different home environments over this period, just as two students who have different school environments, can be expected to show differential gains, although their sophomore achievement was alike.

To address this difference, the analysis shown in table 3.3 can be augmented by incorporating family background characteristics into the analysis.*

Because in the base year study we found considerably different effects of family background in public schools than in the Catholic and other private schools, it appears sensible to allow here also for different effects of family background in the different sectors. This we have done by carrying out three separate regression analyses, regressing senior achievement on sophomore achievement and family background, separately for students in public, Catholic, and other private schools.

Additional measures of individual background beyond those used in the base year are included in the present analysis. These additional measures are: (1) region of the country, (2) respondent's sex, (3) whether or not the respondent planned to go to college when in the 9th grade, and (4) whether or not the respondent was handicapped (according to self-description). These measures of individual background are included in addition to eleven variables which circumscribe the set of background controls that we employed in the base year analysis. The individual measures of income, parental education, and household possessions that we used before are replaced here by a single socioeconomic status (SES) composite variable, which also includes some additional variables that our base year models excluded: father's occupational status, and four additional household possessions. The composite, which is included in the public use data sets, was constructed by standardizing each of the individual component variables and averaging the sum of the components. Ten measures of background which we used in the base year analysis, but which are not included in the SES composite, are also used in the present analyses.

Results are shown in table 3.4, which has the same form as table 3.3 but is based on the analyses including family background and shows the

---

*Expressed as an extension of the equation in the previous footnote, the equation would look like this:

$$y_{2i} - y_{1i} = a + (b_0 - 1) y_{1i} + b_1 z_i + e_i$$

where z is a vector of family background characteristics, and b_1 is a vector of coefficients expressing the effect of family background on achievement growth over the two years.

results when not only sophomore achievement but family background of the average public school student are inserted into each sector equation as described previously.

This table, which includes all six tests, shows that the Catholic and other private increments are reduced for all tests compared to table 3.3. For two tests in the other private schools, there is less growth than in the public sector.

An examination first of the Catholic sector increments shows that the effects remain substantial for four of the six tests. For science and civics, the estimated increments are much smaller. The lack of a substantial Catholic-sector effect in science provides an indirect confirmation of a Catholic-sector effect in the other areas. For as we showed with the sophomore data (Coleman and Hoffer 1983, p. 226), Catholic school students in both academic and general tracks take a considerably higher number of specialized mathematics courses (algebra 1, algebra 2, trigonometry, geometry, calculus), but this was not true for chemistry and physics. Thus, the academic demands in the average Catholic school are considerably greater than those in the average public school in mathematics for students in comparable programs, while this is not so in science.

For the other private sector, the most striking result is the lower growth estimated in both mathematics and science than for students from comparable backgrounds in the public schools. In verbal skills (including reading comprehension, vocabulary, and writing), the other private schools show a positive effect relative to the public schools, though reduced from the effect shown when only initial achievement was statistically controlled (see table 3.3). But for the two technical subjects, mathematics and science, the other private schools show an estimated negative effect relative to the public schools. It should be noted, however, that neither for these estimates nor for the positive estimates in civics and writing, do the estimated effects differ from zero at a statistical significance level of 0.05.

The estimated Catholic and other private sector increments shown in table 3.4 are for students with initial achievement and family background comparable to that of the average public school student. Because this analysis included interactions between sector and family background, and between sector and initial achievement, the increments may differ for other students. For comparison purposes, we will examine effects for the achievement and background of the average Catholic school student. The estimated private sector effects for such a student are shown in table 3.5.

TABLE 3.4

Estimates of Effect of Private Sector on Growth in Achievement of Average Public School Student in Six Tests, Controlling on Family Background[a]

Test	Average number correct in public school at sophomore level	Average growth in public school	Private Sector Increment			
			in items correct		as grade equivalent	
			Catholic	Other Private	Catholic	Other Private
Reading	9.3	1.00	0.49 (0.15)	0.74 (.35)	1.0	1.5
Vocabulary	11.0	1.75	0.74 (0.14)	0.99 (.32)	0.9	1.1
Mathematics	19.1	1.46	0.75 (0.24)	−0.22 (.57)	1.0	−0.30
Science	11.2	0.79	0.05 (0.14)	−0.12 (.32)	0.1	−0.30
Civics	5.9	0.84	0.15 (0.09)	0.27 (.22)	0.2	0.32
Writing	10.5	1.31	0.64 (0.13)	0.40 (.31)	1.0	0.61

[a]Standard errors in parentheses.

TABLE 3.5

Estimates of Effect of Private Sector on Growth in Achievement of Average Catholic School Student in Six Tests, Controlling on Family Background[a]

Test	Average number correct in Catholic school at sophomore level	Predicted growth in public school	Private Sector Increment			
			in items correct		as grade equivalent	
			Catholic	Other Private	Catholic	Other Private
Reading	10.7	0.93	0.42 (0.10)	0.56 (.23)	0.9	1.2
Vocabulary	13.1	1.66	0.44 (0.09)	0.76 (.21)	0.5	0.9
Mathematics	22.1	1.72	0.68 (0.15)	−0.57 (.36)	0.8	−0.7
Science	12.0	0.83	0.10 (0.09)	−0.19 (.20)	0.2	−0.5
Civics	6.6	0.73	0.10 (0.06)	0.10 (.14)	0.3	0.3
Writing	12.1	1.22	0.35 (0.08)	0.15 (.32)	0.6	0.2

[a]Standard errors in parentheses.

This table shows that the increments are smaller for the average Catholic school student, in both the Catholic schools and the other private schools. As figures 3.1 to 3.6 suggest, these smaller absolute increments reflect the fact that students with backgrounds and initial achievements like those of the average Catholic school students are closer to the ceiling on the achievement tests. Equivalently, the Catholic-sector effects are more pronounced for students from lower family backgrounds or with lower initial achievement than they are for students from higher backgrounds and initial achievement. This phenomenon is analyzed in some detail in chapter 5. For the present it is sufficient to note that table 3.5 indicates that the same general results hold as shown in tables 3.2 and 3.3: There are strong positive effects of Catholic-sector schools in reading, vocabulary, mathematics, and writing, (at least four standard error differences) and weak and statistically insignificant effects in science and civics. In the other private schools, there are strong positive effects in reading and vocabulary and statistically insignificant effects in other areas, though estimated to be negative in mathematics and science and positive in civics and writing.

Because our estimates of a Catholic-sector effect on achievement growth in earlier publications (Coleman, Hoffer, and Kilgore 1982a and 1982b; Coleman and Hoffer 1983; Hoffer, Greeley, and Coleman 1985) have been so strongly debated, it appears useful to subject these results to an additional test for selection bias, one proposed by Rosenbaum and Rubin (1983). This test will be carried out only for the comparison between public and Catholic schools, because the number of students in the other private sector is too small for stable results in this test.

Comparing Students with Equal Propensities for Catholic Enrollment

Rosenbaum and Rubin (1983) have proposed a stronger test for elimination of selectivity bias than the linear regression methods just used. They point out that fewer assumptions are made (for example, the assumption of linearity in effects of background variables) if comparisons are limited to those persons who are comparable in their propensity to be selected into the treatment. The method of examining for example Catholic sector effects entails a two-step process of, first, estimating each student's propensity to be enrolled in a Catholic school and, second, comparing the achievement of students in public and

Catholic schools who have the same propensity to be in a Catholic school. In practice, the sample is divided into propensity-score quintiles, and comparisons made within each quintile.* If the sector differences are similar in each quintile, then the inference is that the overall sector effects are in fact applicable for students of all types of background. If these differences are approximately the same as the Catholic sector effect measured with a linear regression model, this confirms the assumptions implicit in that analysis. We have done analyses of the sort that Rosenbaum and Rubin propose for the Catholic sector effects, where the sample size is large enough to allow this.

The analysis of Catholic sector effects involves first giving each student a propensity or probability of enrolling in a Catholic school, based on a logistic regression.† Then, following the recommendation of Rosenbaum and Rubin the sample was stratified into quintiles of the propensity score, and Catholic sector effects were estimated within each of these homogeneous groups.‡

The results of this analysis are shown in table 3.6. Reading across the rows of the table from the lowest propensity quintile (that is, those students who are least likely to enroll in Catholic school) to the highest propensity quintile, there does not appear to be any strong pattern of increase or decline in the estimated Catholic sector effects. The Catholic advantage in mathematics is the most stable set of estimates, fluctuating little between the first and fifth quintiles. In vocabulary, reading, and writing (the other three areas were the overall estimates indicated substantial sector effects), the estimates tend to be quite stable and in the expected direction in the first, second, third, and fifth quintiles, but are sharply lower in the fourth quintile. The reasons for this estimated

*See Rosenbaum and Rubin (1983) for details. If within a quintile, certain variables remain related to achievement, a within-quintile regression may be carried out to control for their effects.

†Students' propensities for Catholic school enrollment are estimated by a logistic regression of sector (Catholic = 1; public = 0) on the set of background measures used in the base year analysis (substituting the composite SES measure for parental education and income, and household possessions) plus a composite measure of 10th-grade achievement. As our analysis of sector entry in the base year (Coleman, Hoffer, and Kilgore 1982a: ch. 3) found that the relationships of background to entry varied for white, black, and Hispanic students, the logistic regression was fit on a stratified basis. Propensity scores (in the form of probabilities of Catholic enrollment) were then obtained for each student.

‡As indicated in the first footnote above, relations of background to achievement remaining within quintiles can be controlled for by within-quintile regression analysis. To determine which variables required further adjustment, a sector by quintile analysis of variance was carried out for each of the twelve predictor variables. Significant main and/or interaction effects of sector within quintiles were found to remain for sophomore achievement, SES, rooms in household, number of siblings, race, and Hispanic ethnicity. These variables were consequently controlled for in within-quintile regressions of 12th-grade achievements used to obtain estimates of the Catholic sector effects.

TABLE 3.6

Catholic Sector Effects on 12th Grade Achievement by Propensity Quintile[a]

			Quintile		
Test	1	2	3	4	5
Reading	0.318 (.47)	0.631 (.34)	0.444 (.27)	0.134 (.24)	0.358 (.19)
Vocabulary	0.402 (.51)	0.613 (.34)	0.555 (.26)	0.045 (.22)	0.410 (.16)
Mathematics	0.634 (.74)	0.751 (.57)	0.642 (.43)	0.765 (.37)	0.665 (.30)
Science	−0.714 (.44)	0.292 (.31)	−0.172 (.23)	−0.027 (.21)	0.085 (.19)
Civics	0.182 (.32)	0.247 (.23)	0.124 (.17)	−0.020 (.14)	0.015 (.11)
Writing	0.856 (.50)	0.490 (.34)	0.557 (.24)	−0.091 (.20)	0.335 (.16)
Average Sample Sizes[b]					
Public	3,323	3,052	3,087	2,964	3,061
Catholic	119	223	328	417	845

[a]Standard errors in parentheses.
[b]Missing values on one or more of the variables used in the logistic regression resulted in deletion of the case from analysis.

drop in verbal achievement gains (a drop which is not at all present in mathematics) are not clear, but the quintiles on both sides of this quintile give confidence that the effects are not confined to those with especially high or low likelihood of enrolling in a Catholic school.

The evidence of table 3.6 indicates that the overall sector effects on achievement estimated in earlier tables continue to be found within homogeneous subsamples defined in terms of propensity for Catholic sector enrollment. And in the two areas of achievement where we found no overall sector effects—science and civics—table 3.6 indicates that the absence of effects holds across the sample as stratified.

The sole exception to this latter generalization is found in the large negative effect of Catholic school attendance on science achievement among those students who are least likely to attend Catholic school, the first propensity quintile. This, however, is a quintile with only a small number (119) of Catholic school students, and the estimate is thus unstable.

Variability of Achievement Growth Among Schools

Another difference in effects of Catholic and other private schools was predicted earlier in this chapter, based on the difference between a functional community surrounding a Catholic school and the value consensus to be found in an other private school. According to this prediction, the values dominant in the Catholic school, and thus the impact of the school on achievement growth, would be relatively impervious to variations in the backgrounds and orientations of the student body as a whole. In the other private schools, the dominance of values directed toward high achievement would be dependent on a consensus among parents and among students, and thus more sensitive to the backgrounds of the student body as a whole.

If this is so, then achievement growth should depend more on the backgrounds and orientations of *other* students in the same school for students in other private schools than for students in Catholic schools. To put it differently, in the Catholic schools the standards and demands are relatively fixed, while in the other private schools, the standards and demands depend on the student body.

To test whether there is such a difference that results in differential achievement, we examined, in Catholic and other private schools separately, the degree to which the student's achievement growth depends on the *average* family socioeconomic status in the High School and Beyond sample, when the student's own family background and prior achievement are statistically controlled.* Achievement growth in verbal skills† and mathematical skills were examined. In both cases, the estimated effect of the student body socioeconomic status on achievement growth was much higher in the other private schools than in the Catholic schools: 0.86 versus 0.49 for verbal achievement growth and 1.72 versus 0.12 for mathematics achievement growth.

These results indicate that the impact of other private schools on achievement growth does depend more on the particular student body than does the impact of Catholic schools. They suggest that in a school that is based on the consensus of a value community, the school's demands depend more on parental values than they do in a school based on a functional community that supports the school's authority.

Achievement of Dropouts: Evidence from a Natural Experiment

In chapter 4, we will examine another outcome of schooling, that of dropping out of school or remaining until graduation. However, at this point the students who dropped out between spring of their sophomore year and spring of their senior year are useful in another way: The dropouts were followed up, and cognitive tests were administered to them, identical to the tests taken by those who were still in school. With the use of these test scores, which allow comparison of their growth in cognitive skills over this two-year period to the growth of those who remained in school, the dropouts (and to a lesser extent, the transfers) make possible a kind of natural experiment of the effect of schooling over these two years. This natural experiment is less valuable for estimating the absolute effects of these two years of school in achievement than it is for estimating the differential effects of these two years in different sectors (or, as we will examine at the

*The analysis was carried out in regression equations in which the following variables were statistically controlled student's own socioeconomic status, sex, handicap, race and Hispanic ethnicity, both parents present, number of siblings, number of rooms in home, mother's labor force participation, frequency of talking with parents, and whether the student planned on eventual college attendance when he or she was in the 9th grade. The values of R^2 in Catholic schools were 0.67 in both verbal and mathematical skills; in other private schools, 0.71 and 0.74, respectively.

†Verbal scores used here and in later analyses combine, by simple addition, the reading comprehension and vocabulary scores shown separately in earlier analysis in this chapter.

end of the chapter, the differential effects for different subjects of study). The reason, of course, is that motivation of dropouts is different from those who remain in school, even if their prior achievement and backgrounds are the same.

The special value of examining achievement of dropouts lies in its aid in separating out apparent differential effects of sectors from differential selection into sectors. If the effects on achievement growth that have been found in the preceding section were a result of selection differences which were not eliminated by controls on background and were not due to differences in school functioning, then the same growth differences among sectors should be found among dropouts after controlling on background.* However, if the effects are true effects, then the dropouts should not differ among sectors (once these same controls for background have been introduced) in achievement growth. The necessity for background controls follows from the rationale for their use when comparing students who remained in school: Young persons will be subject to different environments outside school, and if sector differences in achievement growth are found, these may be the consequence of differences in out-of-school environments for those who are from different sectors.

A first examination may be made of merely the raw achievement growth in each sector, comparing those who remained in school, those who dropped out, and those who transferred. Table 3.7 shows the sophomore and senior verbal scores in the three sectors, for each of these subgroups. Concentrating first on the comparison of the sophomore scores of dropouts and those still in school as seniors, Table 3.7 shows that the dropouts in both Catholic and other private schools were much further below those who subsequently stayed in school than were the dropouts from public schools (6.36 and 6.66 items compared to 4.76 items), but were somewhat higher in level of achievement than public school dropouts (1.86 and 1.95 items, respectively). Thus, the dropouts from both sets of private sector schools were as sophomores further below the rest of the class in verbal achievement than were the dropouts from public school, yet still higher than the latter.

On the basis of these scores, it would appear that if dropping out is largely dependent on achievement levels, some of the private school dropouts would have succeeded in public schools. It suggests also that

---

*This does not make the assumption that the kind of person who stays in school and the kind who drops out is the same in each sector, but does make the assumption that the differences between the kind of person who stays in school and the kind who drops out are the same in each sector.

Achievement Outcomes of Schooling

TABLE 3.7

Verbal Achievement Levels as Sophomores and
Two Years Later for Students Who Dropped
Out of School, Those Who Remained in School,
and Those Who Transferred, by Sector

Verbal Achievement	Grade 10	Grade 12	Gain
Public			
In school	20.28	23.04	2.76
Dropout	15.52	17.15	1.63
Transfer	19.54	21.86	2.32
Catholic			
In school	23.74	27.20	3.46
Dropout	17.38	18.83	1.45
Transfer	21.98	24.23	2.25
Other Private			
In school	24.13	28.05	3.92
Dropout	17.47	20.74	3.27
Transfer	23.70	27.06	3.36

leaving a school depends not only on absolute levels of performance, but also on the level relative to others in the school. It is useful in connection with this to examine the average sophomore achievement in each sector for those who report having left school involuntarily, that is, having been expelled. The dropouts who reported having been expelled are 11.9 percent of the public sector dropouts, 9.0 percent of the Catholic sector dropouts, and 13.5 percent of the other private school dropouts. Their sophomore test scores were, in both the Catholic and other private sectors, considerably below those of the dropouts who were not expelled and, in fact, were below the scores of the public sector expellees: 14.23 in the Catholic sector, 14.59 in the other private sector, and 15.90 in the public sector. This suggests that it is not true that the private sector schools get rid of their failures by expelling them. The private sector dropouts who are above the corresponding public sector dropouts in verbal achievement are those who left school voluntarily. The expellees are below the public school expellees.

When we compare the achievement growth among dropouts and those who remained in school in the three sectors, those who remained in school show the familiar differences presented earlier in table 3.2. However, the comparisons are not the same among the dropouts. First, the growth rates are lower in all sectors (despite the fact that starting points were lower, so that greater gains were possible). But second, the growth rate among dropouts from the Catholic sector is even lower than that from the public sector (though almost identical when measured in logits, a transformation which compensates for the fact that the Catholic starting point is higher).

This constitutes strong evidence that Catholic schools do in fact have achievement effects in verbal skills of at least the size indicated earlier in the chapter, because the dropouts do not gain more than do the public school dropouts—even without controlling on background.

It is valuable in making these comparisons to introduce such a control. This may be done by controlling on sophomore scores and backgrounds of dropouts. Thus, in each sector it is possible to compare the achievement growth of dropouts to the achievement growth of students who had the same sophomore scores as dropouts, and comparable backgrounds, but remained in school. (This will be shown later, in table 3.9.) However, even without this, it is possible to see that the verbal skills of Catholic and public school dropouts grow at quite comparable rates, while the students who remained in Catholic school showed considerably higher achievement growth than did those who remained in public school.

When we turn to the other private schools, the result is quite different. The growth in verbal skills among dropouts from the other private sector is nearly as high as that among those who stayed in school. It is true that the initial scores of dropouts are lower, leaving more room for gain, and it is true that there are no background controls, so the result is not conclusive. Nevertheless, the difference between this pattern and that found in the public and Catholic schools is striking. A subsequent examination will show how much of this difference remains when appropriate statistical controls are introduced; but at this point, the dropout comparisons provide confirmation both for the effects of school itself on achievement growth (in public and Catholic schools), and for a considerably greater effect in Catholic schools than in public schools. There is no confirmation of a differential effect of other private schools on verbal achievement.

An examination of achievement gains among those who transferred to another school gives much the same result, with some additional information. First, the Catholic school students who transfer are somewhat lower in achievement, relative to those who remain, than are those in public or other private schools. Second, the transfers in all sectors have considerably higher sophomore achievement than do the dropouts, though they are slightly lower than are those who remain in the same school. Third, their achievement growth from sophomore to senior level is higher than that of the dropouts, and in two sectors (public and other private), close to that of those who remained.*

Finally, the same pattern of achievement growth is found among Catholic and public school transfers as among the dropouts: The transfers from Catholic schools gain no more than do the transfers from public schools, again indicating that the apparent achievement gain from being in Catholic school depends on actually being there and is not merely an artifact of selection. And again, the transfers throw doubt on the apparent achievement effects of the other private schools.

Before examining these effects with statistical controls for background, it is useful to turn to the comparable evidence from mathematics tests. This is shown in table 3.8. The achievement gains for those who

TABLE 3.8

*Mathematics Achievement Levels as
Sophomores and Two Years Later for
Students Who Dropped Out of School,
Those Who Remained in School, and
Those Who Transferred, by Sector*

Mathematics Achievement	10	12	Gain
Public			
In school	19.09	20.55	1.46
Dropout	13.85	14.05	0.20
Transfer	18.14	19.17	1.03
Catholic			
In school	22.06	24.47	2.41
Dropout	15.71	15.96	0.25
Transfer	19.64	19.87	0.23
Other Private			
In school	23.21	24.86	1.65
Dropout	17.06	17.29	0.23
Transfer	21.96	23.23	2.27

*A more detailed examination (data not shown here) indicates that the lower sophomore scores among the transfers are confined to those who transferred to another school in the same town and may be described as *student transfers,* in contrast to those who transferred to a school in another town, which may be described as *family transfers.* Among the family transfers, the sophomore achievement level in every sector was *higher* than the sector average. These were 84 percent of all the transfers in the public sector, 60 percent in the Catholic sector, and 71 percent in the other private sector. The student transfers (to another school in the same town) were in all sectors slightly higher in sophomore achievement than the dropouts, but only slightly.

remain in the school differ among sectors, as shown earlier in table 3.2. And similar to the case of verbal achievement, sophomore mathematics achievement, that is, before dropout, is much lower among dropouts than among those who stayed. In the public schools, in fact, the average sophomore mathematics score of dropouts is 0.75 standard deviations below those who remained in school, while the verbal score is 0.64 standard deviations below, indicating that dropping out is more related to low achievement in mathematics than to low achievement in verbal skills—a somewhat surprising result.

When the achievement growth among dropouts is compared for the three sectors, a striking result occurs: There is almost no achievement growth in mathematics among the dropouts from any sector. While verbal skills continue to grow outside school, mathematical skills do not. The result is even more striking when we recognize that the dropouts spent, on average, some of the sophomore to senior period in school before dropping out—implying either that their mathematical learning in school had stopped completely by the sophomore year, or that they lost mathematical skills between the time they left high school and the time they were tested.

The absence of growth in mathematical skills among dropouts also provides confirming evidence that the differential growth effects in mathematics found in Catholic schools are true effects and not an artifact of selection.

An examination of the scores of the transfers shows that as in verbal achievement, all are lower as sophomores than those who remain. The transfers from public schools gain somewhat less than those who remain, the transfers from other private schools gain more, and the transfers from Catholic schools gain very little. Taking the dropout and transfer results for mathematics achievement together, they both confirm the greater effect of Catholic schools than of public schools, as found earlier, and the absence of a greater effect of other private schools, compared to public schools, or perhaps even a smaller effect.

In this examination of achievement of dropouts and transfers, there has been no statistical control on background characteristics. Introducing such control takes account of the fact that the background of dropouts may be, quite apart from their sophomore achievement levels, such that lower achievement growth would be predicted, even if they had stayed in school. The question then is just how much less achievement growth, if any, is estimated in each sector not for the average dropout, but for the student of *average sophomore achievement and background* if he or she does not stay in school, but drops out or trans-

Achievement Outcomes of Schooling

TABLE 3.9

Achievement Growth in Verbal and Mathematical
Skills of Students with Sector Average Background
and Prior Achievement in Each Sector, and the
Predicted Deficit in Achievement Growth Due to
Dropping Out or Transferring to Another School[a]

	Public	Catholic	Other Private
Verbal achievement growth for those in school	2.76	3.46	3.92
Predicted deficit due to			
Dropout	−1.43	−2.85	−1.32
Transfer	−0.47	−1.23	−0.82
Mathematics achievement growth for those in school	1.46	2.41	1.65
Predicted deficit due to			
Dropout	−1.49	−2.11	−0.54
Transfer	−0.52	−2.08	−0.20

[a]The variables that are statistically controlled here (in separate regression equations for each sector) are region of the country, rural-urban-suburban residence, race, Hispanic ethnicity, sex, mother's expectation for college, father's expectation for college, own expectation for college in grade 8, and sophomore achievement (verbal or mathematics). The values of R^2 were 0.71, 0.68, and 0.73 in verbal achievement and 0.71, 0.68, and 0.74 in mathematical achievement, for public, Catholic, and other private sectors, respectively.

fers. Table 3.9 shows this for verbal and mathematics achievement in each sector.

The deficits or losses in achievement growth are greatest for dropouts or transfers from Catholic schools, both in verbal and mathematical skills. These deficits can be seen as another estimate of the "value added" or "achievement added" by schools in each sector. The indication is that in both areas, the achievement added is greatest in the Catholic schools. Comparing the public and other private schools shows similarity in verbal skills, but less achievement added in mathematical skills by the other private schools than by the public schools.

Thus by this comparison, the greater effectiveness of the Catholic sector remains apparent; but the other private schools show no evidence of greater effectiveness than the public schools in verbal skills growth, and there are indications of less effectiveness in mathematics achievement. These results, except for the lack of greater effectiveness

of other private schools compared to public schools in verbal achievement growth, are consistent with those discussed earlier in the chapter.
The results do, however, throw doubt on the greater effectiveness of
other private schools in either area.

What Things Are Learned Out of School?

Achievement of dropouts not only helps in discovering the relative
effects of different types of schools on achievement; it can give some
understanding of just how much of different subjects is learned in
school, compared to out-of-school environment. Dropouts are no longer
exposed to English classes, no longer exposed to mathematics classes, no
longer exposed to classes in any of the subjects covered by the tests
given in the study. Just what difference does it make in verbal skills, as
compared to the difference it makes in mathematical skills, for example? Ordinarily, it is not possible to answer questions about the absolute
effect of schooling, because all children go to school. But a study of
dropouts can give some idea of this.

In each of the tests that was given, it is possible to learn, in each
sector, what the estimated achievement is for students whose initial
achievement was at the level of the students who dropped out, but who
remained in school. These can be regarded as the predicted achievement of dropouts if they had stayed in school. Then by comparing the
predicted levels to the actual achievement of those who dropped out,
it is possible to see just how much more was learned in each subject area
by those who had the same sophomore achievement but remained in
school.

Table 3.10 shows this comparison, in each sector. The public school
figures are most reliable because they are based on, by far, the largest
number of dropouts. They are, therefore, most representative of the
population of school dropouts in the United States, and the out-of-school
environments that they find themselves in, having dropped out of
school, are most representative.

Table 3.10 shows that the growth rate in verbal skills for public
school dropouts is something less than half that of their in-school
counterparts. In mathematics, it is only 10 percent of the in-school
growth. In science, it is about 20 percent, and in civics and writing, it
is close to that in verbal skills. The data for Catholic and other private

TABLE 3.10

Relative Achievement Growth of Dropouts
and Students Who Remained in School with
the Same Initial Achievement Levels[a]

Test	In-School	Dropouts	Ratio
Public			
Verbal	3.68	1.63	0.44
Mathematics	1.91	0.20	0.10
Science	1.33	0.30	0.22
Civics	1.32	0.51	0.39
Writing	2.02	0.80	0.39
Catholic			
Verbal	5.17	1.45	0.28
Mathematics	3.15	0.25	0.08
Science	1.56	0.35	0.22
Civics	1.12	0.17	0.15
Writing	2.61	1.48	0.57
Other Private			
Verbal	5.81	3.27	0.56
Mathematics	2.18	0.23	0.11
Science	1.30	0.27	0.21
Civics	1.94	2.03	1.05
Writing	2.71	3.40	1.25

[a]The in-school achievement levels are obtained from the linear regression of senior achievement on sophomore achievement in each sector, and standardization of the regressions equations to the average sophomore levels of achievement obtained by dropouts.

school dropouts generally confirm this (with the exception of civics and writing for other private school dropouts, which we will refer to again shortly).

Thus, it appears that schooling between grades 10 and 12 makes most difference for mathematical skills, next most for science knowledge, and considerably less for verbal skills, civics knowledge, and writing skills. The results across sectors are most consistent for mathematics and science skills, where the dropouts show least growth.

The high growth shown by other private school dropouts in civics and writing suggests (apart from variability due to sample size) that they may constitute a somewhat different kind of high school dropout ("middle-class dropouts") and are subject to a cognitively richer out-of-school environment than the dropouts from public and Catholic schools. But if this is the case, their low growth in mathematics and science indicates that this cognitive richness of out-of-school environments does not provide them with anything more in mathematics and science than is true for the environments of public and Catholic sector dropouts.

A reminder is necessary here. The dropouts are not like those who remained in school, even those who had the same sophomore achievement scores. We do not know how much they would have learned if they had remained in school, simply because they are different, especially in motivation. What allows this comparison between subject matter areas is that it is the same student who took all six of the tests, so that a comparison between subject areas holds constant the motivations of the student. This means that these results can be used to compare the achievement growth over two years for students at the same initial (in most cases, low) achievement levels who were in school and those who were out of school. They do not imply that the students who dropped out would have gained more if they had been forced to stay in school (for example, by raising the age of compulsory education).

Conclusion

RELATIVE ACHIEVEMENT IN EACH SECTOR

These achievement results in the three sectors of American secondary education provide strong evidence about differential achievement growth in different sectors. Both the comparisons of achievement growth across sectors for students who continued in school from the sophomore to senior year, and the comparisons of achievement growth between dropouts and those who remained in school in each sector show strong evidence of greater growth in Catholic schools than in public schools, in both verbal skills and mathematics. The magnitude of the differential effect is about one grade equivalent—with Catholic sector students showing an achievement growth over the two years of about three grade equivalents compared to the two grade equivalents of growth in the public sector. There is no evidence of greater growth in science knowledge or civics in the Catholic schools.

The evidence about relative achievement growth for the other private schools is more equivocal, on several grounds. In examining achievement growth for students who continued in school, there appears to be an extra effectiveness of these schools for verbal skills, at least as great as that found in the Catholic schools, but not for mathematics (or for science), and perhaps a negative effect for mathematics. However, the examination of achievement growth among dropouts raises some question about the estimated greater effectiveness in verbal skills in other private schools, for their growth in verbal skills is closer to that of their counterparts who remained in school than is true for Catholic and public school dropouts. Finally, it is important to recall the earlier warning that whatever is learned about the other private schools in this sample, the sample itself is smaller and probably less representative of the non-Catholic private sector than is true for either of the other sectors.

ECONOMIC RESOURCES VERSUS SOCIAL RESOURCES

These achievement results in the three sectors provide some evidence about the importance of differences among sectors in economic resources compared to the importance of differences in social resources. The evidence is solidly in favor of the social resources. The Catholic sector schools, with least economic resources but with a functional community base which provides social resources, outdistance the other two sectors in overall achievement growth of their students relative to comparable students in the other two sectors. They clearly bring about greater growth than do the public schools in both verbal and mathematical skills, and greater growth than do the other private schools in mathematics. The other private schools may, on average, bring about greater growth in verbal skills than do the Catholic schools, but if so, the differences is not great.

The other private schools, with very similar levels of economic resources as the public schools, but with the social resources of a value community which reinforces the school's demands, show greater cognitive growth in verbal skills, but no greater, and perhaps less, growth in mathematical skills and in science knowledge. This provides slight, but far from conclusive, evidence that the social resources provided by the consensus on values in the other private schools are effective for bringing about greater cognitive growth—at least in verbal skills.

But the absence of a Catholic sector effect in science, and the absence of an other private sector effect in both mathematics and science, suggests a secondary effect of economic resources. It is generally recognized that Catholic schools are deficient in science facilities such as laboratories and experimental apparatus—and in chapter 2 we showed that the extra course work of Catholic school students in college preparatory mathematics courses is not matched in science. This lack of attention to science seems likely to be due in part to the lack of economic resources required for science facilities and for salaries to attract science teachers. In part, of course, it is due to a choice of how to allocate scarce resources, and here the traditionally scholastic, that is, nonexperimental, orientation of Catholic education may play a role.

The choice of allocation of scarce resources may also play a role in the relatively weak showing of other private schools in mathematics and science. In comparison with public schools, schools in the non-Catholic private sector pay lower salaries but have smaller classrooms. In our sample of other private schools, the student-teacher ratio was less than half that in the public (and Catholic) schools.

The lower teacher's salaries in the other private sector probably has more effect in depressing the supply of qualified mathematics and science teachers, for whom there is competition from industry, than it does in depressing the supply of teachers in the humanities. Thus it may be that the non-Catholic private schools' allocation of resources toward small class sizes rather than teachers' salaries has the effect of creating deficiencies in mathematics and science, relative to education in the humanities.

It would seem that if this is so, it should also be true for mathematics in the Catholic schools; yet the Catholic schools' greater effectiveness in mathematics is at least as great as for verbal skills. We can only conjecture about why there is this greater effectiveness despite the low salaries of Catholic school teachers. Our conjecture is that the relative inflexibility of the Catholic schools' curriculum—an inflexibility which the functional community surrounding the Catholic school seems to support—has been able to withstand the curriculum watering-down and course-content watering-down that occurred in American high schools in the 1970s. If this conjecture is correct, it indicates one of the mechanisms through which a functional community surrounding a school has its effectiveness: through providing sufficient reinforcement by the adult community of the school's demands to allow the school to withstand diversionary influences from the outside. And if this conjecture is correct, it indicates a strength in the functional community that surrounds religiously based private schools that does not exist in the value community surrounding independent private schools. The value community is not a true community in the sense of social interaction, but merely constitutes a kind of penumbra of value-consensus surrounding the schools, with parents individually supporting the school's goals. This individualistic value consensus appears weaker than the functional community of the religiously based school in providing support for maintenance of standards in the school.

4

Dropping Out of High School

IN chapter 3, we examined the relative achievement growth that occurs between grades 10 and 12 in public, Catholic, and other private schools. The principal focus was on achievement in the two areas of essential cognitive skills, verbal skills and mathematics skills. Levels of performance in these areas are important for future life, including college admission, as well as getting and keeping a job. But there is another outcome of high school that also has important consequences for a young person's future: completing high school, or failing to do so. In part, because of the credential that high school graduation constitutes for admission to further education or for getting a job, dropping out of high school has strong and long-term effects on a young person's life. And dropping out of high school is not an action that is disappearing from the American educational scene: the dropout rate among American youth has remained around 25 percent over the past fifteen years.

The extensive consequences for a young person of dropping out of high school, and its prevalence for a quarter of American youth, makes its investigation of special importance. We will begin this examination by considering those students who are not doing well in school. There are two general bases for predictions about what will happen to these students in public and private schools. One basis is the different constraints under which public schools and private schools operate. A second is the difference between schools based on a functional community, those without a functional community but containing a value community, and those with neither. These two bases lead to predictions that are almost diametrically opposed.

Hypotheses on What Happens to Students at Risk of Failure

THE DIFFERENTIAL CONSTRAINTS ON PUBLIC AND PRIVATE SCHOOLS

One basis for predicting what happens to problematic students is the greater freedom of action available to a principal or headmaster of a private school, who is not required to keep unsuccessful students, as is a public school principal, but can expel them without the formalities of due process.* These students will end as dropouts or transfers to public school. Public schools must, according to this thesis, take the castoffs and failures from private schools. The predictions implied by this basis are that students who are behavior problems, who do not expect to graduate, or who have low grades will be more likely kept in school to graduate if they are in public school than if they are in a private school. All categories of private schools should, according to this prediction, show higher rates of dropout and higher rates of transfer (to a public school, not a private one) among these problematic students than public schools. The thesis does not distinguish between dropouts from Catholic schools and other private schools.

CONSEQUENCES OF A FUNCTIONAL COMMUNITY AND A VALUE COMMUNITY

A second basis for prediction about what happens to problematic students is based on the social resources provided by a functional community. A general prediction that would be made for schools based on a functional community is that problems students have as sophomores

---

*Legal procedures of due process were not always a constraint in public schools. Their existence is a result of the increasing challenges to authority in public schools that have occurred with decline in community.

would more likely be discovered and responded to in these schools than in others.*

This prediction would imply that for students who had behavior problems as sophomores, or students who had especially low grades as sophomores, some kind of rescue would more likely have taken place in Catholic schools than in public schools. The Catholic school students should be less likely to have dropped out, should be less likely to have transferred to another school, should have higher grades, and should show fewer behavior problems than the public school students. The functional community, according to this thesis, constitutes a social resource that is especially important for those students at risk of dropping out.

The prediction for schools based on a value community is less clear. The value community should generate norms that encourage achievement and discourage antischool behavior, but without the cross-generational social relations of a functional community, the feedback necessary for a response to the problems will be less present, and the responses would depend more on the individual parent. Other private schools, which are more likely to be based on a value community than a functional community, should lie between the Catholic schools and the public schools in their capacity to intervene in the vicious cycle that leads to failing grades, to serious discipline problems, and to dropping out of school.

Further, the response in the other private schools without a functional community is more likely to be an individualistic one on the part of parents, consisting in many cases of transferring the student to another school, public or private. Transfers would be, according to this prediction, more frequent in the other private schools than in the public schools, because these are parents who have already exercised an individualistic choice, in choosing a private school in the first place.†

---

*In a functional community of the traditional residential kind, there would be a prediction in the opposite direction: A community consensus would develop about those students who perform poorly, and the stigma they carry would be stronger than in a more individualistic, anonymous setting. This stigma would reinforce the vicious cycle leading toward failure. But in the functional community based on a single dimension of association, as in a religiously based private school, this effect would be expected to be much less strong. We discuss this again in chapter 8, where we cover the work of earlier sociologists, such as Hollingshead, who examined these stigmatizing consequences in traditional small-town settings of the first half of this century.

†It should be recalled that the sample of other private schools includes a few religiously affiliated schools along with the nonreligiously affiliated ones, so that the test as described is not a pure one. This sample of schools, however, is insufficiently large to separate out these two classes of schools, and thus to carry out a more pure test. Since the Catholic school sample is larger than the other private school sample and more homogeneous than if other religiously affiliated schools were added to it, we decided to maintain the distinction (as used in Coleman, Hoffer, and Kilgore 1982a).

Dropping Out of High School

Thus the prediction based on functional community is that in the schools embedded in a functional community (represented here by Catholic schools), the problematic sophomores will neither have dropped out nor have transferred, but will have survived through the senior year within the same school. The prediction about schools based on a value community (represented here by other private schools) is that the students will have survived rather than dropped out, but more often through an individualistic solution by the parent, that is, a transfer to a different school. In the public school, the problematic students, the potential dropouts, will be more likely than in either of the other cases to have continued on the same trajectory and have dropped out.

These two bases for predictions about problematic students, the "differential constraints" basis and the "functional and value communities" basis, are almost diametrically opposed. The analysis to be carried out in this chapter will provide some evidence on these predictions and thus shed some light on the functioning of public and private schools for students that are not succeeding in school and are at risk of educational failure.

THE EVIDENCE ON DROPPING OUT

The probability of dropping out of school between spring of the sophomore year and spring of the senior year varies greatly among sectors. The tabulation below shows just how great that variation is, according to our sample estimates:

Sector	Percentage Dropping Out
Public	14.4
Catholic	3.4
Other Private	11.9
High-Performance Private	0.0

It should be noted at the outset that our estimates of the proportions dropping out between these two time points is not an estimate of the total dropout rate in American high schools. There are several factors which differentiate these estimates from the overall dropout rate. The most important is that some students, having been held back in school or having turned sixteen before the spring of their sophomore year, will have dropped out before the period covered by this study. Because it is the students who are overage in grade that will be most likely to drop out, and because they will turn sixteen before spring of the sophomore year, we can expect that a large number of dropouts will have occurred before the first data point.

A second, but much more minor, source of difference is the fact that a few students, though labeled "seniors" in the spring of 1982, would not graduate with their cohort and may have left school without finishing. Finally, there is the problem that in the original survey in the spring of 1980, some sophomores were absent both at the time of the survey and on the makeup days that followed. They are missing from the sample and cannot be counted, yet they obviously include a higher proportion of students who will drop out before graduation than does the sample of students actually covered in the survey. As table 4.5 shows, later in the chapter, over half the public school students and other private school students who were habitually absent in the fall of their sophomore year (but present for the survey) dropped out within the next two years.

These sources of discrepancy between the dropout rates shown here and the total dropout rates from high school do not, however, invalidate the comparison between educational sectors. This comparison covers those students who were in school as sophomores in spring of 1980 and not so habitually absent as to be uncountable. The outcomes we examine concern whether they had left school without graduating before the spring of 1982.

Among the three principal sectors, the Catholic sector has sharply lower dropouts than either of the others. The proportion of students in other private sector that drop out is nearly as high as that in the public sector and over three times that in the Catholic sector. The students in other private schools come from higher socioeconomic backgrounds than those in Catholic schools, so clearly something more than the differences among sectors in the average socioeconomic background of parents is involved as a determinant of dropping out. Dropping out of school is an action that results in part from the organizational dynamics of the school itself, and represents (except for those students who never intended to finish high school) failure in that organizational context.

For this reason it becomes particularly useful to examine those students who, in their sophomore year, have shown some signs that may be precursors to dropping out, such as having low grades, or having a history of disciplinary problems, or having been put on probation in high school, or having been extensively absent without being ill.

This examination of what happens to students who are especially at risk of not completing school because of academic or disciplinary problems is especially useful for what it can tell about the functioning of the schools in each of the sectors. The two different bases for predictions

100

Dropping Out of High School

about what happens to students who are at risk of failure—the differential constraints that public and private schools are under to keep students in school, and the functional community surrounding a school which encompasses the families comprising a religious group—are ideas about the ways schools in different sectors function. Evidence about how well these predictions stand up empirically constitutes evidence about school functioning, and, in the end, evidence about how schools that are agents of the larger society and schools that are agents of the family function for the children within them.

A first step in this examination is to see just how likely students who receive different grades in each of the sectors are to drop out of school during this two-year period. The distribution of grades in the different sectors is similar, as shown in table 4.1.* (High performance private schools are included here, but will not be included in subsequent examination of dropouts because no students in our sample from these schools dropped out.)

The distribution of grades in private sector schools shows somewhat higher proportions of the student bodies at the high end, and somewhat lower proportions at the low end, but overall, the distributions do not differ greatly. The fact that grades are comparative measures within the school that tell how well a student is doing scholastically relative to classmates is emphasized by the distribution in the high-performance schools. That distribution does not differ greatly from the distribution in the two other private sectors despite the fact that (as table 3.2 showed) their performance on standardized tests is much higher.

The percentages of students who drop out at each of these grade levels in the public, Catholic, and other private sectors is shown in table

TABLE 4.1

Distribution of Grades by Sector

Grades	Public	Catholic	Other Private	High-Performance Private
A	9.1	13.8	12.8	13.9
A–B	16.9	20.2	21.2	26.0
B	17.6	21.6	20.0	25.8
B–C	26.4	25.4	27.9	21.1
C	15.1	11.9	10.8	9.4
C–D	10.6	5.0	5.9	2.5
D or below	4.4	2.2	1.4	1.3

*Grades are based on self-reports of overall grades in high school up to spring of the sophomore year. Previous research has shown a high correspondence between self-reported grades and transcript grades.

4.2.* Table 4.2 shows that the proportion of dropouts is quite similar in the public and other private sectors, though somewhat less related to grades in the other private sector (a smaller chance of dropping out at the low end of the grade distribution in the other private sector, and a greater chance at the high end). What is most striking, however, is the small likelihood of dropping out among Catholic students whose grades are above *C.* For students with *C* grades or below, the likelihood rises sharply but is still considerably below that of the public and other private sectors.†

This initial result gives some confirmation to the functional community thesis which asserts that the religious community surrounding these schools is able to interrupt the vicious cycle leading toward continued failure and dropping out. However, the prediction of lower dropouts made on the basis of the value community on which the other private schools are organized is not borne out. The dropout rate of students whose grades are low is nearly as high as that in the public schools, despite the fact that the socioeconomic backgrounds of their students is somewhat higher than that of students in the public sector.

A second type of evidence to examine concerns discipline problems. Table 4.3a shows the proportion of sophomores in each sector who reported that they had had discipline problems in high school or had been on probation. Table 4.3b shows another measure of behavior problems, one which has grown greatly in recent years: absence from school.

TABLE 4.2

Sophomore to Senior Dropout by Sector According to Cumulative Grades in High School Up to Spring of Sophomore Year

	Percentage Dropout in		
Grades	Public	Catholic	Other Private
A	1.6	0.8	5.0
A–B	5.1	1.2	7.7
B	6.7	0.7	8.6
B–C	14.0	0.6	13.4
C	18.9	9.5	15.7
Below C	37.0	22.6	35.5

*As in all the analyses carried out in this book, the observations are weighted according to their sampling probabilities, so that the results are estimates of the populations in each sector. The actual numbers of 1980 sophomore students on which table 4.2 is based are 22,496 in the public sector, 2,517 in the Catholic sector, and 496 in the other private sector.

†The bottom two grade categories are collapsed because of the small numbers in private sector schools.

TABLE 4.3

A. *Percentage of 1980 Sophomores Reporting that They Had
Discipline Problems in School or Had Been on Probation,
by Sector*

	Public	Catholic	Other Private	High-Performance Private
Discipline Problems	19.8	15.7	20.3	12.7
Probation	13.1	8.7	12.0	8.7

B. *Percentage of 1980 Sophomores with Various Numbers of Days
Absent in the Fall of Their Sophomore Year, by Sector*

Days absent, other than illness	Public	Catholic	Other Private	High-Performance Private
0	33.5	48.7	34.2	48.5
1–2	29.7	31.6	33.2	37.6
3–4	18.1	12.5	15.6	8.7
5–15	15.4	6.9	14.8	4.7
16 or more	3.2	0.4	2.2	0.5

The table shows the percentage of students in each sector who report particular numbers of absences other than because of illness in the period between September and Christmas of their sophomore year.

Tables 4.3a and 4.3b show that in all sectors there were disciplinary problems and absences, though the frequency was less in the Catholic sector (and among high-performance private schools) than in either the public or the other private sectors. For both the behavior problems and absences, the public and other private sectors show strikingly similar distributions, and the Catholic and high-performance private schools are strikingly similar. This lower level of discipline problems in the Catholic schools (where the socioeconomic status of the student body is on average about midway between that in the public schools and that in the other private schools) is evidence of the stronger discipline imposed in the Catholic schools. It also suggests an impact of the functional community underlying the school, constraining deviant behavior before it gets to the points of disciplinary problems serious enough to be identified by these measures. In the high-performance private schools, it is harder to separate the effects of school from the effects of student background, because of the higher socioeconomic level of the student body.

TABLE 4.4

Percentage of Sophomores Reporting Disciplinary Problems or Having Been on Probation Who Dropped Out Between Sophomore and Senior Years, by Sector

	Percentage Dropping Out		
	Public	Catholic	Other Private
Disciplinary Problems	28.0	13.1	27.1
Probation	32.7	13.3	34.8

The dropout rates for those students who *do* reach these levels of behavior problems are shown in table 4.4 for disciplinary problems and probation, and in table 4.5 for absence.

Again, as with scholastic problems, students who report disciplinary problems are less likely to drop out in Catholic schools, even though they are a smaller minority, while they are about equally likely to drop out in the public and other private schools. Similarly, among those with extensive absences, a much smaller percentage of Catholic students drop out, although, as table 4.3b showed, they constitute a much smaller part of the student body than in the public and other private sectors. In the other private sector, the percentage of habitually absent students who drop out is even higher than in the public sector. (As indicated earlier, none of the students from the high-performance private schools dropped out, though as table 4.3a showed, the percentages reporting these disciplinary difficulties were of similar magnitudes to that in the Catholic sector. As table 4.9 will show,

TABLE 4.5

Percentage of Sophomores with Different Numbers of Absences in Fall of the Sophomore Year Who Dropped Out Between Sophomore and Senior Years, by Sector

	Percentage Dropping out		
	Public	Catholic	Other Private
0 absences	6.3	1.6	5.3
1–2 absences	9.5	4.9	7.4
3–4 absences	16.7	0.4	3.6
5–15 absences	28.3	11.9	36.4
16 or more absences	56.4	38.8	66.6

20 to 30 percent of these students transfer, though they remain in school.)

For students with discipline problems, the difference between the Catholic schools and the other two sectors is even more pronounced than for students with scholastic problems. Although, as table 4.3a showed, fewer students show discipline problems in the Catholic schools than in the other sectors, fewer than half as many of these students who *do* get into trouble and a much smaller fraction of the habitual absentees end up dropping out from Catholic schools than in the other two sectors.

Again this is a confirmation of the prediction made on the basis of the functional community thesis, that students in trouble are more likely to be rescued before dropping out in a school based on a religious community. But again, the other private schools, based on a value community, appear no more effective in this respect than do the public schools. Nor does it appear that the individual actions of their parents, who chose to send them to a private school in the first place, were more effective than the presumably less active parents of the public school students who were at risk of dropping out.

A summary of the dropout rates of problematic students is given in table 4.6, showing the dropout rates by sector for students with course grades below *C*, past discipline problems in school, past probationary status due to disciplinary causes, or with five or more days absent in the fall of their sophomore year. The dropout rates for these problematic students are very similar in the other private and public sectors; the Catholic sector is sharply lower than either, for both scholastic and disciplinary reasons.

Up to this point, the thesis that a functional community rescues students at risk of failure is strongly supported by the evidence, with

TABLE 4.6

*Percentage of Sophomores Dropping Out Among
Those with Scholastic or Disciplinary Problems,
by sector*

	Percentage Dropout in:		
Problem	Public	Catholic	Other Private
Grade below C	37.0	22.6	35.3
Discipline problems	28.0	13.1	27.1
Probation	32.7	13.3	34.8
5 or more absences	33.2	13.3	40.3

respect to the religious based private sector, while the value community thesis is not. The latter, which depends more nearly on individual actions by parents of a problematic student, appears to offer no greater protection than does the public school.

The thesis that asserts that the rate of dropout from the private sector should be greater than from the public sector because the private schools can easily expel their problems students is not supported by this evidence. The evidence from the Catholic schools and the high-performance private schools is directly opposite to this, and the other private schools show no higher dropout rates than do the public schools among these problem students, though not lower rates either.

TRANSFERRING OUT

There is also other evidence that is important to examine. Pushing problematic students out and back into the public sector is an action that, according to the differential constraint thesis, is one way the private sector disposes of their problems. We have no direct evidence of this, but whether a student transferred between sophomore and senior years provides indirect evidence. Some transfers have nothing to do with schooling but are for family or other reasons. But others do; and particularly the comparison of transfer rates for students who are at risk of failure as sophomores with those who are not can provide indirect evidence about transfers due to poor performance.

The overall estimated numbers of transfers in the student population and percentages transferring from each sector into public and private sector schools is shown in table 4.7. The transfers shown in table 4.7 are only those transfers who are still in school, though a different school than the one attended as a sophomore. A student who has transferred and then dropped out is counted among the dropouts from the school attended at the time of the first data collection. Thus, among those transfers made because of scholastic or disciplinary problems, those who dropped out of the school they transferred to are already counted among the dropouts of the school they transferred from.

Table 4.7 shows that about ten times as many public school students transfer to other public schools as to the private sector, and that, from both of the private sectors, there is a higher transfer rate into public schools than into private school. Part of this discrepancy is to be expected, of course, since the private sector constitutes only about 10 percent of the total high school population. If there is to be the same number of students moving from private to public as from public to

TABLE 4.7

Estimated Numbers and Percentages of Transfers to Public and Private Sector Schools Between Sophomore and Senior Years, by Sector

Original School	Transfer to:							
	Public		Private		Total		Total	
	Number	Percentage	Number	Percentage	Number	Percentage	Number	Percentage
Public	204,417	6.0	18,549	0.5	222,966	6.5	3,419,000	100.0
Catholic	18,664	8.1	4,208	1.8	22,872	9.9	230,329	100.0
Other Private	18,425	14.3	10,283	8.0	28,708	22.4	128,240	100.0

private, the percentages of the private sector student bodies transferring to the public sector must be nine or ten times as great as the percentages of public school students transferring to the private sector. But as table 4.7 shows, these percentages are considerably greater than ten times as high (8.1 and 14.3, compared to 0.5), resulting in just about twice as many students moving from private to public between grades 10 and 12 as there are students moving from public to private. This raises even more directly the question of whether these transfers are especially likely among students who are at risk of failure, particularly in the private sector.

Table 4.8 shows the percentage of students transferring from each sector into public schools and into private schools for students at each point in the course grade distribution. The relation between grades and transfer is near zero in the public sector. For the public sector, about 6 to 7 percent of students transfer, almost independent of grades. Also nearly independent of grades is the destination of those who transfer from a public school. There is only a small relation between grades and the sector of the destination school, with a slight tendency for the high-performing students to have a private school destination more often than do the low-performing students.

This absence of the relation of grades to transfer rate and transfer destination is far from true for the private sector schools, however, as table 4.8 shows. In the Catholic sector, the other private sector, and in the high-performance private sector, the likelihood of transferring to a public sector school increases sharply for students whose high school grades are low. Transfers from Catholic schools to another private school are unlikely at any point in the grade distribution. This probably

TABLE 4.8

Percentage Transferring to Public and Private Sector Schools Between Sophomore and Senior Years, by Grade and by Sector

	Percentage transferring to a public school				Percentage transferring to a private school			
Grade	Public	Catholic	Other Private	H.P. Private	Public	Catholic	Other Private	H.P. Private
A	5.4	1.2	9.2	10.0	0.8	1.7	21.1	0
A–B	5.4	0.4	10.0	0	0.4	0.9	12.1	0
B	5.1	8.4	17.0	3.6	0.8	3.4	4.9	8.0
B–C	6.5	11.8	15.9	6.4	0.6	1.2	6.0	2.4
C	7.2	15.6	15.0	15.3	0.3	3.2	1.3	11.7
Below C	6.7	16.7	25.6	39.5	0.4	0.4	0.0	23.7

reflects the neighborhood or parish basis of most Catholic schools, with the local public school as ordinarily the only other option in the neighborhood.

Transfers from high-performance private schools to other schools in the private sector are primarily among students who are doing badly in coursework, presumably to a less demanding private school. The transfers to the private sector from other private schools are, in contrast, from the upper end of the grade distribution, presumably to a *more* demanding private school.

It is, however, in the transfers to the public sector that the interest lies. There is a strong relation of these transfers to grades, in both Catholic and other private sectors. It is true that only about 17 percent of the Catholic school students with grades below *C* transfer to a public school, and only about a quarter of the other private school students. However, the figure shows that it is the students who are at risk of scholastic failure that are most likely to transfer to the public school. This evidence is consistent with the thesis that asserts that the lesser constraints in private sector schools allow them to dispose of their failures in the public schools.

A similar question arises with respect to students who are disciplinary problems. Do disciplinary problems in private sector schools also lead to transfer from the private to the public sector? Table 4.9 shows that the answer appears to be: Not much. In some comparisons, there is a relation. Students in Catholic schools who have been on probation, those with high absence rates in the other private sectors, and those with discipline problems in the high-performance private schools, all show elevated transfer rates to public schools. But for most of the comparisons, behavior problems show little relation to transfer into the public sector. The generally higher transfer rate of the students in the other private sector is evident, but with the exceptions mentioned, there appears much less effect of discipline problems than of scholastic problems in bringing about transfers into the public sector. (It is quite possible also that some of the higher rates of transfer in the comparisons just mentioned are due to low grades, which are often associated with discipline problems.)

Yet this is not quite the complete picture of transfers between public and private sectors. There is an extensive shift among sectors between elementary and high school. According to our estimates, shown in table 4.10, the Catholic high schools have over 20 percent of their students from public elementary schools, and the other private high schools have almost as many students from public elementary schools as they do from

TABLE 4.9

Percentage Transferring to Public or Private School Among Those with Disciplinary Problems, by Sector

		Percentage transferring to a public school				Percentage transferring to a private school			
		Public	Catholic	Other Private	High-Performance Private	Public	Catholic	Other Private	High-Performance Private
Disciplinary problems	Yes	7.8	8.1	13.6	20.3	0.5	3.2	7.9	0
	No	5.4	7.5	13.9	4.4	0.6	1.6	7.7	4.5
Probation	Yes	7.6	9.7	16.8	19.2	0.4	2.9	4.5	10.5
	No	5.7	6.5	13.5	5.2	0.6	1.8	8.1	3.3
Absences	0-4	6.4	7.9	11.5	6.7	0.6	1.9	9.6	2.9
	5 or more	8.1	9.4	29.1	0	0.6	0.9	0.4	23.1

Dropping Out of High School

TABLE 4.10

*Composition of Enrollment, Graduates, Dropouts, and Transfers
to the Other Sector Among Public, Catholic, and Other Private
Students, According to Sector of 8th Grade Enrollment*

8th Grade Origins	Enrollment (%)	Graduates (%)	Dropouts (%)	Transfers to other Sector (%)
(Public Sophomores)				
Public	94.0	93.9	95.1	89.4
Private	6.0	6.1	4.9	10.6
	100.0	100.0	100.0	100.0
(Catholic Sophomores)				
Public	21.7	20.0	40.1	37.2
Private	78.3	80.1	59.9	67.8
	100.0	100.0	100.0	100.0
(Other Private Sophomores)				
Public	47.1	44.1	61.0	49.8
Private	52.8	55.9	39.0	50.2
	100.0	100.0	100.0	100.0

private sector elementary schools. Similarly, public high schools contain a small proportion of students who were in a private sector school in the 8th grade.

The number of public elementary students who go to other private high schools and are there at grade 10 is approximately equal to the number of students from non-Catholic (other private) elementary schools who go to a public high school and are there at grade 10. The numbers are unequal in the Catholic-public exchange: About three times as many Catholic elementary students are in a public high school at grade 10 as public elementary students are in a Catholic high school at grade 10. Table 4.10 shows the composition of each sector according to the sectors of attendance in grade 8.

The diverse elementary school origins of the private sector students makes the matter of dropouts and transfers more complicated than it has appeared so far. As it turns out, the public school elementary students in private sector high schools contribute disproportionately to the dropouts and the transfers to the public sector, as table 4.10 shows. The public school 8th graders are overrepresented among dropouts and are overrepresented in transfers to the public sector, greatly so in Catholic schools and slightly so in other private schools. In the Catholic sector the public school 8th graders constitute only 20 percent of the gradu-

111

ates, but 40 percent of the dropouts and 37 percent of the transfers to the public sector. In the other private sector, they are 44 percent of the graduates, but 61 percent of the dropouts and 50 percent of the transfers to the public sector. In the public sector, the transfers from private schools are underrepresented among the dropouts (6.1 percent of the graduates, but 4.9 percent of the dropouts), though they are overrepresented (10.6 percent) among the transfers.

The problem of students who transfer after 8th grade from the public sector to the private sector can be seen in another way. Table 4.11 shows the percentage of students in each sector with disciplinary problems, probation, high absence rate, and low grades, according to the sector they were in at the 8th grade. In the Catholic schools, the students who were in public school at grade 8 have greater disciplinary difficulties, more of them show high absence rates, and more of them get low grades than do students who were in the private sector (nearly all in Catholic schools) in the 8th grade. In the other private sector, there are essentially no disciplinary differences, and only small differences in the percentage with low grades, but absence rates are much higher. The private sector transfers to public school show little difference from those who had been in public elementary school.

There is some indication, then, from tables 4.10 and 4.11 that students who transfer from public sector elementary schools to the private sector, particularly to the Catholic sector, contain a high number who were doing poorly, scholastically or behaviorally, in public elementary school. They have more scholastic and disciplinary problems in high

TABLE 4.11

Percentage of Students from Public and Private 8th Grades Who by Grade 10 Had Disciplinary Problems, Probation, High Absence Rate, or Low Grades, by Sector of Enrollment at Grade 10

| | 10th Grade School | | | | | |
| | Public | | Catholic | | Other Private | |
8th grade school:	public	private	public	private	public	private
Percentage with disciplinary problems	19.5	21.6	18.7	15.0	21.4	19.5
Percentage on probation	12.7	15.1	13.9	7.4	11.7	12.3
Percentage with 5+ absences, Fall 1980	18.8	17.7	9.6	6.7	27.9	12.3
Percentage with high school grades below C	14.8	15.8	9.2	6.6	7.9	6.8

school, as table 4.11 shows, a disproportionate number drop out between sophomore and senior years, and a disproportionate number transfer back to the public sector after grade 10. The student transfers from private elementary schools to public high schools appear to be below the private school average, scholastically and behaviorally, but about at the public school average.

Thus, the case that the private sector is sending its scholastic failures back to the public sector appears less clear. Rather, it appears to be sending back to the public sector students who came into the private sector from a public elementary school and were scholastically unsuccessful. The public sector in turn appears to be sending a number of its failures to the private sector, where they sometimes succeed and sometimes do not.

The especially high contribution of the public elementary school transfers to discipline problems, scholastic problems, dropouts and transfers in the Catholic sector suggests another aspect of the functional community: Its degree of closure as a community makes it less valuable as a support for newcomers than for longer-term members of the community. The protections against failure that religiously affiliated schools appear to provide for their students may be less effective for newly arrived students. This will be examined at greater length in chapter 5 when we examine achievement and dropout in Catholic school among students of different religious backgrounds.

DROPOUTS AND TRANSFERS TOGETHER

It is useful at this point to go back to the original question, "What happens to students at risk of failure?" and to examine their destinations in each of the sectors. Table 4.12 summarizes the destinations in the public, Catholic, and other private sectors of students who had grades below *C,* those who reported having had discipline problems, those who reported having been on probation, and those with five or more absences.

Table 4.12 shows first that dropout is lower for all these high-risk groups in the Catholic schools than in the public or private schools, which are very similar in dropout rates for these students. Among these high-risk groups, the other private sector has higher proportions who transfer, while the Catholic sector is between the other private sector and the public sector. The fraction still in the same school or having graduated early is highest in the Catholic sector and lowest in the other private sector.

TABLE 4.12

Destinations of Students at Risk of Failure, by Sector

	Public	Catholic	Other Private	High-Performance
Percentage dropouts among those with:				
Grades below C	37.0	22.6	35.3	0
Discipline problems	28.0	13.1	27.1	0
Probation	32.7	13.3	34.8	0
5 or more absences	33.2	13.3	40.3	0
Percentage transfer among those with:				
Grades below C	7.1	17.1	25.6	63.2
Discipline Problems	8.5	11.3	21.5	20.3
Probation	8.1	22.5	21.4	29.2
5 or more absences	8.7	10.4	29.5	23.1
Percentage in same school or graduated early:				
Among those with:				
Grades below C	55.9	60.3	39.1	36.8
Discipline Problems	63.5	75.6	51.4	79.7
Probation	59.2	64.2	43.8	70.3
5 or more absences	53.34	76.2	30.2	76.9

These results generally support the predictions based on the functional community thesis, but do not support the thesis that the value community on which a school in the other private sector is based offers special protection for those at risk of failure. There is some support for the prediction based on the differential constraint thesis that the private sector schools can get rid of their failures back to the public sector, but this support is reduced by the fact that disproportionate numbers of dropouts and transfers from the private sector were public school elementary students.

Effects of Performance on Dropping Out with Statistical Controls

A final step in this analysis of dropouts and transfers is to examine the effect in each sector of scholastic and disciplinary problems, when other aspects of the students' background and performance are statistically controlled. This will show the basic levels of dropouts in each sector for students of comparable backgrounds, as well as the degree to which the probability of dropping out is augmented by scholastic and disciplinary problems. The analysis is carried out through a logistic regression in which background items as well as scholastic performance and disciplinary behavior are included.

Table 4.13 shows the strong effects of discipline problems, grades, and absences on dropping out in each of the sectors, independently of one another and independently of background factors. It is clear that both academic and behavior problems contribute independently and strongly to dropping out.

Grades are an especially powerful determinant of dropping out of Catholic schools, while behavior problems are especially important for dropping out from other private schools. There appears to be no special effect of a functional community in the Catholic schools in reducing the effects of these school problems in amplifying the probability of drop-

TABLE 4.13

*Expected Dropout Rates in Each Sector for Students
Differing in Disciplinary Behavior, Grades, and Absences,
in Each Case Controlling on Background and Other
Aspects of Status in School*

	Public (%)	Catholic (%)	Other Private (%)
Discipline problems and probation			
Neither	11.5	2.5	8.5
Both	22.1	7.4	28.2
Grades			
Above B average	7.4	1.2	9.2
Below C average	26.7	22.9	14.2
Absences			
None	9.3	2.7	4.9
5 or more	20.6	5.0	35.9

These expected rates are based on weighted logistic regressions for public school students (random sample 4,000), Catholic school students (2,386), and other private school students (470). Variables in the equation are SES, race, Hispanic ethnicity, both parents in home, mother worked before child attended school, frequency of talking with parents about personal matters, mother's college expectation, father's college expectation. For the samples used in this analysis, the dropout rates in each school were lower than for the total sample, because the logistic regression program required listwise deletion of cases. The rates are 12.7 percent, 3.1 percent, and 10.6 percent for the three sectors. The High School and Beyond code for "above B average" was taken as 2; for "below C average" was taken as 6; for "5 or more absences" was taken as 4.5.

ping out, except that the overall level of dropout that is reached among students with discipline problems or high absences is only a third to a seventh of that for comparable students in the public or other private schools. The impact of the functional community lies in part in the reduced incidence of the behavior problems themselves, in part in the very low level of dropouts for all groups of students.

Conclusion

This chapter has examined an important outcome of secondary school, continuing to graduation or dropping out. We began with two conflicting bases for predicting sector effects on dropping out (and transferring out). One was the thesis that the lesser constraints on private schools to keep students who perform poorly academically or who are discipline problems would result in a higher rate of dropouts and transfers among private sector students who are at risk in either of these ways than among public school students. The other was that the social resources provided by a (religious) functional community surrounding the Catholic schools would reduce the rate of dropout and transfer below that in the public schools, and that the value community augmented by parental resources, which characterizes other private schools, would reduce dropout rates from these schools, though it would also lead to elevated transfer rates.

The most striking result in the chapter is the much lower dropout rate from Catholic schools than from either of the other sectors. This very low dropout rate is evidence that the functional community surrounding the Catholic school does provide social resources which keep students from dropping out. This effect is strong at all levels of scholastic performance and discipline-related behavior. It does not, however, keep in school those students performing at especially low academic levels as sophomores—though it does differentially keep in school students who have exhibited discipline problems as sophomores. Those with sophomore grades below C remain much less likely to drop out than those with comparable grades in public or other private schools, although they are much more likely to drop out than Catholic school students with higher grades.

The second most striking result is the relatively high dropout rate from other private schools, almost as high as that from public schools even though the socioeconomic status of students from other private schools, as well as their performance on cognitive tests, is higher than that of public school students. When family background, cognitive skills, and school performance are statistically controlled, the dropout rate is even higher than the rate for public schools. The value community that characterizes other private schools appears not to constitute a social resource to prevent dropping out. Furthermore, in other private schools, dropping out of high school is less related to scholastic performance than in the public schools or (especially) than in the Catholic schools. Dropout in the other private schools seems to stem in greater part from matters other than poor scholastic performance, while in Catholic schools it seems to stem almost wholly from that.

Transferring to another school is higher in both private sectors than in the public sector and is much more highly related to poor scholastic performance, giving some confirmation to the thesis that reduced constraints on private school principals and headmasters allows them to push their failures into the public sector. However, when we look at transfers between sectors that occurred at the end of elementary school, we find that transfers from private elementary to public high school have a *lower* than average chance of dropping out of high school, while transfers from public elementary to private high schools have a *higher* than average chance of dropping out.

Looking at all destinations of those who as sophomores have a high risk of dropping out due to poor scholastic performance or disciplinary problems shows that students from Catholic schools have the highest likelihood of remaining in the same school until graduation, while those in other private schools have the lowest likelihood.

Altogether, these results on dropouts provide a strong confirmation of the importance of social resources provided by a functional community in preventing dropouts. But it does not provide any support for the notion that schools which are agents of the family are by that fact better able to carry their students through to graduation than are schools which are agents of the state. There is no evidence that choice of school per se reduces the chance of dropout among children of those families who have exercised choice to leave the public sector. That reduction appears to be confined to the Catholic schools, or if the hypothesis is correct that their success is based on the religious functional community surrounding them, to those schools surrounded by a functional community.

5

Achievement and Dropout in Disadvantaged and Deficient Families

WHAT schools do for children from disadvantaged backgrounds or deficient families is of special importance in designing education for the future. First we must make a distinction between family backgrounds that we will call "disadvantaged," and those that we will call "deficient."

The backgrounds we will term disadvantaged are those marked by low education and low income. These are the resources in the child's background traditionally regarded as important for the educational development of a child. Children of racial and ethnic minorities are also often regarded as "disadvantaged," the minority status serving primarily as an indicator of low education, low income, and the lack of other resources valuable for educational development. The fact that minority ethnic or racial status is merely a correlate of disadvantage and not a direct measure is indicated by the academic success of children from various immigrant groups throughout American history.

118

Achievement and Dropout in Disadvantaged Families

All this is nothing new. To distinguish what is new, we will use the term "deficient," meaning certain resource deficiencies that were once, but are no longer, largely confined to families of low education and low income. An increasing fraction of families has structural and functional deficiencies. The structural deficiencies lie primarily in what were once called "broken homes," but are now called "single-parent families." It lies secondarily in the increasing involvement of women in the corporate world, the world of work institutions from which children and youth are excluded. The functional deficiencies lie in the increased self-interest of parents, the decreased personal investment in activities of the family as a unit, and the decreased parental involvement with the children. The two principal indicators of structural deficiency in this study are single-parent households and working mothers. The major indicators of functional deficiency as it affects acquisition of cognitive skills is the question of how often the child talks to mother or father, and whether the parents hold expectations for the child's going to college. Obviously a study designed for the purpose of investigating these questions would have better measures, but here we must rely on these indirect indicators.

The importance of treating traditional disadvantage separately from deficiency lies in several points. First is the reduced relation between educational or economic disadvantage and these resource deficiencies. Second is the fact that although the traditional measures of disadvantage are decreasing (as both average education and average real income increase), the structural deficiencies just described are increasing. Thus, to examine the potential problems of education in the future requires examining these growing deficiencies, not merely the traditional disadvantages. It is important to know just what kinds of schools will function well for children of the family of the future—for the family of the future will be marked by these structural deficiencies more often than has the family of the past.

Children from disadvantaged backgrounds or deficient families will make up an increasing fraction of future cohorts of children in the United States. The birth rate of black and Hispanic minorities is larger than in the past, relative to that of non-Hispanic whites, and the fraction of women of childbearing age who are members of these minorities is larger than in the past. The birth rate for women of higher socioeconomic status is less than in the past, relative to that of women of lower socioeconomic status.

Similarly with deficiencies of families as childrearing institutions. An increasing proportion of children grow up living with only one parent.

Families in which both parents are at work outside the home all day are deficient as childrearing institutions; and the proportion of children who are from such households is increasing.

Altogether, the capabilities of the family of the average American child as an institution for raising children and equipping them for modern society is declining, giving special relevance to the questions raised in this chapter. And because the schools in the three sectors are differently grounded in the social structure and have different designs, it seems reasonable to expect that they have different capacities for educating children from these disadvantaged or deficient family backgrounds.

A portion of the questions to be examined in this chapter have already been studied in earlier research using these same data. The examinations were almost entirely confined to the public-Catholic comparison and were concerned only with achievement on standardized tests, not with dropouts. The first examinations (Coleman, Hoffer, and Kilgore 1982a and Greeley 1982) were based wholly on crosssectional data obtained in 1980. In our earlier analysis of the High School and Beyond base year data (Coleman, Hoffer, and Kilgore 1982a, pp. 143–46), we discovered that the effects of measured family background (parental education, race, and Hispanic ethnicity) on achievement in vocabulary, reading, and mathematics were weaker in the Catholic schools than in the public schools. For the other private schools, only the effects of parental education could be tested, but these appeared to be at least as great as in the public schools.

Moreover, we found that the effects of these background characteristics were generally smaller for the 1980 Catholic seniors than for the 1980 Catholic sophomores, while this was not true in the public schools. This suggested that the Catholic schools were functioning to diminish the effects of background, so that the Catholic schools more closely approximated the "common school" ideal of American education than did the public (or the other private) schools (Coleman, Hoffer, and Kilgore 1982a; chap. 6). Approaching the problem in a different way and using different methods of analysis, Greeley (1982) came to similar conclusions in comparing public and Catholic schools.

These results indicate that Catholic schools are differentially effective in increasing achievement on standardized tests for children from backgrounds conventionally regarded as disadvantaged. They are silent concerning the other private schools, they are silent on other outcomes of schooling, in particular dropout, and they are silent concerning children of deficient, rather than disadvantaged families.* It is these questions we will examine here, and from the answers to them, attempt to gain a better understanding of how the different grounding of these three sectors affects their capacity to educate children from disadvantaged or deficient families. In the following analysis, we will first examine effects on standardized achievement, and then effects on dropout.

Achievement Effects

We will focus our examination on growth in verbal and mathematics achievement. As was shown in chapter 3, there appear to be negligible sector effects for science and civics, and the positive effects of Catholic schools on the writing tests does not add substantively to the comparably positive effects on other verbal tests. Thus, we start with the general result that both Catholic schools and other private schools show substantially greater growth in verbal achievement for the average student than do public schools, and that the Catholic schools show substantially higher growth in mathematics achievement than either the public or other private schools—with the latter showing perhaps slightly lower growth than the public schools in mathematics achievement. These results are shown in row 1 of table 5.1. The figures in row 1 are the levels of additional achievement growth beyond that in public schools for Catholic and other private students with background and sophomore achievement equal to the average public school student.† These figures serve as a basis for comparisons with the growth of students from different backgrounds in each sector.

*Two recently published papers test the Coleman, Hoffer, and Kilgore (1982a) and the Greeley (1982) findings with the 1982 High School and Beyond longitudinal data. The results of one of these studies, by Hoffer, Greeley, and Coleman (1985), are incorporated into this chapter. The results of the second paper, by Alexander and Pallas (1985), contradict the Hoffer, Greeley, and Coleman (1985) results, but appear to be methodologically flawed. Critiques of the Alexander and Pallas analysis are found in Hoffer, Greeley, and Coleman (1985, p. 95) and in Jencks (1985).

†Achievement growth was calculated by regressing senior achievement (verbal or mathematics) on sophomore achievement (verbal or mathematics), composite SES, number of siblings, rooms in home, both parents present, mother's labor force participation during pre-elementary years, frequency of talking with parents, father's and mother's college expectations (1980), region (three dummies), respondent's 9th grade college expectations, sex, and handicap status. All regressions were estimated separately by sector; for the analysis of differential effects of race and Hispanic ethnicity we stratified the sector samples into two groups: blacks and Hispanics, and others. The others are called non-Hispanic whites in the text. The other analyses are based on the full sector samples, and included controls for race and ethnicity.

TABLE 5.1

Public and Private School Achievement Growth Differences for Students with Less-Advantaged Backgrounds.[a]

Student	Verbal		Mathematics	
	Catholic Minus Public	Other Private Minus Public	Catholic Minus Public	Other Private Minus Public
Average Public Student	1.11	1.66	0.77	−0.23
Racial-Ethnic				
Black	1.59 (.75)[b]	NA	0.88 (.66)	NA
Hispanic	1.85 (.60)	NA	1.69 (.49)	NA
Non-Hispanic white	0.78 (.22)	NA	0.54 (.28)	NA
Socioeconomic Status				
Low SES	1.21 (.33)	1.68 (.97)	0.84 (.28)	−0.35 (.85)
High SES	1.00 (.36)	1.64 (1.01)	0.70 (.30)	−0.10 (.86)

[a]Measures of growth are for students with backgrounds like that of the average public school student (excluding the indicated dimension), except for the racial-ethnic groups. Then, the backgrounds of blacks and Hispanics are like the average minority (black or Hispanic) public school student, and the average non-Hispanic white public school student, for non-Hispanic whites.
[b]Standard errors in parentheses are adjusted for an assumed design effect of 1.5.

The remainder of the table shows the achievement benefits or costs of attending a Catholic school rather than a public school, or attending an other private school rather than a public school, not for the student of average background, but for students who differ according to measures of traditional disadvantage of background. The first comparison, which can be made only for the Catholic and public schools, concerns minority racial and ethnic status.* Rows 2, 3, and 4 in table 5.1 compare the achievement benefits of Catholic school attendance for black, Hispanic, and non-Hispanic white students. As the comparisons show, the achievement benefits of Catholic school are considerably greater for black and Hispanic students than for non-Hispanic whites. The Catholic advantage for black and Hispanic students is more than double the item increment for whites in verbal achievement. In mathematics, Catholic school blacks learn about 0.9 of an item more and Catholic school Hispanics learn about 1.7 more items than their public school counterparts, while non-Hispanic whites learn only about 0.5 of an item more in Catholic schools.

A second measure of traditional disadvantage is family socioeconomic status, a combination of parental education, occupation, and income.

*The other private schools are excluded from these comparisons due to the combination of a small overall sample size in this sector and small proportions of blacks and Hispanics in their enrollment.

Here, both the Catholic-public comparison and the other private-public comparison are possible. Examining first the Catholic-public comparison, rows 5 and 6 show that the greater effectiveness of Catholic schools for achievement growth is also higher for students from low SES backgrounds than for those from high SES backgrounds. Designating students one standard deviation below the public school average on the SES composite variable as "low SES," and those one standard deviation above as "high SES," the comparison shows that the low-SES students realize greater additional growth in the Catholic schools, for both verbal and mathematics skills than do the high-SES students.

The comparison between other private and public schools shows that the additional other-private growth in verbal skills is about the same for low and high SES students. In mathematics, where a slight decrement is estimated for other private schools, that decrement is estimated to be *larger* for low SES students than for high.

Altogether, the results of table 5.1 show that the achievement benefits of Catholic schools are greater both in verbal skills and in mathematics skills for students from traditionally disadvantaged backgrounds. This is consistent with the cross-sectional results of Coleman, Hoffer, and Kilgore (1982a) and Greeley (1982), and with the longitudinal results of Hoffer, Greeley, and Coleman (1985). However, the other private schools, which show a verbal achievement benefit for the student of average background, show about the same degree of benefit for students from traditionally disadvantaged backgrounds and students from advantaged backgrounds. There is an indication that in mathematics, where other private schools show a slight achievement cost compared to public schools, that this cost is greater for students from disadvantaged backgrounds than for those from advantaged backgrounds. Thus there is a differential benefit to students from traditionally disadvantaged backgrounds in attending a Catholic school, but no such differential benefit in attending another private school.

The same kind of question can be asked about students from deficient families. Is the achievement benefit of Catholic schools in verbal and mathematics skills and the achievement benefit of other private schools in verbal skills greater or less for families with these deficiencies than for those without? The answer is given in table 5.2, which shows the estimated achievement growth of a student who has a public sector average background, except for the structural and functional deficiencies discussed earlier. In row 1 is the estimated achievement for students without such family deficiencies, and row 2 is the estimated achievement for students from families with these deficiencies. The

TABLE 5.2

Achievement Growth of Public and Private School Students with and without Family Deficiencies, with Backgrounds Otherwise Equal to the Public School Average

	Public	Catholic	Other Private
Verbal Achievement Growth			
Without family deficiencies	3.28	3.98	5.06
With family deficiencies	2.00	4.11	3.21
Deficit	1.28[*]	−0.13	1.85[*]
Mathematics Achievement Growth			
Without family deficiencies	1.96	2.65	2.66
With family deficiencies	0.75	1.58	−0.24
Deficit	1.21[*]	1.07[*]	2.90[*]

[*]Predicted deficit statistically significant at $p < .05$.

differences between estimated achievement growth of students from nondeficient families and that of students from deficient families can be termed the achievement deficit of students from these deficient families in each sector.

For verbal achievement, students from deficient families are estimated to show no deficit at all in Catholic schools, a substantial deficit (less than two-thirds the achievement growth of those from nondeficient families) in the public schools, and an even greater deficit in the other private schools. In mathematics achievement, the order is the same: least deficit in Catholic schools, greatest deficit in other private schools. In the other private schools, the deficit is so great as to wholly account for the slightly negative effect of other private schools in mathematics. Students from families without these deficiencies learn more mathematics in the other private schools than the public schools.

These achievement results for students from deficient families show the same Catholic sector "equalizing" effect compared to public schools as found for students from traditionally disadvantaged backgrounds. But where there seemed little or no differential effect in the other private sector by disadvantaged background, there is a strong "unequalizing" effect by deficient family. Thus the two private sectors are on either side of the public sector: Catholic schools produce more equal outcomes independent of family deficiencies, and other private schools produce more divergent outcomes between those students with and without family deficiencies.

These striking differences between the two private sectors raise questions about their different functioning and perhaps more generally of the different functioning of religiously based private schools and the independent private schools. Given both the different grounding of schools in these two sectors, and their differences in design, the question arises why these two sectors (and the public sector) are so different in their functioning for students with family deficiencies. But before examining evidence on that question, we will discuss dropping out among students from disadvantaged and deficient families.

Dropouts, Disadvantage, and Deficiency

We will ask similar questions about the effect of public, Catholic, and other private schools on student dropouts from backgrounds that differ in their degree of disadvantage, and families that differ in their degree of deficiency. In doing so, it is important to keep in mind the fact that the achievement data examined in the preceding section was limited to those students who were in the same school as sophomores and seniors. The school's impact on the dropout rate is an independent measure of the school's effect, because the dropouts and transfers are not counted in examining achievement growth. But although the measures are independent, school policies may affect both, and certain policies might well affect them in opposite directions. For example, a policy of rigorous demands might increase the achievement growth of those who remain in school, but at the cost of bringing about more dropouts. There is no reason, therefore, to expect that schools with higher achievement growth in verbal and mathematical skills among those who remained in school would show lower dropout rates than would schools with lower achievement growth.

Second, it is important to keep in mind that dropping out of school is a phenomenon that appears to have two major sources. One can be seen in the noncompletion of high school as the normal termination of education in order to go to work at a job not requiring a high school education. This has been, in recent generations, limited to a fraction of the youth from lower socioeconomic backgrounds. And as the jobs not requiring a high school education have become fewer and fewer, this reason for dropping out has become much smaller. This source of dropout is associated with what we have called traditional measures of disadvantage, low socioeconomic background and being a member of a disadvantaged racial or ethnic minority. A second source of dropout, which accounts for an increasing fraction of all dropouts, is what can be regarded as failure—which of course, may arise in a number of different ways, but in general is less associated with traditional measures of disadvantage than is the first source. One of these ways, which became more important in the 1970s, is a general disaffection with education which cuts across socioeconomic status and has been called "middle-class dropout."

Recognition of these two different sources of dropout is important because of their different relation to traditional disadvantage and to deficient families. The first reason for dropout is almost wholly limited to the disadvantaged and may be an important source of dropout among some Hispanic immigrant groups whose parents have had little education. The second reason for dropout is not limited to the disadvantaged, for it is a change in course of students whose parents fully intended them to complete high school (and perhaps more) and who themselves intended to do so. If, on the other hand, family deficiencies (apart from socioeconomic or minority disadvantage) have an effect on dropout, it is an effect on this second source of dropout. In examining dropout in the different sectors, we can expect to find not only the first source of dropout, but also the second, and thus a possible relation to family deficiencies, apart from traditional disadvantage.

Because dropping out of school is one extreme in the continuum of academic success, it would be appropriate also to compare the relative effects of the three sectors on the other extreme of success, such as, for example, the percentage whose sophomore cognitive achievement scores were at or near the upper limit. Thus, when we compare the percentages dropping out in each sector for students with and without specific disadvantages in background, we are examining only one end of a continuum of academic success. The results say nothing about differential sector effects for students from various backgrounds toward the other end of the continuum of academic success.

THE EVIDENCE ON DROPOUTS

As chapter 4 showed, dropout rates are strikingly lower among Catholic sector students than among students in the other two sectors. Catholic schools appear to provide a much more effective protection against dropping out of high school than does either the public or the other private sector. Here we ask how that protection against dropping out differs for students from different backgrounds. First we examine measures of traditional disadvantage, racial and ethnic minority status, and

126

Achievement and Dropout in Disadvantaged Families

socioeconomic status. Table 5.3 shows the percentage dropping out in each sector, for blacks, Hispanics, and non-Hispanic whites. The rates are highest in all sectors for Hispanics, next for blacks, and least for non-Hispanic white.

In each sector, the percentage dropping out of Catholic schools is much lower than for the other two sectors. The absolute size of the Catholic sector reduction, relative to public schools, is least for Hispanics and greatest for blacks, while the percentage reduction is greatest for whites.

Thus there is a strong staying-in-school benefit to being in a Catholic school for all three groups, though the benefit is least strong for Hispanics. Insofar as dropouts in all three groups (quite apart from race and ethnicity) are from more disadvantaged backgrounds than nondropouts, the Catholic sector brings about a protection against dropout for students from disadvantaged family backgrounds. But as table 5.3 shows, this protection is less strong for Hispanic students than for others. Thus, for this first measure of traditional disadvantage, there is not the same result as for achievement growth. It is not the case that the higher dropout rate among disadvantaged minorities is suppressed in Catholic schools, relative to that in public and other private schools. The dropout rate from Catholic schools is much lower in each group than in public or other private schools, but not differentially lower among minorities than among whites. For other private schools the rates are comparable to those in public schools, though the black and Hispanic sample sizes are too small for strong inferences.

A second measure of family disadvantage is family socioeconomic status. Family SES (table 5.4) has a strong association with dropping out in the public and Catholic schools but has a much less strong impact in

TABLE 5.3

*Percentage of Students Dropping Out of High
School by Race-Ethnicity and School Sector*

| Race-Ethnicity | School Sector | | |
	Public	Catholic	Other Private
White	13.1	2.6	10.8
	(18,062)	(1,703)	(508)
Black	17.2	4.6	14.4
	(3,468)	(415)	(15)
Hispanic	19.1	9.3	22.9
	(4,565)	(591)	(55)

Sample sizes in parentheses.

127

the other private schools. The effect of SES in other private schools also appears inconsistent, but the low estimate of dropout among low-SES other private students, 7.2 percent, is based on a small sample of students (N=36) and is likely to be unstable. Of the various components of the SES composite variable used here, parental education, particularly mother's education, is the dominant factor in the dropout decision. Additional analysis (not tabulated here) indicates that the critical distinction is whether or not the mother completed high school: The dropout rate among students whose mothers completed high school or more is much lower than for those whose mothers did not complete high school.

Socioeconomic status is strongly related to dropping out in the public and Catholic schools. The Catholic dropout rate is much lower among students in each SES quartile, although the relation of dropping out to SES is greater than in either of the other sectors. Catholic school students in the lowest socioeconomic quartile are over four times as likely to drop out than those in the next lowest quartile. It is clear that the high school completion benefits conferred by Catholic sector schools on their students are not especially great for students disadvantaged by the socioeconomic criterion but are in fact less than for those in the upper three-quarters of the socioeconomic scale. Once again, as for racial and ethnic minorities, and in contrast to the results for achievement, Catholic schools do not show differential benefits for students from backgrounds that are traditionally disadvantaged. They show very strong benefits for all students, but the benefits appear to be greater for those of higher socioeconomic levels.

TABLE 5.4

Percentage of Students Dropping Out of High School, by Composite SES Quartiles and School Sector

| SES Quartile | School Sector | | |
	Public	Catholic	Other Private
1 low	22.3	14.9	7.2
	(6,251)	(368)	(36)
2	13.2	3.3	15.8
	(5,780)	(553)	(75)
3	10.7	0.2	14.3
	(5,450)	(655)	(115)
4 high	7.1	1.7	8.9
	(5,087)	(951)	(277)

Sample sizes in parentheses.

Achievement and Dropout in Disadvantaged Families

This result is especially curious since the other private schools show the *lowest* relation of dropout to socioeconomic status. If the other private schools showed benefits vis-à-vis dropout compared to the public schools, this relatively flat relation of dropout to socioeconomic status would be grounds for saying that the other private schools are differentially beneficial for students from low socioeconomic status. As it is, however, the rates are *higher* in other private schools than in public schools, at all socioeconomic levels except the lowest, where the sample size is small. It is almost as if one must say that the other private schools are differentially harmful for students from higher socioeconomic status. Such a statement, however, can hardly be made in view of the fact that the sample showed no dropouts at all (among sophomores) from the high-performance private schools, which have the students from the highest socioeconomic backgrounds.

Some insight concerning this puzzling difference between the distribution of effectiveness of the Catholic sector and the other private sector in cognitive skill growth and dropout can be gained by examining the second measure of disadvantage, that is, deficient families. Tables 5.5, 5.6, and 5.7 show the relation of dropout to families that are structurally deficient, to families that are functionally deficient, and to family deficiency overall. All three of these tables show a striking result: The Catholic sector benefits are especially great for students from families with deficiencies, whether structural, functional, or combined. The relation of dropout to deficient families is small or absent in Catholic schools, which show very low dropout rates for students from all types of families. In contrast, the public sector and the other private sector show strong relationships of dropout to family deficiencies, whether structural, functional, or combined. The other private sector shows an even higher relation of dropout to family deficiencies than does the public sector.

We can also examine the effects of traditional disadvantage and modern family deficiency with statistical controls for each of these aspects of background. In table 5.8 the results of logistic analyses are shown for each of the three sectors, in which all the background variables discussed are included. The first two rows of table 5.8 show the expected dropout rates in each sector for students from socioeconomic status 1 standard deviation above and one standard deviation below the sector mean.* In the public and Catholic sectors, a higher socioeconomic status reduces the chance of dropout. The reduction is slightly greater in the public sector, though only 3 percent. The effect of SES in the other

---

*The standard deviation of SES in the public sector, 0.341, was used.

TABLE 5.5

Percentage Dropping Out of High School Between Sophomore and Senior Year From Families with Varying Degrees of Structural Deficiency[a]

	Public	Catholic	Other Private
Neither	12.1	3.4	8.9
	(11,972)	(1,414)	(285)
One	15.8	3.9	12.7
	(11,788)	(1,058)	(261)
Both	20.3	0.8	28.0
	(2,335)	(237)	(32)

[a]Sample sizes in parentheses.

TABLE 5.6

Percentage Dropping Out of High School Between Sophomore and Senior Year From Families with Varying Degrees of Functional Deficiencies[a]

	Public	Catholic	Other Private
Neither	8.2	2.1	6.3
	(9,755)	(1,452)	(290)
One	16.9	4.9	16.2
	(12,402)	(1,053)	(246)
Both	22.5	4.1	24.4
	(3,938)	(204)	(42)

[a]Sample sizes in parentheses.

TABLE 5.7

Percentage Dropping Out of High School Between Sophomore and Senior Year From Families with Varying Degrees of Functional or Structural Deficiency, by Sector

Deficiencies	School Sector		
	Public	Catholic	Other Private
None	6.8	2.7	9.5
	(5,086)	(823)	(109)
1	11.8	3.1	5.1
	(8,704)	(1,006)	(200)
2	18.5	4.6	13.4
	(9,284)	(675)	(175)
3 or 4	24.3	4.1	40.2
	(3,020)	(205)	(34)

Sample sizes in parentheses.

Achievement and Dropout in Disadvantaged Families

TABLE 5.8

*Expected Dropout Rates in Each Sector for
Students Differing in Socioeconomic Status, in
Family Structural Deficiencies, and Family
Functional Deficiencies, in Each Case
Controlling on Other Aspects of Background*

	Public (%)	Catholic (%)	Other Private (%)
SES			
1 SD Above	12.0	1.8	10.0
1 SD Below	14.8	4.5	9.4
Structural Deficiencies			
None	11.8	3.3	7.2
Both	18.8	1.6	18.6
Functional Deficiencies			
None	8.9	2.5	4.4
Both	20.7	3.4	28.4

These expected rates are based on weighted logistic regressions
for public school students (random sample 4,000), Catholic school
students (2,478), and other private school students (491). Variables in the equation are SES, race, Hispanic ethnicity, both parents in home, mother worked before child attended school,
frequency of talking with parents about personal matters,
mother's college expectation, father's college expectation. For
the samples used in this analysis, the dropout rates in each school
were lower than for the total sample, because the logistic regression program required listwise deletion of cases. The rates are
13.3 percent, 2.9 percent, and 9.7 percent for the three sectors.

private sector is almost absent; the higher SES students are even slightly
more likely to dropout when the other background characteristics are
controlled statistically.*

The third and fourth rows of table 5.8 show the expected dropout
rates for students from families with and without the two structural
deficiencies described earlier. The absolute effects are strong in the
public schools, extremely strong in the other private schools, and small

*Effects of race and Hispanic ethnicity are not shown in the table. The estimated
dropout rates are as follows:

	Public	Catholic	Other Private
Non-Hispanic White	12.6	1.7	11.2
Black	16.7	2.9	18.7
Hispanic	19.9	4.9	32.8

For both blacks and Hispanics, the other private estimates are based on small numbers
of cases.

and even slightly reversed in the Catholic schools. The bottom two rows show the effects of functional deficiencies. Here the effects are stronger than the effects of structural deficiencies in the public schools and the other private schools, with the expected rate rising to 28 percent in the latter schools for students who did not talk to parents about personal matters and whose parents had no college expectations. In the Catholic schools, there is only a small effect of these deficiencies.

These analyses show the powerful effects of these modern family deficiencies in the public schools and especially in the other private schools, indicating that it is principally these structural and functional deficiencies of the family, rather than the traditional disadvantages, that are responsible for much of the dropout from high school in modern society. The analyses shows also the relative imperviousness of students in Catholic schools to these family deficiencies.

If we set aside for the moment the overall lower rate of dropout in the Catholic sector than in either of the other two sectors, the two private sectors function quite differently with respect to students who are traditionally disadvantaged and those whose families have structural or functional deficiencies. The public schools are in between on both measures. The Catholic schools show the strongest relation of dropout to the basic measure of traditional disadvantage, that is socioeconomic status, and the other private schools the weakest relation. Their positions are reversed for students from deficient families: The other private schools show the strongest relation of these family backgrounds to dropout, while the Catholic schools show little or no relation —again with the public schools in between.

This provides a rather strong indication that dropout from Catholic schools is largely limited to what we described earlier as the first source of dropout, that is, dropout which does not represent a sharp change of course but constitutes a termination of education to pursue jobs that do not require a high school diploma. Dropout from the other two sectors, however, and particularly from the other private sector, appears to stem from the second source, involving a sharp change of course, dropping out of an activity that one had intended to complete.* This source of dropout, with a low relation to the traditionally disadvan-

*Confirmation of this inference is provided by the fact that, by spring of 1984, two years after the normal point of graduation, only 18.6 percent of Catholic school dropouts had obtained a high school equivalent diploma, while 50 percent of other private school dropouts and 22.6 percent of public school dropouts had done so. It seems clear that the educational aims of the public and other private school dropouts were, on the average, higher than those of the Catholic school dropouts. Because of the very low rate of dropout from Catholic schools, this still left a smaller proportion who had dropped out and not obtained a diploma than in the other private sector or the public sector.

taged, has been called as suggested earlier, "middle-class dropout." Middle- and upper-class students (and as chapter 4 showed, students with intermediate and even high levels of sophomore achievement) tend to drop out of the other private and public schools at much higher rates than in the Catholic schools. It is useful to ask what lies behind this source of dropout, and why it is not present in the Catholic schools. The state of affairs appears to be not that the first source of dropout is higher in Catholic schools than in the other private and public schools, for it seems to be somewhat lower, but that the second source of dropout, the "middle-class dropout," which is often regarded as stemming from alienation, is almost absent in Catholic schools. The question is, why the difference.

MIDDLE-CLASS DROPOUT, EGOISM, AND ANOMIE

Behind the similarity in the pattern of dropouts in the public and other private sectors may be two different processes. In the public sector, the integrative structures of the school tend to be pluralistic, with a variety of relatively independent bases available for students to become attached to: sports, advanced academic specialties, vocational interest clubs, and a wide array of other extracurricular activities. In larger schools, which are the norm in the public sector, these units serve as the principal mechanisms through which students are able to feel a part of the school, and which require a certain commitment to the school on the part of the student. Opportunities for such involvement are limited, however, and largely dependent on the student's own initiative. Students who do not participate in these groups may not find the support and structures of obligation that function to keep one in school. A student may be psychologically and administratively "lost" in a large public high school. A student who does not have a concretely based sense of belonging to the school is likely to, at least, be very familiar with the temptation to drop out, if not actually to do so.

Strong families are often able to fill this void, but if families are not strong there is often no functional community to provide backup support and insure that the student becomes reintegrated into the school.

In the other private schools, a different set of structures and forces may be operative. These schools tend to be small and organized around a specific value orientation. Recruitment of students is ordinarily more selective than in the Catholic schools, and almost all students who enroll are involved in extracurricular activities. These engender a school-based community within the student body. Students are hardly likely to become administratively "lost." How might the relatively high drop-out rates in these schools be accounted for then? One possibility is that the school is not surrounded by a functional community, in which each family's child is the responsibility of all. If a student becomes alienated from the dominant norms of the school-based community (which because of school size are more likely to be monolithic than in the public school), there are few forces, apart from family, to prevent dropping out. There is a certain irony here, for these schools tend to be the most "child-centered" in terms of ideology and day-to-day practice. The school may do all that it can to help the students, but this institutionalized help is not a substitute for the integration that would be provided by a functional community among the families with children in the school. The individualistic character of enrollment in and attendance at these schools may well lead to social isolation. Despite the school's efforts, a student, without socially integrative forces surrounding the school, may come to see no alternative to dropping out, finding no happiness in being there.

The students in these schools are not (except in private schools in unusual setting such as a university-based school attended primarily by children of faculty) drawn from a single neighborhood, but from various neighborhoods in the city. The parental choice is a highly individualistic one, and neighborhood friendships of students are often truncated by this choice. Thus, neither the neighborhood-based friendship groups that form in childhood, nor a community of adults attentive to the activities of all members' children, surrounds the student. If the student is not integrated into the school, integration into the family and support from the family becomes especially important if the student is to find sufficient social rewards to merit staying in school.

The phenomenon of substantial dropout rates in public and other private schools among students with satisfactory cognitive skills and those without disadvantaged backgrounds recalls Emile Durkheim's study of anomie and egoistic suicide (1951). Durkheim showed that suicide rates were much higher among persons whose own social integration into a family was low and in cultures which emphasized individualism at the expense of social integration. Indeed, Durkheim found that areas of Europe in which Catholicism was dominant showed lower suicide rates than those in which Protestantism was dominant, and attributed the result to the individualistic character of Protestantism. Here, of course, we cannot separate out the effect of a religious community surrounding the school from the communal or individualistic character of that religion and have interpreted the effect as due to that of the religious community per se. It remains for further research, with a sufficient sample of schools with religious orientations other than Catholic, to separate out these two elements.

It is clear, however, that many public high schools, as well as most independent private schools, constitute a setting without a set of social resources outside the family from which a young person can draw. Large public high schools often constitute such a setting, if the school is not an outgrowth of a residential community. Small private high schools are not an anonymous and individualistic setting, and some attempt to create a community within the school. But the out-of-school social settings for other private school students often approximate the individualistic and isolating social setting that Durkheim investigated.

For Whom is the Catholic School's Functional Community Effective?

Among the students attending a Catholic school, not all are Catholics. Among the Catholics in the school, not all are involved in the religious community. What about the effectiveness of the Catholic school for these students? Does the functional community operate only for those near its center or also for those on the periphery? Is there differential effectiveness depending on the family's involvement in the functional community? A direct examination of these questions can be gained if the Catholic sector effects on achievement growth are estimated separately for Catholics and non-Catholics, holding constant other aspects of background. The results of this test indicate that students who are Catholic do benefit more from a Catholic school education than do non-Catholic students. Table 5.9 shows that Catholics in Catholic schools learned over 1 additional verbal item and 0.76 additional mathematics items compared to public school Catholics, while non-Catholics in Catholic schools learned only 0.69 additional verbal items and 0.28 additional mathematics items compared to their public school counterparts. The indication, then, is that Catholic schools are most beneficial for students who are members of the Catholic religious community. At the same time, it is not the case that nonmembership constitutes a liability, for non-Catholics in Catholic schools are still learning more than they would in a public school.

But church membership does not necessarily involve active partici-

TABLE 5.9

Predicted Achievement Growth in Public and Catholic Schools of Catholic and Non-Catholic Religion Students with Backgrounds and Sophomore Achievement Otherwise Equal to the Average Public School Student[a]

	Sophomore-to-Senior Growth		Catholic Advantage
	Public	Catholic	
Verbal Achievement			
Catholic religion	2.92	3.98	1.06 (.35)
Non-Catholic religion	2.66	3.39	0.69 (.60)
Mathematics Achievement			
Catholic religion	1.61	2.37	0.76 (.29)
Non-Catholic religion	1.39	1.67	0.28 (.54)

[a]Standard errors in parentheses.

pation in the church, and it may be the case that nonparticipants are effectively penalized in schools organized around a religious community, even though they are nominal members of the community. We can gain an idea of the extent to which this is true by making use of a question from the base year survey that asked students how frequently they attended religious services. The possible responses ranged from "more than once a week" to "never." Estimated achievement growth in public and Catholic schools for Catholic students with backgrounds otherwise like that of the average public school student who responded at the extremes to this question is shown in table 5.10.* The benefits of Catholic school attendance for Catholic-religion students are greater for those who attend religious services more frequently. Infrequent attenders still realize a benefit from Catholic school compared to their public school counterparts, but the benefits are only about half of those realized by frequently attending Catholics. For mathematics achievement growth, those who never attend religious services show in fact slightly less achievement growth than was shown for non-Catholics in table 5.9 (though the difference is not statistically significant).

The greater achievement effects of the Catholic schools for Catholics than for non-Catholics and the greater effects for those Catholics who are integrated into the religious community than for those who are not

*Estimated achievement growth was calculated from regressions of senior achievement on sophomore achievement, the set of background variables listed in the footnote on p. 121, a Catholic religion dummy variable, the frequency of religious service participation, and an interaction of Catholic religion and service particiaption.

Achievement and Dropout in Disadvantaged Families

TABLE 5.10

*Predicted Achievement Growth in Public and Catholic Schools of
Catholic Religion Students Who Attend Religious Services
Frequently and Infrequently with Background Otherwise Equal to
the Average Public School Student[a]*

	Sophomore-to-Senior Growth		Catholic Advantage
	Public	Catholic	
Verbal Achievement			
Catholic religion students			
Attend church often	3.01	4.29	1.27 (.44)
Never attend church	2.82	3.53	0.71 (.50)
Mathematics Achievement			
Catholic religion students			
Attend often	1.99	2.84	0.86 (.39)
Never attend	1.21	1.51	0.29 (.46)

[a]Standard errors in parentheses.

provide strong confirmation of the effect of integration into a functional community on student achievement. But the dropout rate should provide an even more sensitive test, for two reasons: First, dropout is more closely related in content to lack of social integration than is achievement on standardized tests. Second, Catholic schools, based on a religious community and public or other private schools, which are not, differ much more in dropout rates than in achievement growth of those who remain in school. Thus, on both theoretical and empirical grounds we would expect to find dropout rates reflecting the degree of integration into the religious community. Table 5.11 shows the dropout rate for Catholics and non-Catholics in Catholic schools. Both are equally low, offering no confirmation of the effect of integration into the religious community on dropout rate. Table 5.12, however, shows that the dropout rate among Catholic students who rarely or never attend

TABLE 5.11

*Dropout Rate of
Catholic and
Non-Catholic Students
in Catholic Schools*

Catholics	Non-Catholics
3.4%	2.9%
(2,065)	(455)

TABLE 5.12

*Dropout Rate of Catholics from Catholic Schools
According to Frequency of Attendance at
Religious Services*

Often (1/week or more) (%)	Sometimes (%)	Rarely or Never (Never or 1 to 2/year) (%)
2.7	5.3	6.2
(1,421)	(340)	(278)

church is over twice that of those who attend once a week or more. It is much lower than that of Catholics in the public or other private schools who rarely or never attend church (6.2 percent versus 17.6 percent and 34.9 percent, respectively), but it is much higher than those in Catholic schools who do attend church.

There are additional pieces of evidence about the role of functional communities in affecting a student's likelihood of dropping out of school. One is the rather strong relation of dropping out of school to nonattendance at religious services. In each sector, the dropout rate is about twice as high among those who rarely or never attend church as among those who attend once a week or more, as shown in table 5.13. This suggests that integration into a religious community per se, even when there is no link between the religious community and the school, provides the kind of social-psychological resource which sharply reduces the likelihood of dropping out of high school. Another piece of evidence supports this. The Catholic church as a religious community appears to exercise a stronger integrative force than do most other

TABLE 5.13

*Dropout Rate of Students from Public,
Catholic, and Other Private Schools According
to Frequency of Attendance at Religious
Services*

	Often (%)	Sometimes (%)	Rarely or Never (%)
Public	9.1	14.9	19.5
	(8,945)	(3,686)	(7,688)
Catholic	2.6	4.4	5.9
	(1,552)	(419)	(374)
Other	8.1	14.3	16.1
	(241)	(68)	(156)

Achievement and Dropout in Disadvantaged Families

religious groups. Those Catholic students who attend school outside this community (that is, in a public or other private school) and who do not attend church, relative to those who are integrated into the community in one or both of these ways, would then be especially vulnerable to the psychosocial resignation that constitutes dropping out of high school. As table 5.14 shows, each of the two forms of integration is strongly related to the likelihood of dropping out. Only 2.7 percent of those students integrated into the community in both ways drop out, while 21.1 percent of those who are not integrated in either way drop out of high school.

The evidence from tables 5.13 and 5.14 indicates a role of religious observance that goes beyond the discussion so far. These data indicate that attendance at religious services, independent of the school's connection to the religious body, provides social support for remaining in school, and thus protects against dropping out of school. Religious attendance in this interpretation, then, constitutes an involvement in a locally based functional community, and that functional community, even without a formal connection to the school, provides the support, norms, and constraints that lead high school students to complete their schooling rather than to drop out. Religious groups are, of course, only one of the bases for a functional community that cuts across generations, but, with the waning of other bases, it is one of the most important, perhaps the most important, that remains.

Taken all together, the results of this section give strong support for the hypothesis that integration into a functional community exercises a strong impact on students' school outcomes. It is precisely those students who are most integrated into a school grounded in a functional community—Catholics who attend church most regularly—that benefit

TABLE 5.14

Dropout Rate Among Catholics According to Two Measures of Integration into the Catholic Community: School and Church

	Church		
School	Attend often (1/week or more) (%)	Sometimes (%)	Rarely or Never (Never or 1 to 2/year) (%)
Catholic school	2.7% (1,421)	5.3% (340)	6.2% (278)
Public or other private school	6.5 (3,399)	13.6 (1,217)	21.1 (2,262)

most from Catholic school attendance. And, more generally, those students who are most integrated into some religious community, whether connected to the school or not, are more likely to complete high school than those who are not.

What About Religiously Based Schools in the Other Private Sector?

The differences between the Catholic schools and the other private schools that are apparent in the preceding analyses are extensive. This is true particularly for dropouts but also for other outcomes of schooling, such as growth in cognitive skills in mathematics. The theoretical ground on which some of these results were explained was the religious community surrounding the Catholic schools and the absence of such a community—indeed, the extreme individual-choice basis of enrollment that characterizes many of the independent private schools. But if this explanation is correct, religiously based schools other than Catholic schools should show the same general outcomes as found for the Catholic schools. There are some schools of this sort in the sample of other private schools. If it is true that the religious community surrounding a school serves, among other things, to inhibit the tendency to drop out of high school, then those schools surrounded by a religious community should show low dropout rates like those of Catholic schools. These schools may be distinguished from the others by the name, containing some denominational or religious reference. However there are two types of schools, which, though they contain such a reference, do not serve primarily a religious community. One type is established independent schools that serve a nondenominational clientele. Schools that were founded as Episcopal schools and schools founded as Friends schools are the most frequent such cases. Second, there are recently founded schools, sometimes called "Christian Schools," often begun as an escape from desegregation, that do not serve a religious community but contain students from various religious groups. The criterion that distinguishes both of these groups of schools from those that serve primarily a religious community is the religious affiliation of the student body. Eight of the other private schools that contained some religious reference in their names had over 50 percent of their student bodies from a single denomination.

Achievement and Dropout in Disadvantaged Families

These schools were smaller than average, so that although they constituted eight of twenty-seven schools, they represented only 19 percent of the student bodies of other private schools in the population.* Three were Baptist, two were Jewish, and one school each for three other Christian denominations.†

Fifteen schools of the twenty-seven in the sample of other private schools are independent schools, although a few of these have a religious affiliation but have become secularized over time. In addition, four schools have a religious reference in the title (three of them nondenominational) but do not have a majority of students from a single denomination.

For these three sets of schools, there was not only a difference in homogeneity of religious affiliation, there was a substantial difference in degree of religious observance of the students. In the homogeneous religious schools, the average reported frequency of attendance at religious services was once a week; in the heterogeneous religious schools, the average was half-way between once a week and two to three times a month; and in the independent secular schools, it was once a month.

Table 5.15 shows the dropout rates for these three sets of schools in the sample.

This tabulation shows that the religious schools with a homogeneous student body (over 50 percent from a single denomination) did show a very low dropout rate, comparable to that of the Catholic schools. Both other sets of schools draw their students on an individual basis, and both

TABLE 5.15

Dropout Rates Between Sophomore and Senior Years

	Religiously Homogeneous	Religiously Heterogeneous	Independent Secular
Percentage	3.7	25.7	8.0
Number of Cases (Unweighted)	(162)	(48)	(368)
Number of Schools	(8)	(4)	(15)

*There was not stratification of the sample by religious affiliation, so that this does not imply that 19 percent of the non-Catholic private sector is in schools that are religiously homogeneous. The 1978–79 estimate of students in religiously affiliated schools is 43 percent of the non-Catholic private sector (see Coleman, Hoffer, and Kilgore, 1982, table 2.5). Many of these, however, like some religiously affiliated schools in our sample, do not have religiously homogeneous student bodies.

†There were in addition three nonreligiously affiliated schools with slightly more than 50 percent of their student bodies from a single denomination, two Baptist (in the South) and one Presbyterian.

show a higher dropout rate. The especially high rate shown by the religiously based but heterogeneous schools may, of course, be due to the especially small sample size, but it may also be due to the very small size and consequent instability of some of these schools. We have not addressed until now the potential instability of very small private sector schools and the possible consequences of small size. However, this tabulation suggests a very possible consequence: If the school is not large enough to be maintained as a going concern, then students will of necessity face leaving because of the school's instability; this can increase chances of dropping out rather than transferring.

This examination of the types of other private schools confirms the inferences made earlier from the low dropout rates in the Catholic schools: The religious community surrounding the high school provides social support that inhibits the extreme action of dropping out of high school. Simultaneously, this examination reinforces the conception of dropping out as an act brought about by social isolation, an act with much the same psychosocial roots that Durkheim found in suicide.

It is useful also to examine another major difference that was found between the Catholic schools and the other private schools: The difference in the amount of mathematics learned between sophomore and senior years. If the generalization is to be made from the sample of other private schools to the independent secular private schools (as was implicit in the discussion prior to this section), then the achievement growth should be examined for the three sets of schools shown in table 5.15 separately.

Table 5.16 shows the sophomore and senior test scores in verbal skills and mathematical skills for the three sets of schools. The table shows that the independent schools have almost identical achievement growth in mathematics that was shown earlier for the other private sector as a whole (1.67 compared to 1.64 from table 3.2), much less than that shown by the Catholic schools (2.39). This tabulation provides no basis for modifying the conclusions drawn elsewhere in the book about the relative inattention to college preparatory mathematics in the other private schools. It does not, however, lessen the caution that must be applied in generalizing about independent private schools, because the sample is small and the diversity among independent private schools is great.

TABLE 5.16

Verbal and Mathematics Achievement Scores for Students in Each of Three Types of Other Private Schools as Sophomores and Seniors, for Students Who Remained in the School

	Religiously Homogeneous	Religiously Heterogeneous	Independent Secular
Verbal			
Sophomore	23.21	22.29	24.73
Senior	27.11	25.08	28.83
Gain	3.90	2.79	4.10
Mathematics			
Sophomore	23.03	19.42	23.85
Senior	24.90	20.59	25.52
Gain	1.87	1.17	1.67
Number of Cases (Unweighted)	(127)	(32)	(300)

How Does a Functional Community Act Through the School?

The preceding pages provide evidence that the functional community on which Catholic schools are based constitutes effective social resources for young persons' learning. These social resources are especially important when the resources of the family itself are low. However, this does not tell the school practices and policies through which these social resources have their effect.

A school with a strong supporting adult community can impose greater academic demands on its students than one without. It can impose stricter disciplinary standards. The support that such a school has can allow a variety of policies intended to strengthen learning. This leaves open, however, *which* policies are most important in strengthening the achievement of students from disadvantaged backgrounds. In this section, we will examine some ways in which public and Catholic schools differ in the learning experiences they provide for minority youth, that is, black and Hispanic students, and the effects of these differences.

Earlier, we discussed the possibility that the academically focused curriculum of private schools is especially effective in raising the achievement of less-advantaged youth. The fact that the other private schools, with the most academically focused curriculum, do not show this special effectiveness indicates that this possibility does not generally hold. However, it is useful to examine just how much of the Catholic sector effectiveness for disadvantaged students can be accounted for by curriculum and academic demands. It is quite possible that a non-college preparatory curriculum, in which many public school minority youth find themselves, has the consequence of lowering the expectations placed on general and vocational students and hence their achievement growth.

One way to examine these effects is to include measures of academic demands in the regressions used in table 5.1. This will allow estimating how much of the differential effectiveness of Catholic schools for disadvantaged students can be accounted for by differences in academic demands placed on black and Hispanic students.

A second set of school policies concerns discipline. The stronger discipline maintained in Catholic schools may be especially effective for students from disadvantaged backgrounds. The effects of these policies can be examined in the same way as those involving academic demands.

To arrive at estimates of the effects of academic demands and discipline, it is first necessary to separate the effects of the student's own background from the effects of school sector on these variables. Table 5.17 presents predicted public-private differences on the schooling variables, separately for minorities and whites, controlling on family background and sophomore achievement.*

Table 5.17 shows that on most of the dimensions of academic demands, blacks and Hispanics in Catholic schools realize greater advantages than Catholic school non-Hispanic whites compared to their public school counterparts. The relative advantages are greatest for placement in an academic program of study, homework, English coursework, and the number of advanced mathematics and science courses completed.

This differential does not hold, however, for most disciplinary demands. Catholic school minorities exhibit no relative advantage in this respect compared to whites in Catholic schools, and in fact do not have substantially better attendance than their public school peers. Similarly, although both Catholic school minorities and Catholic school non-Hispanic whites perceive their schools to be more orderly places than do public school minorities and whites, they do so to about the same degree. The Catholic school advantages for whites and minorities on the extent of absenteeism, class cutting, students fighting, and students threatening teachers are similar in magnitude.

*The controls for family background used in this analysis are the same as those described in the footnote on p. 121.

TABLE 5.17

Predicted Levels of School Experience Variables, for Minority and Non-Hispanic White Students with Average Public Minority and White Background and Sophomore Achievement, by School Sector

	Minority			Non-Hispanic White		
	Public	Catholic	Catholic Advantage	Public	Catholic	Catholic Advantage
Probability of Academic Program Placement	0.29	0.55	0.27*	0.54	0.72	0.17*
Hours of Homework/Week	3.76	5.01	1.25*	4.72	5.62	0.90*
Semesters of Coursework						
English	3.67	4.32	0.65*	3.72	3.82	0.10
Foreign language	1.12	1.56	0.44*	1.42	1.87	0.45*
Mathematics	2.37	2.64	0.28	2.66	2.92	0.26*
Number of Advanced Math and Science Courses	1.93	2.84	0.91*	3.61	4.15	0.54*
Attendance						
Absenteeism	2.48	2.35	-0.13	2.40	2.04	-0.36*
Class cutting (1 = cut sometimes, 0 = do not cut)	0.36	0.31	-0.05	0.40	0.21	-0.19*
Perceived Problems of Other Students in School (Higher values mean fewer problems)						
Absenteeism	1.58	2.09	0.49*	1.62	2.27	0.65*
Class cutting	1.50	2.18	0.68*	1.56	2.28	0.72*
Fighting	2.01	2.48	0.47*	2.11	2.56	0.45*
Teachers threatened	2.76	2.92	0.16*	2.86	2.93	0.07*
School Average Sophomore Achievement and Social Composition						
Verbal achievement	17.97	20.48	2.51	21.01	23.40	2.39
Mathematics achievement	16.88	19.14	2.26	19.81	21.89	2.08
Proportion with college plans in 9th grade	0.60	0.75	0.15	0.58	0.76	0.18
Average SES	-0.26	0.09	0.35	0.00	0.31	0.13
Proportion Hispanic	0.20	0.25	0.06	0.10	0.10	0
Proportion black	0.29	0.19	-0.10	0.06	0.04	-0.03

*Catholic advantage significant at $p < .05$ level.

The lowermost panel of figures in table 5.17 shows the Catholic advantages for minorities and whites on a number of aggregate school characteristics. These variables can be seen as measures of the peer group resources that students have, as well as measures of the "raw materials" that the schools have to work with in their day-to-day tasks of teaching. Minorities and whites differ substantially in both sectors on most of these variables. There are also large sector effects on most of the variables, but the sector effects are comparable for minority and white students. Catholic students of both types attend schools that have higher levels of sophomore achievement and schools where more of the incoming sophomores planned to eventually go to college. The average Catholic school student, white or minority, has classmates with a higher average SES—about one-third of a standard deviation on the composite scale for minorities and about one-eighth higher for whites. The Catholic-public differences in minority composition are not consistently higher for either minorities or whites.

To what extent can these differences in school experiences indexed by the variables in table 5.17 account for the greater effectiveness of Catholic schools with minority students? To answer this question, we have calculated the amounts of extra achievement growth that the average public school minority and white students would realize from attending a school that provided the same experience as Catholic school minorities and whites have. The results of these calculations are presented in table 5.18.

Table 5.18 shows that the greater effectiveness of Catholic schools for black and Hispanic students is explained in large part by the more rigorous academic demands that Catholic schools place on these students. For both verbal and mathematics achievement, the Catholic sector achievement advantage is nearly twice as great for minorities as for non-Hispanic whites. Comparing the total estimated effects of these demands with the growth differences shown in the bottom row of table 5.18 suggests that if public schools were as likely to place minorities in academic programs as were Catholic schools, assign as much homework as Catholic schools, and require students to take as many semesters of academic coursework as Catholic schools, then public school minorities would do as well as Catholic minorities in mathematics and would reduce the Catholic advantage in verbal skills by almost one-half. The stronger discipline of Catholic schools, in contrast, appears to explain little of the Catholic minority students' achievement advantages.

Catholic school blacks and Hispanic do realize some benefits, but small ones, from attending schools that have higher average SES, lower

Achievement and Dropout in Disadvantaged Families

TABLE 5.18

Achievement Differences Between Public and Catholic School Minority and White Students Due to Differences in School Functioning

	Minority Students		Non-Hispanic White Students	
	Verbal	Mathematics	Verbal	Mathematics
Academic program	0.275	0.210	0.158	0.123
Hours of homework per week	0.079	0.122	0.032	0.041
Academic coursework	0.459	0.985	0.250	0.680
Total, academic demands	0.813	1.317	0.440	0.844
Attendance	0.008	0.021	0.022	0.070
Perceived student discipline	−0.216	−0.193	0.161	0.210
Total, discipline demands	0.208	−0.172	0.183	0.280
Total, background and soph. achievement composition	0.198	0.113	−0.105	0.190
Total explained	0.802	1.258	0.518	1.314
Total to be explained[a]	1.722	1.290	0.784	0.535

[a]This row is taken from the calculations on which rows two and three (combined) and row four of table 5.1 are based.

proportions of blacks and Hispanics and higher average sophomore achievement. But they do not realize uniformly higher benefits from school social composition than do whites.

The overall result of this examination then is that the principal policy differences through which Catholic schools bring special achievement benefits to black and Hispanic students are the extra academic demands placed on them, not through the extra disciplinary demands nor through the social composition of the schools. This does not imply that public schools are in a position to impose those demands, because many of them lack the social resources outside the school that are provided for Catholic schools by the religious community.

Conclusions

This chapter has found that Catholic schools are more effective than public or other private schools in raising the academic achievement of subpopulations that traditionally achieve at lower levels: blacks, Hispanics, children from families that provide lower levels of parental support, and children from families with lower socioeconomic standing.

147

They are also more effective at increasing achievement of students with less traditional family deficiencies in structure or function. Other private schools, in contrast, appear least effective in increasing achievement of either the students from traditionally disadvantaged backgrounds or those from families that are structurally or functionally deficient.

The proximate reason for the Catholic schools' success with less-advantaged students and students from deficient families appears to be the greater academic demands that Catholic schools place on these students. But the ability to make these demands appears to follow in large part from the greater control that the school based on a functional community is able to exercise. In the Catholic schools, the cognitive achievements depend least upon the characteristics of the family, either traditional disadvantages or "modern" family deficiencies, and in the other private schools they depend most upon these characteristics. It is not the case that only members of the religious community benefit, though the benefits are greatest for those who are most integrated into the community, both through religious identification and through involvement in the religious community.

The examination of dropouts among students from different backgrounds shows especially striking results. Here the communal character of the Catholic community appears to reduce very sharply the likelihood of dropping out of school. As in Durkheim's examination of suicide rates in social environments that are integrating and those that are isolating, this examination of dropout rates shows the powerful effects of a socially integrated community in reducing the likelihood of leaving the system. Furthermore, this community constitutes a social resource that compensates for family deficiencies, having its greatest effect in reducing the dropout rate among students from families with structural or functional deficiencies.

In contrast, the individualistic settings of the other private schools increase the likelihood of "middle-class dropout" even above that for comparable students in public school. Students from families with structural or functional deficiencies are particularly at risk in these schools.

6

Beyond High School: The Path Chosen

THE preceding chapters have given an indication of what difference it makes for a high school student to attend a public school, a private school based on a functional community (a religious community in the analysis as carried out), or a private school based on a value community that does not have a functional base. We have not yet examined what difference it makes, if any, for the young persons' lives after school.

A person's life is shaped in many ways by the first few years beyond high school. For some, it is a period during which a lifetime's occupational career will be established. For others, it is a period of continued preparation for later occupational decisions, and for many, it is a period of floundering, either in the labor force or in college. Some of those in the labor force move from job to job or have spells of unemployment, while some of those in college do poorly, finding themselves ill-equipped or unmotivated. Some get married, some have children.

These activities and experiences are in part a result of what happened in high school. And what happened in high school depends in part on what high school one attended. In this chapter, we will examine just how one aspect of a young person's high school—whether it was in a public high school, a high school based on a religious community, or a private high school that is not based on a religious community—affects these activities and experiences.

What Is Success Beyond High School?

We have written of "success beyond high school" as if this were a well-defined outcome. Success *in* high school is relatively well defined, even though there are several dimensions of success. This simplicity of definition gives no forewarning of the complexity that follows high school.

High school is the last institution in life through which all pass (or at least enter) and for which there is a common set of dimensions of success. We have examined several of those in the last two chapters: dropping out, achievement in basic cognitive skills, and achievement in other cognitive areas (for example, science, civics). But there is nothing comparable to these measures beyond high school. Paths diverge; aspirations differ. Some young persons select an undemanding college and receive high grades. Others select a more demanding college and receive low grades. Still others choose not to attend college at all but to hold down a job. Who is more successful? Some choose an occupation that provides immediate income and requires no further schooling. Others aim higher and are less successful in reaching that goal. Which has the greatest measure of success?

The central difference in defining success during high school and success beyond high school lies precisely in this area of path selection. Until the end of high school, a young person's path, as it concerns formal institutions, is largely defined by others. Whether the school is a private school or a public school makes little difference: It is a school, its occupants are students, and they follow a path through this institution that is largely prescribed by others.

Once a young person leaves high school, the path is no longer externally prescribed. It may be into the labor force, in any of a number of kinds of jobs; it may be into any of a variety of different kinds of educational or training institutions; it may be having and raising children. If external support is forthcoming, it may be traveling or other diversions.

In one sense of success, then, measurement is only possible once the path is determined. In this sense, success can be compared only among that set of young persons who has, for example, directly entered the labor force. Or success can be compared among those who have chosen to go to a four-year college. But it cannot be compared across these sets of persons, because their paths are different.

By another sense however, comparison among paths is possible, for some paths, if successfully pursued, will lead to greater success in the directions that school prepares for than will others. With few exceptions, a successful pursuit of a bachelor's degree in college will result in an occupation that brings higher income, higher status, and more chance for advancement than direct entry into the labor force with no education beyond high school.

One reasonable way, then, of approaching the question of success beyond high school is to divide it into two parts: the choice of paths and success within that choice. Attendance at a religiously based or other private high school may affect either of these, both, or neither. Or it may affect success within certain paths, but not others. It will not be possible, according to this approach, to give a single answer to the relative effectiveness of schools in different sectors for success beyond high school. The answer must be two-dimensional, consisting of answers to two questions. The first question is the choice of paths: What is the effect of school sector on college attendance and on level of educational aspirations beyond high school? Second, for those persons who take a particular path what is the effect of sector on success in pursuit of this path? Before examining the evidence on these questions, it is useful to pose them a little more carefully, and to indicate some possible predictions about the effects of schools in different sectors.

The Choice of Paths: Definition and Measurement

One way that high school affects success beyond high school is in one's aspirations. Ordinarily the "level" of these aspirations is the level of formal education that they imply. This is not wholly congruent with level of occupational aspirations, for there are some adult occupations or activities that bring high status or high income or both, for which formal education is not important. Movie stars and other entertainment stars are examples. Yet these are exceptions; the correlation between educational level of an occupation and the status of the occupation is very high, and that between education and income, though less high, is nevertheless reasonably strong. The correlation also between the educational level of an occupation and the growth in income that this occupation brings with age is a high one. Quite apart from these correlations, the most predictable or methodical path toward better occupation and higher income is further education. Most other paths have a high degree of uncertainty in bringing occupational success.

For this reason, a good measure of the effect of a high school on the path one chooses is its effect on educational level embarked upon at the end of high school. This does not mean, of course, that for a given student, higher educational aspirations are necessarily better. Those aspirations may be unrealistic, given one's level of preparation and cognitive skills. Only the second measure of success, that is, how well a student succeeds in the path embarked upon, will determine that. Thus, a high school that has graduates with very high educational or occupational aspirations but with very high rates of failure in what they attempt is not producing better outcomes than one whose graduates have lower aspirations, but with high rates of success in what they attempt.

Recognizing that the effect of a high school or a high school sector on raising levels of aspirations or paths embarked on at the end of high school cannot be evaluated as "good" or "bad" without measurement of rates of success in the paths embarked on, we will nevertheless examine first the effect upon path. In the next chapter, we will turn to the question of success.

How Should the Different Orientations of Different Sector Schools Affect the Path Taken After High School?

Schools are, as we have described in the first chapter, agents of family, community, and the larger society. Public schools come closest to being agents of the larger society, Catholic schools closest to being agents of the (religious) community of which the family is a part, and nonreligious private schools come closest to being agents of the individual family, the parents of the students attending them.

Chapter 2 showed some of the differences that this difference in orientation means for the design and functioning of schools in the three sectors, and some of the differences among parents who choose to send their children to a Catholic or other private school, rather than to accept the local public high school. In a similar way (and in part at least through the differences in design and functioning of the schools), the different orientations should lead to different postsecondary paths.

It is true, of course, that parents are not always able to guide their children onto the paths they would choose, even with the help of a school that reflects their interests. The fact that children are as likely to drop out of the other private high schools in our sample (but not Catholic ones) as are children from comparable family backgrounds in the public schools gives ample evidence of this. Another indicator is the phenomenon of "middle-class dropouts from the system" during or after the end of high school that was especially evident in the decade 1965–1975 and is apparent in both the public and other private schools in this study. As these dropouts indicate, certain effects of the bases on which schools are organized are quite independent of the intentions of those who organize them, for they have their effect through the social structure they bring about in the school and surrounding it. Whether through conscious intentions or independent of them, these different orientations expressed by schools in the three sectors should be evident in the postsecondary paths taken by their graduates.

As was apparent both in the design of high schools and in the orientations of those parents who choose private schools, the overwhelming choice of parents who send their children to private school (whether religious or independent) for their child's path after high school is toward further education.* The fact that they have already invested money in their children's education means that they have both an interest in their children's education and the resources to send their children to college. The greater interest and resources of the average private sector parent should have an effect in increasing the likelihood of their child's college attendance quite apart from what transpired during high school.

But as shown in chapter 2, this college preparatory orientation is also manifested in the design and functioning of private sector schools. They keep children in an academic track and academic courses far more often than does the average public school, even when their family background and parental interest in further education are comparable.

---

*This can be seen in other countries as well. A good example is Japan, where education is more highly competitive than in the United States and where selection into a vocational secondary school rather than an academic one has irreversible consequences. There, many parents put their children into private academic schools rather than have them assigned to a public vocational high school. In Japan, the private sector constitutes about 30 percent of the total, three times as high as in the United States.

TABLE 6.1

Percentage of 1980 Men and
Women Seniors Enrolled
Full Time in a Four-Year
College Before Spring 1982,
by Sector

	Men	Women
Public	28.2	31.1
Catholic	51.4	50.5
Other private	60.3	51.9

They demand and get more homework from children of comparable backgrounds and parental interest, and they produce greater growth in cognitive skills, as shown in chapter 3.

We should find, then, that high school seniors in both the Catholic and other private sectors are more likely to attend college than are their public school counterparts with the same degree of success in high school (as measured by grades and behavior). Without looking at background or success in high school, the gross college attendance rates are, as one might expect, considerably higher among students in the private sectors than those in public schools. Table 6.1 shows the rates of enrollment in a four-year college by sector, for men and women separately. The differences are very great; slightly larger for men than for women. Table 6.2 shows that the difference remains, though it is greatly reduced, when students in an academic program and those not in an academic program are examined separately.

Comparing the likelihood of college attendance among sectors for those children whose success and behavior in high school was similar shows that enrollment in college is generally higher from the private sectors. Table 6.3 shows that it is higher in the Catholic and other

TABLE 6.2

Percentage of 1980 Seniors Enrolled
Full Time in a Four-Year College
Before Spring 1982, by Academic or
Nonacademic Program in High School

	Academic	Nonacademic
Public	57.4	15.4
Catholic	63.3	21.5
Other private	69.5	23.1

Beyond High School: The Path Chosen

TABLE 6.3

Percentage of 1980 Seniors Enrolled Full Time in a Four-Year College Before Spring 1982, by Average Grades in High School

	A	A–B	B	B–C	C	C–D	D or lower
Public	67.0	42.0	32.6	18.2	9.5	5.8	1.5
Catholic	79.5	64.9	51.6	34.5	13.7	6.5	—
Other private	75.3	54.5	59.6	57.2	16.1	25.4	—

Average grades are obtained from student self-reports to a question asked in spring, 1980.

private sectors at nearly every level of grades in school. Tables 6.4 and 6.5 show that there is higher college attendance among private sector students regardless of their absence levels, disciplinary behavior, or homework. At almost every level of grades and disciplinary behavior, students from either of the private sectors are more likely to enroll in college than are students from public sector schools.

There is, however, a second result shown in tables 6.3 through 6.5. There is a lower relation of success in high school to college attendance in the private sectors than in the public. This is especially true for the other private sector. In these areas, the relation of performance in high school to enrollment in college is lowest in the other private sector, highest in the public sector, with Catholic schools intermediary. This suggests that whether it is through the schools or independent of them, parents who have shown a willingness to pay for their children's education in high school will be more willing to provide college support to their children with mediocre high school records than will either the state or parents for children with mediocre records in public school. Thus, there is a suggestion that continuing education beyond high school is at least in part due to a different orientation and resources on the part of parents of private school students, and not wholly to some-

TABLE 6.4

Percentage of 1980 Seniors Enrolled Full Time in a Four-Year College Before Spring 1982, by Absenteeism and Disciplinary Behavior

	Scale of Seriousness of Absenteeism and Behavior						
	1	1.125	2	2.25	3	3.375	4
Public	36.8	20.3	29.6	5.4	21.9	12.1	11.2
Catholic	60.2	34.3	32.6	0	44.4	—	49.4
Other private	60.6	—	60.4	—	47.8	—	5.2

TABLE 6.5

*Percentage of 1980 Seniors Enrolled
Full Time in a Four-Year College
Before Spring 1982, by Hours of
Homework Done Per Week*

	4	3	2	1
Public	50.5	35.3	22.6	15.6
Catholic	66.5	52.0	34.9	28.7
Other private	63.3	57.8	42.3	44.3

Hours of homework are student-reported average
hours per week spent on homework, from the 1980
questionnaire.

thing the schools themselves do. At the same time, it should be recalled
that there is an effect of attending a private sector school on the very
behaviors that were taken as given in tables 6.3 through 6.5. Private
sector students are less likely to be absent, do more homework, and are
better behaved in school than are students from comparable backgrounds in public schools. These differences are particularly marked for
Catholic schools.

Thus, there is a real difference in college attendance at all levels of
school performance between public sector students and private sector
students. Some of this is due directly to differences in parent orientations and resources, but it is not clear just how much. Part should be due
to events that occur within the school itself or as an outcome of those
events. Part, for example, should be due to the higher levels of achievement in basic cognitive skills produced by the private sector schools for
students from comparable backgrounds (as shown in chapter 3). Part
should be due to their being in an academic track rather than a vocational or general track and to their taking harder courses and doing
more homework (assuming that enrollment in an academic track,
harder courses, and more homework have effects toward college attendance apart from effects on cognitive skills). Part should be due to
the stronger discipline that private schools demand and get from students regardless of background. And part may be due to still other
attributes of private sector schools.

To separate out these different effects, it is useful to order the events
or factors that may affect postsecondary activity, recognizing that prior
events or factors may affect any subsequent ones. At the broadest level,
family background characteristics are prior to school sector, school sector is prior to activities and outcomes in the school, and all are prior to
postsecondary activity. This can be pictured in figure 6.1.

Beyond High School: The Path Chosen

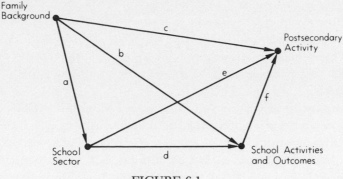

FIGURE 6.1

Temporal Ordering of Influences on Postsecondary Activities

In this characterization, family background factors may influence postsecondary activity through the school a child is sent to (arrow *a*), through effects on what the child does in school in whichever sector (arrow *b*), or independently of either of these two routes (arrow *c*). If the effect is through the school sector and independent of background, this may in turn happen in either of two ways: through the sector effects on school activities and outcomes (arrow *d*) or independently of these (arrow *e*).

Yet from each of the intermediate points, there are effects that are not due to the prior factors: Those properties of school that are embodied in the term "school sector" are only in part shaped by the family backgrounds of the children in them, and thus exercise an independent effect [either through the activities and outcomes measured in this study (arrow *d*) or apart from them (arrow *e*)]. Similarly, a child's activities and outcomes in school are only in part shaped by family background and by the kind of school attended. Thus, they exercise effects (arrow *f*) that are in part independent of these two prior influences.

The overall differences in postsecondary activity by students in different sectors as shown in table 6.1 include both those associated with the different family backgrounds of students in each sector, and the actual effects of the sector that are independent of family background (arrows *e* and *d–f*). For example, among 1980 seniors, 28 percent of boys and 31 percent of girls from public high schools enrolled in a four-year college within the first two years after high school (most of them directly, a few after staying out a year). (What is measured here is college enrollment of the 1980 seniors after high school, if it occurred before spring 1982, at the time of the first followup.) Among Catholic seniors, the comparable percentages were 52 percent for boys and 51 percent for girls. This is a difference of 24 percent for boys and 20 percent for girls. How much of this difference is due to differences in background, and how much can be attributed to the school sector itself? And of that due to the school sector, how much can be explained by the difference between sectors in the various activities and outcomes that have been measured?

To answer this question requires "unpacking" the various elements that go into what is labeled school activities and outcomes. Later we will look at the amount of school sector differences that can be accounted for by different parts of these two bundles, but at this point, it is sufficient merely to know what goes into each. In addition, it is useful to unpack the various elements that go into what is labeled family background.

The bundle called "family background" as measured here consists of three components, and each of these in turn consists of two or more elements. The three are location of residence, family resources, and parental orientations to postsecondary education. The following list the elements that go into each of these three components:

1. Location of residence:
   (a) Region (Northeast, North Central, South, West)
   (b) Rural, urban, suburban
2. Parental resources:
   (a) Race and ethnicity: Hispanic, black, and other (labeled here as non-Hispanic white)
   (b) Socioeconomic status, based on family income, father's occupation, and mother's and father's education
3. Parental orientations to postsecondary activity
   (a) Mother's expectations that the child will or will not attend college
   (b) Father's expectations that the child will or will not attend college
   (c) Child's expectations of attending college at grade 8 (as recalled at grade 12). (This is included as an additional measure of family orientations toward college prior to high school.)

The bundle of school activities and outcomes that are affected by both the child's background and the school sector (and in turn may affect postsecondary activities) we have partitioned into three components: school program, coursework and homework, and out-of-class activities. These in turn include several elements, as follows.

1. Academic program:
   (a) Enrollment in academic program in the school
2. Coursework and homework:

158

(a) Number of advanced mathematics and science courses taken
(b) Number of hours of homework done each week
(c) Grades in school
3. Out of class activities:
(a) Absences, probation, and "disciplinary problems"
(b) Number of extracurricular activities
(c) Number of hours worked at a job per week in preceding semester

The way the overall differences between each of the private sectors and the public sector break down can be illustrated by breaking down the 24 percent difference between Catholic and public school senior boys:*

24 percent total difference
13 percent due to family background and not through the school, either directly (path *c* in figure 6.1) or indirectly (path *b–f*).
11 percent due to sector independent of background (through path *e* or path *d–f*).
Of this 11 percent sector effect independent of background, there is:
9 percent due to sector differences in measured activities and outcomes, independent of family background (path *d–f*).
2 percent residual effect of sector independent of family background and unexplained by school activities and outcomes (path *e*).
The principal division is between the 13 percent, which can be thought of as a spurious effect of sector, due to prior background differences, and 11 percent, a true effect of sector, not due to the prior differences. A secondary division is according to the *way* that sector effect comes

*The components of difference between sectors described in the text and in tables 6.6, 6.8, 6.9, and 6.11 are obtained by least squares regressions of four-year college enrollment on various subsets of variables, for each sex separately. The percentages reported as "due to" each set of variables is the difference between the sector regression coefficient when that set of variables is not included in the equation and the sector regression coefficient when that set of variables is included. For each set of variables lower in the hierarchy, the variables above it are included in the equation.

For example, in accounting for the 24 percent difference between Catholic and public school:
1. The Catholic school coefficient is 0.24 when only Catholic, other private, and high-performance private variables (all 0, 1) are in the regression equation.
2. The Catholic coefficient is reduced to 0.11 when the background variables described in the text are added to the equation described under 1.
3. The Catholic coefficient is reduced to 0.02 when the measured activities and outcomes of school are added to the equation described under 2.

A similar procedure is used for examining sequentially the effects of various elements within each of the bundles of variables.

Because the dependent variable, four-year college attendance, is a qualitative response variable, with values 0 and 1, nonlinear methods, such as logistic regression, are desirable. But because the proportion in each sector is not near 0 or 1, ordinary least squares is a satisfactory substitute and is used here.

about, in this case 9 percent through the measured activities and outcomes, and 2 percent through some other, unknown factors.

This kind of analysis for full-time enrollment in a four-year college in the first or second year after high school is shown in table 6.6 for men and women separately, and for Catholic and other private schools relative to public schools. This table shows first of all that about half the difference in enrollment is due to background factors that existed before high school, either acting through differences in the way the schools function (*b* through *f* in figure 6.1) or independently (*c* in figure 6.1), and about half is an effect of the sector independent of the student's background. This effect is greater for men in both sectors, but especially so in the other private schools, where it is estimated as 18 percent more going to college. Of the sector effects, nearly all the Catholic sector effect is accounted for by measured differences in school activities and outcomes, but only about half of the other private sector effect can be accounted for in this way. This last difference again suggests that especially in the other private sector, parents' willingness to send their children to college, and the children's interest in going, is less dependent on (or has less effect on) the child's performance in high school. It is in accord with the lower relation of college enrollment in the other private sector to the various activities and outcomes in high school, as shown in tables 6.3 through 6.5.

As table 6.6 indicates, the private sector effects on enrollment in a four-year college are quite strong, even though they constitute only about half the overall sector difference. One objection to this interpre-

TABLE 6.6

Components of Sector Differences in Full-Time Enrollment of 1980 Seniors in a Four-Year College Before Spring 1982

	Men 28%		Women 31%	
	Catholic (%)	Other Private (%)	Catholic (%)	Other Private (%)
Public High School				
Total increment	24	34	20	21
Due to background[a]	13	15	11	9
Independent of background	11	18	9	12
Due to measured activities	9	8	7	6
Independent of activities	2	10	2	6

[a]The t = values of the estimated sector effects with controls for background are: Catholic men, 3.1; other private men, 3.7; Catholic women, 2.8; other private women, 2.9. A design effect of 1.5 is assumed in the calculation of these t = values.

tation, however, lies in the fact that the student's verbal and mathematical ability before high school is not taken as part of background resources, because this cohort was studied for the first time as seniors. The only measures of cognitive skills for these students is a measure at the end of high school, as seniors. Since we know from chapter 3 that there is a differential effect on the growth rate in cognitive skills in the three sectors, it is possible to approximate a control for cognitive ability by first overcorrecting (including senior cognitive skills as part of background resources) and then adjusting for the differential growth rates in public, Catholic, and other private schools. When verbal and mathematical skills as measured by senior tests are included as part of family resources, the estimate of the Catholic sector effect remains the same for boys at 11 percent, and declines from 9 percent to 7 percent for girls. The estimate of the effect of the other private sector declines from 18 percent to 17 percent for boys, and from 12 percent to 8 percent for girls.*

However, when the differential growth rate is taken into account, then the estimated effects come back up to their original values.† This does not mean, of course, that verbal and mathematical skills make no difference in college enrollment; it means only that when we have already taken account of both parents' expectations about college attendance, the student's own 8th grade expectation, and the various background resources described earlier, the public-private differences in cognitive skills tell us nothing more about sector differences in four-year college enrollment.

What About Two-Year Colleges?

The preceding examination was confined to four-year college enrollment. Are there still these great sector effects when enrollment in two-year colleges is counted as well? A comparison of table 6.1 and table

---

*This result is based on including two additional variables in the regression equation, the mathematics test score and the combined vocabulary and reading test scores.

†The differential growth rates are obtained from table 3.3, which shows 1.65 added growth in verbal skills and 1.29 in mathematical skills in the Catholic sector, 2.26 in verbal skills and .56 in mathematical skills in the other private sector. These are then multiplied by the regression coefficients for verbal and mathematical skills in the equation containing all background variables and sectors, to obtain the amount to be restored to the estimated effects. In every case, the resulting estimate matched or slightly exceeded the original estimate without cognitive skills, indicating that the parental resource and expectation factors that were already taken into account more than controlled for differences in sophomore-level cognitive skills.

TABLE 6.7

*Percentage of 1980 Seniors
Enrolled Full Time in a
Four-Year or Two-Year
College Before Spring 1982,
in Each Sector*

	Men	Women
Public	42.1	46.6
Catholic	65.8	67.6
Other private	63.0	64.1

6.7 suggests that there must be reduced effects, at least in the other private sector for boys, because the enrollment is only 3 percent greater by this expanded definition, while it is 14 percent greater in the public sector. Table 6.8 shows the estimates of these effects.

The Catholic sector effects are not much changed; the effect for boys has declined from 11 percent to 9 percent, and that for girls has increased from 9 percent to 11 percent. For the other private schools, however, the estimated sector effects are sharply less. For boys, the effect is reduced nearly to zero, and for girls, it is reduced from 12 percent to 8 percent. Thus, the large effect of the other private schools on boys' enrollment in four-year colleges does not hold true when two-year colleges are included as well. What appears to be true is that the Catholic schools and public schools are similar in the mix of four- and two-year colleges attended, once differences in background are taken into account, and that girls from other private schools are not

TABLE 6.8

*Components of Sector Differences in Full-Time Enrollment in a
Four- or Two-Year College Before Spring 1982*

Public School	Men 42%		Women 47%	
	Catholic (%)	Other Private (%)	Catholic (%)	Other Private (%)
Total Increment	25	22	22	18
Due to background	16	20	11	10
Independent of background	9	2	11	8
Due to measured activities	8	7	6	5
Independent of activities	1	−5	5	3

greatly different either; but boys from other private schools seldom enroll in two-year colleges after high school. Since a major difference between the average four-year institution and the average two-year institution is in costs, this may reflect the same willingness to spend money on their son's further education as is evidenced in the parents' willingness to pay high school tuition. (Recall that a large portion of the estimated effect of other private schools in boys' four-year college enrollment is unaccounted for by activities and outcomes in high school; that may be simply due to a greater willingness of parents to spend income on their son's enrollment in a four-year college.) Why it is not evident in girls' enrollment patterns at four- and two-year colleges is not clear.

It is useful to point out the meaning of the negative residual sector effect of −5 percent for boys in the other private sector. What this means is that for boys in the public and other private sectors who were alike in both background and high school activities, there would be 5 percent fewer of the other private boys attending a four- or two-year college than there would public school boys. This does not mean that the overall sector effect is negative, because as the figure indicates, the other private school brings about activities and outcomes that increase the chance of going to college. It is to these activities and outcomes that we now turn.

Unpacking the Sector Effects: What Activities and Outcomes Contribute to the Difference?

In the examination to this point, we have divided the estimated sector effects into a part which is accounted for by activities and outcomes that make the private sector schools different from the public sector schools, and a residual part which cannot be accounted for in this way. It is useful now to ask which of the activities and outcomes that were discussed earlier make the important differences.

In answering this question, we again assume a causal ordering among the three components, as shown in figure 6.2. First, are there any sector effects that can be accounted for by sector differences in students from comparable backgrounds being in an academic (rather than a vocational or general) program? Then, are there sector effects that cannot be accounted for in this way but can be accounted for by students in

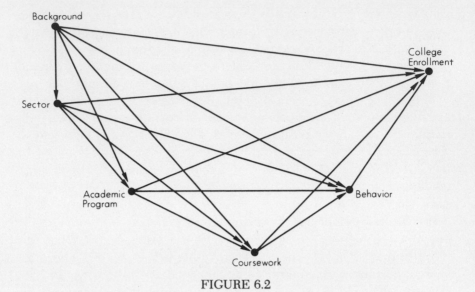

FIGURE 6.2

Assumed Causal Ordering of Influences on College Enrollment

the same program taking harder courses, doing more homework, and getting better grades? Finally, are there sector effects that cannot be accounted for in this way but can be accounted for by out-of-class activity differences between sectors for students from comparable backgrounds, in the same program, with the same coursework, homework, and grades? These out-of-class activities include behavior problems (which reduce college enrollment), extracurricular activities (which increase enrollment), and working outside school (which decreases enrollment). The components that are farther along in this causal sequence can be expected to account for decreasing amounts of the difference in college enrollment, because they are constrained to explain differences among students who are alike in all the prior aspects of background and school activities, as well as school sector.

Table 6.9 shows that over both sexes and in both sectors, somewhere between 5 and 8 percentage points in the sector differences in four-year college enrollment can be accounted for by the greater likelihood of students from comparable backgrounds to be enrolled in academic programs. This is half to two-thirds of the sector effect for Catholic schools, and a third to a half of the sector effect for other private schools. Enrollment of a much broader range of students in an academic program is, as became apparent in chapter 2, one of the marks of a school in the private sector.

164

Beyond High School: The Path Chosen

TABLE 6.9

Components of Sector Effects on Full-Time Enrollment of 1980 Seniors in a Four-Year College Before Spring 1982

	Men		Women	
	Catholic	Other Private	Catholic	Other Private
Sector differences	(%)	(%)	(%)	(%)
Independent of background differences (from table 6.6)	11.3	18.4	9.1	12.4
Due to academic program	7.8	6.1	4.9	6.6
Independent of program	3.5	12.3	4.2	5.8
Due to coursework	0.7	0.0	2.5	−0.8
Independent of coursework	2.8	12.3	1.7	6.6
Due to out-of-class	0.8	2.0	−0.3	0.4
Independent of out-of-class	2.0	10.3	2.0	6.2

The remaining effects, independent of program but explainable by coursework or out-of-class activities, are small; however, there are some interesting differences between sectors. If we were to unpack the coursework component further, a striking difference between the Catholic and other private sectors would become apparent. Taking the total sector effect that is independent of program as 100 percent (that is, expanding the 3.5 percent, 12.3 percent, 4.2 percent, and 5.8 percent from table 6.9, each to 100 percent), we can ask how much of this remaining sector difference can be accounted for by a greater likelihood of a student in that private sector to take mathematics and science courses that are preparatory for college than is true for a student in the public sector in the same program and with the same family resources and orientations. The answer for boys from the Catholic sector is 26 percent of the remaining difference, and for girls, 48 percent of the remaining difference. Catholic sector boys from comparable backgrounds and in the same program are somewhat more likely to take those mathematics and science courses that lead to college than are public sector boys, and girls are especially more likely to do so. When we turn to the other private schools, the remaining sector effect for boys is raised very slightly if we know the mathematics and science courses he took, meaning that for students of the same background and program, a boy from a private sector school was slightly less likely to take college preparatory mathematics and science courses than was a boy from a public school. For girls, the difference is striking: The remaining sector effect is raised 26 percent, meaning that a girl from a private

165

sector school was much *less* likely to take college preparatory mathematics and science courses than was a public school girl from a comparable program and background.

This lack of attention to mathematics and science in the curriculum of schools in the other private sector is manifested in the slightly negative, though not statistically significant, effects of the other private sector on growth in mathematics and science skills shown earlier for the sophomore cohort in table 3.4. We may ask just what the consequences of this are for the fields of study chosen by college students from the three sectors. There are two sources of information about this. One is the 1980 high school senior cohort, which was in its fourth year of college in October 1983, the last time they were asked about their field of study. The other is the 1980 sophomore cohort. Those who followed the normal sequence of high school graduation in 1982 were in their second year of college in October 1983. In table 6.10 are shown selected fields of study among all those enrolled in a four-year college program, for each sector. The first two sets of fields are those which require a good background in mathematics: physical or biological sciences, and engineering or computer sciences. Though there are some differences between cohorts, in both cohorts and for both of these areas of study, the college students who had graduated from high schools in the other private sector are less likely to be in these programs than college students who were from either public or Catholic high schools. The percentage in engineering or computer sciences is particularly low, less than half that in either of the other sectors for both cohorts.

Two other fields of study shown in table 6.10, humanities and the

TABLE 6.10

Among Students Enrolled in a Four-Year College, the Percentage in Each of Selected Fields of Study in October 1983, by Sector

	Physical or Biological Sciences (%)	Engineering or Computer Sciences (%)	Humanities (%)	Social Sciences (%)
1980 Seniors				
Public	7.0	13.7	15.7	13.2
Catholic	11.3	12.1	10.8	15.6
Other private	4.1	5.2	25.4	33.0
1980 Sophomores				
Public	8.3	15.8	14.7	10.8
Catholic	7.8	15.0	14.8	13.2
Other private	7.0	6.8	23.9	28.7

social sciences, show where the students from the other private sector are disproportionately located. They are one and a half to almost three times as likely to be found in these fields as are college students whose high school was public or Catholic.

Some caution is necessary in concluding that students in the schools of the non-Catholic other private sector in the United States avoid those fields of study that use mathematics and gravitate to the humanities or social sciences. The sample of other private schools is deficient, as we have mentioned earlier. This is less damaging for studies of changes within a cohort (as in chapters 3, 4, 5, and parts of this chapter) than for cross-sectional comparisons of the sort shown in table 6.10.

Although there is a need for caution about generalizing to the sector as a whole, the data clearly show that for *these* schools in the other private sector, a weakness in college preparatory mathematics and science is associated with a reduced number of college-bound students taking these courses, which in turn is associated with comparatively less growth than in verbal skills, and finally with fewer college students majoring in fields where mathematics is important. Beyond this, if the generalization from this sample to other private schools as a whole does hold, there is a rather strong suggestion from the evidence of chapter 3, and from the evidence in this chapter on coursework and choice of fields of study, that schools in the other private sector are deficient in mathematics and the natural sciences, relative to the education and motivation they give for the humanities and social sciences. This may be in part a consequence of small size, for, as table 2.6 shows, the average size of other private schools is much smaller than either the average Catholic school or the average public school.

In chapter 3, we showed also that Catholic schools were little or no more effective in physical sciences than public schools for students from comparable backgrounds; but their effectiveness for mathematics appears, on the basis of courses taken and fields of study chosen by college students, to be strong. (It should be recalled that Catholic-school students are about 10 percent more likely to be in a four-year college than are public school students from comparable backgrounds, so the students who constitute the basis for table 6.10 are a larger fraction of the Catholic school cohort than of the public school cohort, even standardizing on family backgrounds.)

Unpacking the final set of school activities and outcomes in table 6.9, that is out-of-class activities, indicates one other noticeable difference between Catholic and other private schools. Students with high participation in extracurricular activities are somewhat more likely to attend college than students who are like them in all the other ways described earlier, but do not participate. Because students in other private schools have higher participation in extracurricular activities than do comparable students in public schools, this activity explains a part of the remaining difference in enrollment in a four-year college, both for men and for women. In Catholic schools, where participation is no higher than among comparable students in the public sector, none of the college enrollment difference can be accounted for by extracurricular activities in high school.

It is possible to sort out the components that are causally prior to sector, that is location of residence, family resources, and parents' orientations to college to show the amount of public-private difference due to each of these components. Although these are not *effects* of the sectors, they do show something about the different components of backgrounds of Catholic and other private school students that make them more likely to attend a four-year college than a public school student. Table 6.11 shows the results of this unpacking. First, location accounts for a small part of the Catholic extra enrollment, because more Catholic schools are located in areas from which college attendance is slightly higher (urban and suburban areas, Northeast and North Central regions). The other private schools in our sample (which is not very locationally representative of the population of these schools) are located less in these areas, so they contribute negatively to the other private-public difference.

Nearly all the other private-public difference that is accounted for by

TABLE 6.11

Components of Sector Differences in Full-Time Enrollment of 1980 Seniors in a Four-Year College Before Spring 1982 Due to Different Components of Background

	Boys		Girls	
	Catholic (%)	Other Private (%)	Catholic (%)	Other Private (%)
Sector Differences				
Due to measured background (from table 6.6)	13.0	15.2	10.8	8.8
Due to location	2.5	−1.4	2.8	−0.9
Independent of location	10.5	16.6	8.0	9.7
Due to resources	3.9	13.7	4.2	9.7
Independent of resources	6.6	2.9	3.8	0.0
Due to orientations	6.6	2.9	3.8	0.0

TABLE 6.12

College Plans or Attendance at Various Points Before, During, and After High School:
All Students Combined

| | Grade 8 planning to attend college[a] | Grade 12 proportion who expect college degree or more | Two Years After | | | Four years after Proportion who expect college degree or more |
			Proportion who have enrolled in four-year college	Proportion who have enrolled full-time in two or four year college[a]	Proportion who expect college degree or more	
Men	0.60	0.47	0.31	0.43	0.44	0.51
Women	0.66	0.45	0.33	0.48	0.49	0.48

[a]Question was: Did you expect to go to college when you were in the following grades? No was scored as 0; not sure or hadn't thought about it as 0.5; yes as 1.0.

background is due to the greater resources of families in this sector: higher income, higher occupations, higher education. Once these elements are known, very little more is accounted for by parents' orientations toward college: 2.9 percent for boys, and none for girls. In the Catholic sector, the differential resources account for much less, since incomes are less high than in the other private sector, occupations are lower, and parents' education is lower, though they are all higher than for the average public school student. The end result is that some, but not much, of the Catholic-public difference in four-year college enrollment is accounted for by greater parental resources. Much more, compared to the other private sector, is accounted for by the greater likelihood that parents with comparable resources will expect their son (or less often, their daughter) to go to college. Again, the difference between the backgrounds of students in the Catholic and other private sectors is apparent. The Catholic school parents are more likely to be lower middle class, with fewer objective resources that contribute to college attendance of their children, but strong expectations that their children attend college. The other private parents are more often upper middle class, with sizable resources for college and with college expectations for their children, but expectations that are little more than congruent with their objective resources.

Another way of examining the relative impact of public, Catholic, and other private schools on college plans and college attendance is to see the movement over a sequence of time points. The points that can be examined are: (1) college expectations in the 8th grade (as recalled by 12th graders); (2) college expectations as reported in the 12th grade; (3) actual college enrollment (four-year colleges, or four- and two-year colleges combined), within the first two years after high school; (4) plans for educational attainment at that point; and (5) finally plans for educational attainment four years after high school (in 1984). Table 6.12 shows the trend over time for all students, although only the second, fifth, and sixth points are based on identical questions and can be directly compared. The numbers show interesting differences, with the men showing slightly greater proportions planning to graduate, but women showing slightly greater proportions planning to attend in grade 8 and actually enrolled.

In all these measures of college enrollment or aspirations, the Catholic and other private schools can be expected to be considerably higher than public schools, because of the greater family resources and higher parental expectations for their children's education. When we control on our measures of these resources and expectations, that increment is sharply reduced, as was evident in the analysis of the preceding section. But then two questions arise: Does an increment remain after these resource and parental expectation differences are taken into account? And how do the public-private differences in expectations at grade 8 change over the course of high school and in the years following? The first of these questions has been answered for enrollment in college after high school, but neither question has been answered fully.

Table 6.13 shows that at grade 8, the student's own expectations for college are 8 percent higher for boys in Catholic schools than for their counterparts with the same background resources and parental expectations in public schools, but there is essentially no increment due to the other private sector, at 8th grade. The second column shows that a substantial increment develops in the Catholic schools when the question at grade 12 is graduation from college, but that there is only small growth in the other private schools. Columns 3 and 4 show that in terms of actual enrollment within the two-year period after high school, the Catholic increment remains at about the level of the 12th-grade college graduation expectation. For students from other private schools, the increment increases sharply, if only enrollment in four-year colleges is considered (column 3), but does not, if enrollment in two-year colleges is included as well (column 4). The increments in expectations of college graduation at two years after high school remain about the same for the Catholic-public comparison, but increase somewhat for the other private-public comparison.

The changes in relative positions of the three sectors between grade 8 and grade 12 give some indication of the effects of the school in influencing its students toward further education, as against other effects, such as the effects of youth culture, pulling in other directions. The comparison of columns 1 and 2 in table 6.13 indicates that the Catholic schools seem best able to exercise such an effect, with the other private schools only slightly better than the public schools.

Another indication of the schools' resistance to influences outside the home acting against further education is a comparison of parental expectations for college on the part of the child, as reported by the child in grade 12, and the child's own expectations, as reported at the same time. In the Catholic schools, mothers were 12 percent more likely to have college expectations for their sons, and 8 percent more likely for their daughters, than were mothers of public school students when the families were equated on background resources. In the other private schools, the comparable increments were 6 percent and 1 percent, respectively. But then the boys in Catholic schools were 21 percent

TABLE 6.13

Catholic and Other Private Increments over Public School Students in College Plans or Attendance with Background and Parental Expectations for College Statistically Controlled[a]

	Grade 8 expect to attend	Grade 12 expect to graduate	Two Years After			Four years after expect to graduate
			Attend four-year college full time	Attend two- or four-year college full time	Expect to graduate	
Men						
Catholic	0.08	0.14	0.13	0.11	0.12	0.11
Other private	0.01	0.04	0.19	0.02	0.11	0.10
Women						
Catholic	0.02	0.12	0.10	0.12	0.12	0.14
Other private	0.00	0.05	0.13	0.08	0.07	0.05

[a]Increments reported are regression coefficients for dummy variables for Catholic schools and other private schools in ordinary least squares regression equations with controls for region and rural-urban-suburban residence, race and Hispanic ethnicity, SES, mother's expectation for college, and father's expectation for college.

more likely to report expecting to graduate from college than were boys from public schools with backgrounds equated in the same way, and girls were 16 percent more likely. The increment in students' expectations were 9 percent and 8 percent more than those of parents. In the other private schools, the increments in own expectations were only 1 percent and 4 percent greater than the increments in mothers' expectations.

Thus, on the basis of both of these indicators, estimated changes in educational expectations over the period of high school and estimated differences between mothers' expectations about college and students' own expectations, the sectors seem to be ordered from high to low in their ability to counter influences against further education, with Catholic schools strongest and other private schools only slightly stronger than the public schools. Although we have no direct measure of the effect of the functional community of adults surrounding a religious school, this difference is quite consistent with such an effect. It seems quite likely that a portion of the effect of the Catholic school toward higher education is a consequence not of the internal functioning of the school, but of the community surrounding it, and its relation to the school.

How and Where Do Intentions Lead to Action?

Another way of assessing the different functioning of schools in the public, Catholic, and other private sectors is to ask how intentions for further education come to be realized in action in the three sectors. In particular, just what difference do college plans make in the taking of courses?

Table 6.14 shows the number of language courses and the number of college preparatory mathematics and science courses taken by the average student in each sector, together with two effects: the effect of parents' expectations about college attendance when the student was a sophomore and the effect of own college expectations at grade 8. The amount of language taken by the average public sector student is about half that taken by the average student in either private sector, and the effect of parents' and own college expectations is less than that in the private sectors. The result is that the amount of languages taken by the average public school student who plans to attend college and whose

TABLE 6.14

Effect of Plans to Attend College on Coursework in Languages and College Preparatory Mathematics and Science, in Each Sector, with Sophomore Verbal and Mathematics Skills Controlled

	Public	Catholic	Other Private
Years of language by average student	0.8	1.5	1.5
Effect of parents' expectations	+0.3	0.5	0.4
Effect of own expectations in grade 8	+0.2	0.3	0.4
Effect of bringing soph. achievement to Catholic level	+0.2	0	0
Total	1.5	2.3	2.3
Years of college prep math, science by av. student	2.6	4.0	3.8
Effect of parents' expectations	+0.8	0.8	0.3
Effect of own expectations in grade 8	+0.4	0.4	0.2
Effect of bringing soph. achievement to Catholic level	+0.5	0	−0.1
Total	4.3	5.2	4.2

parents hold similar plans remains considerably below that taken in either private sector. Included in the table is the effect on coursework in languages of bringing the achievement level to that of the average Catholic sector student. Doing this allows comparing the years of language taken by students whose sophomore verbal and mathematics achievement are like those of the average Catholic sector student, and whose parents and self have plans for college. The years of language taken by such a public sector student fall considerably short of those in both private sectors, which have comparable levels.

The comparisons for mathematics and science give quite different results. As with languages, the average public sector student takes considerably fewer of these courses than does the average private sector student. But parents' expectations about college make much more difference for public school students than was true for languages, as they do in the Catholic sector. In the other private sector, parents' and own college expectations make *less* difference than they do for languages. When the students are equated in sophomore achievement to the average Catholic sector student, the mathematics and science courses taken by these college-bound public school students is as high or higher than that in the other private sector, though still below that in the Catholic sector.

These results indicate first that neither college plans nor school policy does much to lead to foreign language preparation for college-bound students in public schools. Although the average public school student has little language preparation, neither plans to go to college nor higher cognitive skill levels do much to differentiate the language coursework of the student who plans to go to college from that of the student who does not.

In contrast, college plans and cognitive skills do much more to lead the public sector student who is college-bound to take college preparatory mathematics and science courses. College plans have a similar effect in Catholic sector schools; but they have little effect in other private schools.

This result indicates once more that the other private schools are considerably more humanistically oriented than they are oriented to mathematics and science. The same lack of attention to mathematics and science that was apparent in achievement growth in chapter 3, and was apparent in college majors earlier in this chapter, is apparent here. Once more, however, a warning must be introduced: This sample of other private schools may not be representative; while these results are true for the sample of schools in the study, they are only suggestive of what may be true for non-Catholic private schools as a whole.

Conclusions

There are very large differences in the percentages (about 20 to 35 percentage points) of public, Catholic, and other private high school graduates who attend a four-year college, and still sizable, though smaller, differences in the percentages who attend either a two- or four-year college. For both Catholic and other private schools, and for both boys and girls, about half of this difference can be accounted for by differences in background characteristics. For graduates of other private schools, most of the difference in background is due to differences in family resources, particularly socioeconomic status. For graduates of Catholic schools, most is due not to differences in resources, but to differences in orientations and expectations of parents toward college attendance.

Of the public-private school difference in college attendance that is not accounted for by family background, most (in Catholic schools) or about half (in other private schools) is accounted for by differences in what goes on in school. Of this, a large part is accounted for by the higher likelihood of students from comparable backgrounds being enrolled in an academic program (rather than a general or vocational program) in Catholic and other private schools. Small additional amounts are accounted for by students from comparable backgrounds and in the same program taking more academic courses and doing more homework in Catholic and other private schools than in public schools. A smaller amount is accounted for by out-of-class differences: fewer discipline problems, less after-school work, and (in other private schools) more extracurricular activities.

For those planning to attend college, both Catholic and other private school students are more likely to take a foreign language than public school students, even when parental college expectations and own pre-high school expectations are the same. But among these same students, students in other private high schools are no more likely to take college preparatory mathematics and science courses than are public school students when parental college expectations and own pre-high school expectations are the same.

An apparent effect of the last result is that graduates of other private high schools who attend a four-year college are considerably less likely to major in physical or biological sciences or in engineering or computer sciences than are public or Catholic school graduates. They are much more likely to major in humanities or the social sciences.

7

Success in College or Work

THE questions posed in the preceding chapter concerned entry into college and did not address, except in an oblique way (tables 6.12 and 6.13), the question of success. Here we will take up the question of success for those students who entered a four-year college at some point in the four years following high school and those who had no college during this period. This excludes seniors who went to a two-year college but never attended a four-year college, and it excludes those who dropped out of high school before their senior year. For the two groups which are examined, we do not follow them in detail through the period, but ask only about certain activities. Thus, the examination of success is quite selective, but it does focus on success in college and in work.

The rate of enrollment in four-year colleges is about 20 percent greater for girls in either private sector than in the public sector, and even more for boys, rising to more than a 30 percent difference for boys from the other private sector (table 6.1). For comparable backgrounds (including cognitive skills), about 10 percent more Catholic school and other private school students enter a four-year college than do public school students (table 6.6), an increment that rises to nearly 20 percent for boys from other private schools.

This considerably greater college enrollment for private sector students from comparable backgrounds and cognitive skills means that the public and private entrants to college are more alike in background than are the senior classes as a whole in the two sets of schools. In grade point averages, college entrants from private high schools are even slightly below college entrants from public high schools. Does this result in a lower success rate in college for private sector graduates? Or does the stronger coursework preparation, better homework, and disciplinary habits that students get in private sector schools (or perhaps something else) lead to greater success for the private sector students? Or alternatively, does the smaller size of private high schools or the closer community of Catholic high schools make the size and impersonality of college a greater shock than to the public school student? Or finally, does the diversity among colleges throughout the country lead students from whatever sector to choose colleges that equally well fit them, thus leading, and with whatever level of performance within sector, to comparable success rates in college? It is not at all clear what prediction is warranted.

Similarly, it is not clear just what prediction is warranted concerning success in the labor force for those who do not attend college. The narrower focus of private sector schools, their orientation toward preparation for college and virtual absence of a vocational program, suggests that those who go directly to work without further education may be poorly prepared. Because other private schools are more narrowly focused in this way, their graduates might be expected to be least well prepared for the world of work.

In addition to predictions stemming from the different orientations of schools in the three sectors, there are various popular conjectures about the way one's high school affects success in college or in the labor force immediately following high school. They are related, but not the same. An approximate statement of each is as follows:

1. Doing poorly in high school, either scholastically or behaviorally, is related, either causally or symptomatically, to success in the post-high school years. Concretely, this conjecture states that a boy or girl who has poor attendance in high school, has disciplinary problems, or gets poor grades, will have difficulties in the labor market or in postsecondary education. Conversely, a boy or girl who gets good grades and has no serious discipline problems will be successful.

2. Weak preparation in high school, in terms not of grades in school, but of measurable basic skills, leads to difficulties in the labor force or in postsecondary education. Poor study habits, whether because little

178

homework was assigned or because one chose to spend little time on homework, also leads to difficulties in college.

Because these attributes are interrelated and are related to family background, they sometimes are all assimilated to a single general proposition: "Children from better social backgrounds do better in school and do better after school." But as the preceding chapters have indicated, social background is far from the whole explanation. Background has an effect on success in school and afterwards, but the high school attended makes a difference as well.

Chapters 3, 4, and 5 showed how a student's educational outcome in high school depends on whether the high school is public, Catholic, or other private. In basic cognitive skills, students from comparable backgrounds show somewhat greater educational growth in Catholic schools than in public schools. Students from other private schools show greater growth in verbal skills, but not in mathematics, where the growth may be less than in public schools for comparable students. In study habits, students from both private sectors do considerably more homework than students from comparable backgrounds who are in public schools. There are fewest absences in Catholic schools, and the most in public schools for comparable students. Participation in extracurricular activities is slightly greater in the other private schools than in Catholic and public schools.

As chapter 5 showed, the functional community on which Catholic schools are based intensifies the relative effectiveness of Catholic schools for young persons from lower socioeconomic backgrounds. In all these areas of performance and achievement during high school, a student from a background with lesser resources—either objective socioeconomic resources or subjective volitional ones on the part of the parent—is benefited more by attending a high school based on a functional community (represented in this research by Catholic schools) than is a student from a background with greater resources. In the other private schools, however, effectiveness in both achievement and staying in school was weaker for children from disadvantaged backgrounds and for children from families with structural or functional deficiencies.

These results suggest that if comparable effects held beyond high school, then the success beyond high school of students from disadvantaged or deficient family backgrounds should be most dependent on which kind of high school they attended, and the success of those with strongest families least dependent on high school sector.

If the first of the two popular conjectures with which we began is true, young persons from similar social backgrounds should have a greater degree of success beyond high school if they attended a Catholic high school than if they attended a public high school or an other private high school. Catholic school students have better attendance, get slightly better grades, and have fewer disciplinary problems in high school than is true for students in other sectors. If the second popular conjecture is true, then young persons from comparable backgrounds should have greater success beyond high school if they had attended either a Catholic or an other private high school. They have better study habits and higher levels of achievement on standardized tests than do students from comparable backgrounds in public schools.

If the conjectures are not true, then it does not matter for future success that a student has had disciplinary problems or low grades in high school or has graduated from high school with a low level of basic cognitive skills. And if the conjectures are true, but the high school performance and achievement is merely a symptom or indicator of some underlying traits, then the impact of the student's high school on discipline, staying in school, cognitive achievement, and study habits merely affects the symptoms or indicators but not the underlying traits. If this is the case, then we should find that homework or cognitive achievement or good discipline were artificially elevated in Catholic or other private schools, and for given levels of these performance and achievement variables at the end of high school, students from the private sector would be less successful beyond high school than those from the public sector. That is, behavior and skills would revert to their normal levels, and the effect of the educational sector would prove to be merely a temporary one.

This possibility may sound somewhat convoluted and improbable, but there are popular beliefs that exemplify it. For example, it is believed by some college admissions officers that a high score on the SAT tests (similar in content to the standardized tests in reading, vocabulary, and mathematics used in this study) by a student from a private school does not mean as much as a high score by a student from a public school, because more of the private school student's "potential" will have been drawn out in the private school and measured by the SAT test, while the public school student's potential remains partly hidden, not measured by the SAT test. Or as another example, it could be that the better disciplinary behavior and higher attendance among Catholic school students is held in place only by the constant pressure of the school and does not represent habits that will carry over beyond high school. Once out of high school, the behavior might revert to its "normal" level (or even worse, if there is a reaction against the suppression during high school).*

These are two examples of the way the sector of a young person's high school attendance might make no difference even though the two conjectures with which the chapter began are true. As these conjectures indicate, it does not directly follow from the results of chapters 3, 4, and 5 that there is a lasting effect on a young person's success of attending a Catholic or other private high school. In both cases, the words "potential" and "normal" point to underlying traits that may be uninfluenced by school, and may be the true causes of success beyond high school.

To test just whether there is such an effect, there are two ways of proceeding. One is to test first the conjectures about the relation of success *in* high school in the several dimensions mentioned to success *beyond* high school, and then to examine whether a given level of success and good habits in high school leads to the same level of success beyond high school for students from a Catholic or other private school as for students from a public school. If the answer is yes on both these tests, this means that the greater demands made and better performance exacted from students has a lasting impact. But if the same level of cognitive skills, good grades, and good habits leads to less success beyond high school, this suggests that high school merely modified the levels of the symptoms, but did not change the underlying traits which determine success beyond high school. The second way of proceeding is, of course, to test directly the relation between high school sector and success beyond high school.

There are defects to both of these ways of testing the effects of school sector on success beyond high school. A defect of the second method is that much less is learned about the process through which success in high school affects success beyond high school. If there is no sector effect on success beyond high school, this may be either because the two conjectures with which the chapter began are wrong (that is, the measures of success and behavior in high school that are affected by sector are not related to success beyond high school), or that these are merely artificially improved by schools in the private sector, while it is the underlying traits that determine post-high-school success. If there is a sector effect, it may be through these factors or independent of them. For example, the functional community underlying Catholic schools

*These possibilities receive some empirical support from a recent case study by Jensen (1986), which finds that Catholic school students tend be less conforming to legal and informal norms outside of school, while maintaining greater conformity within school.

may constitute an aid (or be an impediment) to occupational success of graduates of Catholic high schools.

The first way of proceeding in testing the effect of school sector on success beyond high school also has defects. If it shows no sector effect through these factors, this does not imply that a sector effect is absent, for the effect may occur through other factors. For example, it is commonly felt that occupational success of private preparatory school graduates is in part due to the school's effect on "whom they know" rather than its effect on "what they know." If this is true, then the behavioral and cognitive factors we examine may have no effects, yet the sector has an effect.

For these reasons, we will use a combination of these two approaches in examining sector effects on success after high school. We will examine both the effects of those factors of high school experience that earlier chapters showed to be affected by high school sector, and the effects of sector directly on the various measures of post-secondary success.

Success in College

We will use two classes of measures in determining the effects of high school sector on success in college. One class is grades in college. The 1980 seniors reported grades at two points in time, spring of 1982 and spring of 1984, that is in the spring of the second and fourth year out of high school. The 1980 sophomores reported grades at one point in time, spring of 1984, spring of the second year out of high school.

A second class of measures is continuation in college without dropping out. There are various measures in this class. One is survival in the first college entered after high school; the data make it possible to track that survival month by month. A second is the proportion who enroll in a second school rather than dropping out entirely, based on those who fail to survive in their first college. A third measure is the proportion who are still in their original school by spring of their fourth year out.*

*The data of the study allow estimation of parameters of a model that mirrors this process, in which each student has a transition rate toward dropping out of college, which may depend on background and on type of high school attended. (See Cox, 1972; Coleman, 1981; Tuma and Hannan, 1984; and Heckman and Singer, 1985 for discussion of these models). Use of such a model would allow more efficient estimation of the effects of school sector than use of the various measures we shall use. However, it would give somewhat less rich descriptive information about what happens to students from different sector schools than the several measures we will use.

Success in College or Work

Survival in College

We will first examine the survival measures among those who entered a four-year college, and after that the grades. Table 7.1 shows, for all those who enrolled in a four-year college in fall 1980, the percentage who left this college in or at the end of the first year, second year, and third year, and the remaining percentage who continued into their fourth year. The table shows that among those who entered college directly following high school something over half survived in their first institution into their fourth year. The survival was somewhat higher for students from the Catholic sector, where about 60 percent survived, and from the high-performance private schools, where about 80 percent survived.* Thus, survival into the fourth year is similar in all sectors, with the exceptions indicated.

However, these survivors constitute very different fractions of the overall student body of seniors in each of these sectors: only about 16 percent in the public sector, 31 percent in the Catholic and other private sectors, and 80 percent among students who were from the high-performance private schools. Based on the number who were present as sophomores in high school, the disparities are even greater, because of dropouts between sophomores and senior years. Assuming that dropouts for the 1980 cohort were the same in each sector as for the 1982 cohort, the survival rates reduce to 14 percent for public, 31

TABLE 7.1

For All Students Enrolled in a Four-Year College by Fall 1980, the Percentage Remaining by Spring 1984, and Percentage Leaving in Each Year, by Sector of High School

	Public (%)	Catholic (%)	Other Private (%)	High-Performance Private (%)
Remaining, Spring 1984	54.3	60.2	55.6	81.4
Left in third year	7.7	5.2	2.0	5.0
Left in second year	12.7	13.4	10.9	0.6
Left in first year	25.3	21.2	31.5	12.9
Number of cases	(3,029)	(557)	(146)	(54)

*Data for men and women are combined because of the small sample sizes in some sectors. Tabulations for men and women separately show no large and systematic differences except as discussed subsequently. Later figures show rates for men and women separately.

percent for Catholic, 29 percent for other private, and 80 percent for high-performance private.

The paths toward differential survival appear to be somewhat different in the different sectors. In the Catholic sector, the losses are lower the first year, but in the second and third year are similar to those of public school students. In contrast, graduates of the other private schools show highest losses of all sectors in the first year, and then lower losses in the second and third years. Losses among graduates of high-performance private schools, though small, are also concentrated in the first year.

These paths can be seen in more detail in figures 7.1 and 7.2, which show the month-by-month survival in the first institution for men and women separately. These figures include data not only for those who entered college in fall 1980, but for all students who had entered a four-year college by spring 1984 and are thus not directly comparable to those in table 7.1.

Looking first at figure 7.1 for men, it is evident that there are strong differences in survival paths between sectors. The first large losses occur at the end of the first year in college, shown here as the eighth and ninth months. As table 7.1 indicated, losses at the end of that year, as well as those during the year, are very similar for graduates of public and other private schools, with even greater losses by the end of the year for other private school graduates than for public school graduates. The losses among Catholic school graduates are much less both during the year and at the end, with the result that at the end of the first year (after ninth month) only 13 percent of men from Catholic high schools had left the colleges they entered, while 24 percent of public high school graduates and 26 percent of other private school graduates had left. The men from high-performance private schools showed losses at the end of the first year similar to those of the public and other private graduates, though smaller losses during the year.

But *after* the first year, the survival curves of the public and Catholic school graduates are almost parallel, so that by the fourth year (from the thirty-third month on) the college cohort of Catholic school graduates remains the same distance (between 10 percent and 15 percent) above the college cohort of public school graduates as at the end of the first year. The college cohort of other private school graduates, in contrast, shows much better survival after the first year than either the public or Catholic cohort. At the end of the first year, it is below the public school level of survival. By the fourth year, it is close to the Catholic level. The high-performance private cohort shows an even flatter survival curve after the first year.

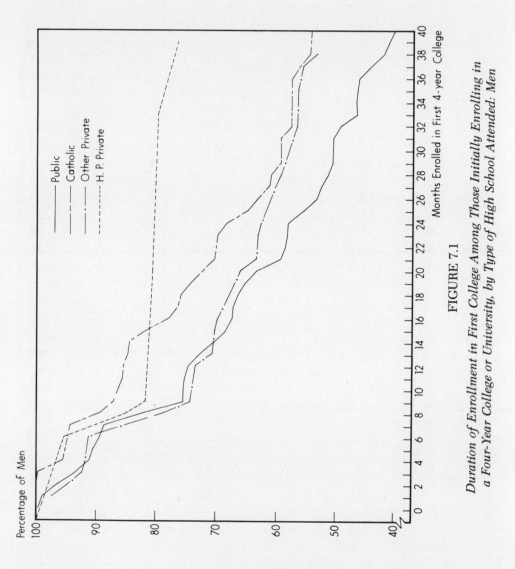

Percentage of Men

—— Public
—·—— Catholic
—·—· Other Private
------ H. P. Private

Months Enrolled in First 4-year College

FIGURE 7.1

*Duration of Enrollment in First College Among Those Initially Enrolling in
a Four-Year College or University, by Type of High School Attended: Men*

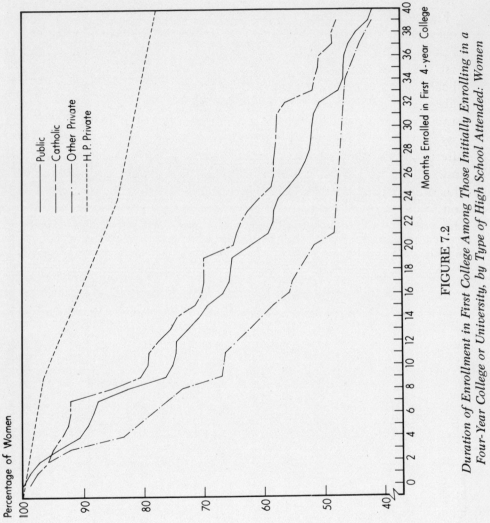

Percentage of Women

Public
Catholic
Other Private
H. P. Private

Months Enrolled in First 4-year College

FIGURE 7.2

Duration of Enrollment in First College Among Those Initially Enrolling in a
Four-Year College or University, by Type of High School Attended: Women

Success in College or Work

Thus, the public and other private graduates are similar in the first year out of college, while the men from Catholic high schools show higher survival rates. Then in subsequent years, the remaining men from Catholic and public schools show very similar survival rates while the other private school graduates show much higher survival rates.

Figure 7.2 shows data for 1980 women seniors who entered a four-year college from each of these sectors. For the women, the graduates of public and Catholic schools show quite similar patterns, both in the first year and throughout (though Catholic school survival rates are about 5 percent higher throughout), while the graduates of other private schools are very different. First, they show strikingly greater losses during and at the end of the first year, resulting in a 9 percent greater loss than for Catholic school graduates. But in the third and fourth years after high school, (twenty-one months and beyond), their losses are much lower. The end result is that they are at about the same point as the public school graduates by the spring of the fourth year. A comparison of the men's and women's survival curves for each sector would show that in the public sector, men and women left at almost identical

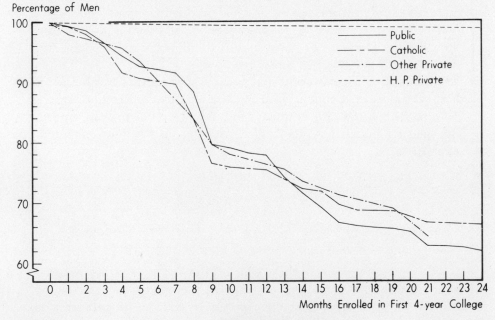

FIGURE 7.3

Duration of Enrollment in First College Among Those Initially Enrolling in a Four-Year College or University, by Type of High School Attended: 1982 Senior Men

rates throughout the period, while for both Catholic and other private sectors, women's survival was lower, averaging about 5 percent below men for Catholic school graduates and over 10 percent below for graduates from other private high schools. Thus, women from the private sector high schools fared less well in the college they entered than did men.

We can also examine survival rates for the first years out of high school in the cohort that is two years younger, that is, those who were sophomores in 1980. Figure 7.3 shows that for men in this cohort the order of sectors at the end of two years was the same as for the 1980 seniors: highest survival rates among Catholic school graduates, next among those from other private schools, and lowest among public school graduates. However, the patterns of loss do not correspond to those of the 1980 graduates. The only generalization that holds for men in both cohorts is the order of the sectors in survival rates at the end of two years: highest survival among Catholic school graduates, lowest among public school graduates—but with a difference in survival rates of less than 10 percent overall.

For women, figure 7.4 shows that the pattern of the 1982 high school graduates differed from that of the 1980 graduates, as was true for the men. Again the Catholic school graduates showed the highest survival rates, but the survival rate for women from other private schools was higher than that for public sector women.

From these four cohort and sex groups, the most that can be said is that survival rates in college appear somewhat higher for graduates of Catholic schools than for graduates of public or other private schools. The rates for public and other private schools do not show consistent differences.

What Happens to Those Who Leave Their First College?

A next question concerns those who left the first college they entered without finishing. Did they go back to college within the period covered by the followup surveys, or did they leave college altogether? The question is complicated by the fact that only about 70 percent of the boys and 75 percent of the girls who entered a four-year college did so by the October of their first year after high school. To simplify the question, we will restrict it to this set of students who went to a four-

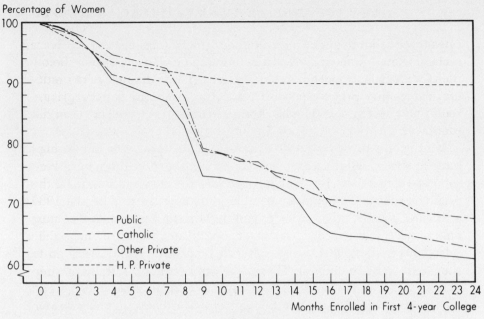

Percentage of Women

Months Enrolled in First 4-year College

FIGURE 7.4

Duration of Enrollment in First College Among Those Initially Enrolling in a Four-Year College or University, by Type of High School Attended: 1982 Senior Women

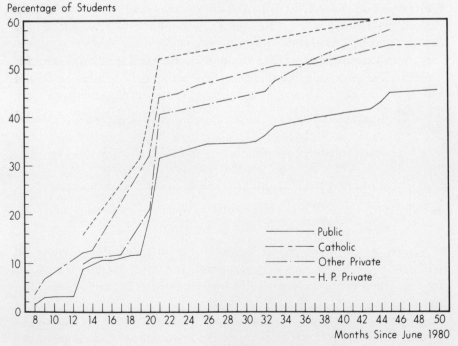

Percentage of Students

Months Since June 1980

FIGURE 7.5

Rates of Reentry into College Among Students Who Entered a Four-Year College Immediately After High School and Subsequently Dropped Out, by Type of High School Attended

year college immediately after high school. For those students, we can examine college reentrance patterns for those who left during or at the end of their first, second, or third years. Those who left by the end of their first year had a period of thirty-three months between June of 1981 and March of 1984 when they were reinterviewed in the second followup.* Those who left during or at the end of the second year had about twenty-one months after June 1982; and those who left during or at the end of the third year had about nine months after June 1983.

The reentry patterns of these students are shown in figure 7.5. The data for men and women are combined because the numbers are small (in the Catholic, other private, and high-performance private schools there were in these three years 142, 68, 50; and 47, 20, 5; and 11, 1, 2 dropouts from the first college entered, respectively, in the three years, for both sexes combined). There appeared to be no systematic differences between the sexes when analysis was done separately.

Figure 7.5 also shows that the reentry patterns (though not the levels of reentry) are quite similar for students in each sector. Between 10 percent and 20 percent of those who left enter a new college during the first year out of high school. Most of the remainder who are going to reenter during this three-year period do so at the beginning of the next academic year. The principal difference is in the proportions who finally do reenter during this total period: about 45 percent for the public sector, and about 55 to 60 percent for each of the two private sectors (and much higher for the high-performance private schools).

Table 7.2 shows the overall rates of reentry for those who leave in the

TABLE 7.2

Reentry Rates into a Four-Year College by March 1984 for Those Who Entered College by October After Their Senior Year in High School (October 1980) and Left by the End of the First Year, Second Year, and Third Year[a]

	Public	Catholic	Other Private	High-Performance Private
First year	45.3	54.9	57.9	60.6
	(863)	(142)	(47)	(11)
Second year	49.9	58.6	67.9	b
	(386)	(68)	(20)	(1)
Third year	45.6	38.2	b	b
	(219)	(50)	(5)	(2)

[a]Numbers of cases are in parentheses.
[b]Number of cases too small to estimate.

*Some interviews were completed in months following this date.

first, second, and third years, by sector. Although small sample sizes preclude strong statements, it appears that the public-private differences hold for these later leavers as well, and that the later leavers reenter in roughly the same proportions as the first year's leavers.

The overall conclusion from examining reentry is that nearly all the reentry occurs in the year after leaving the first college, and that the reentry rates are between 40 percent and 50 percent for public school graduates, and between 50 percent and 60 percent for private school graduates.

Why the Differences Among Sectors in Survival and in Reentry?

In chapter 6, we examined the high school activities that lead to greater likelihood of going to college for students from different backgrounds—activities that partly account for the sector differences in college attendance by students from comparable backgrounds. But once students are in college, are there aspects of their high school experience that make a difference in their survival in college they choose? And if so, are they aspects of high school that were differentially present in schools in the different sectors? We will examine those factors that had some importance for entry into college: absenteeism in high school, discipline problems, high school grades, homework, and verbal and mathematical test scores. Do these factors matter for survival in the first college and for grades in college?*

The very first point is that all these school factors together, plus socioeconomic status, race, Hispanic ethnicity, sex, region of the country, rural-urban residence, do not account for much of the variation in durations. Only 11 percent of the variance in duration of college enrollment is explained by all these factors together (not reported here in the

*This examination of durations was carried out through ordinary least squares (OLS) regression for the cohort as a whole, for each sex separately, and for each sector separately. A partial likelihood technique which mirrors the process would have been preferable for unbiased estimation, because the durations are not normally distributed, and the process is censored; but the OLS procedure captures the major effects. Also, the partial likelihood method assumes that censoring is independent of the factors that affect survival, but here the time of censoring depends on time of entry into college, and late entry (=early censoring) is related to some of the factors that affect survival. A maximum likelihood procedure which models the censoring itself would solve this last problem; but for the qualitative inferences made here, these refinements are unnecessary. See Coleman (1981, chapter 5) for a discussion of these last points.

TABLE 7.3

Percentage Leaving by the End of the First Year Among All Those Who Enrolled in a Four-Year College by the Fall Following High School (Fall 1980), by Grades in High School, Verbal Scores, Mathematics Scores, and Homework

	Grade Average in High School		
Below *B*	*B*	*A–B*	*A*
39.7	28.8%	23.5%	13.6%

	Verbal Scores (Number Correct)		
Lowest Sixth	Next Lower Third	Next Third	Highest Sixth
33.0	29.7	21.1	17.2

	Mathematics Scores (Number Correct)		
Lowest Sixth	Next Lower Third	Next Third	Highest Sixth
37.9	29.7	21.0	14.9

	Homework in Hours Per Week		
Less than 1	1–3 Hours	3–5 Hours	More Than 5 Hours
41.9	30.6	23.8	18.9

figures or tables). Putting aside for a moment the school factors and examining the background factors, with each of these other variables statistically controlled, blacks and students from higher socioeconomic status backgrounds remain slightly longer, and students who went to high school in small towns or rural areas survive a shorter time. Among women, those who live in the West have shorter survival in college than those from the other regions of the country.

These variables are not, however, as strong in accounting for length of survival as are factors having to do with high school and performance in high school. While background factors play a very important role in high school dropout, their role in dropout from college in greatly reduced.

If we compare the effects of the school factors listed previously, survival in the first college entered after high school is most strongly related to grades in school. Of next importance is cognitive skills, which are, of course, strongly correlated with grades; but they have a strong effect on survival, independent of grades.

Beyond these measures of academic performance relative to others in the high school, and cognitive skills measured on a scale that is independent of high school, other factors are less important. The amount of homework done in high school is the most important of these noncognitive measures. The fact that homework in high school is important for survival in college, even when high school performance, partly a result of that homework, is statistically controlled, suggests that high school work habits themselves make a difference. This inference is reinforced by the fact that absences in high school also reduce the likelihood of survival, but by a smaller amount. Disciplinary problems in high school appear to have a weak effect in reducing survival, consistent across sexes and sectors.

The preceding statements are based on examining the relation of these factors to duration of enrollment in first college with all the other factors mentioned statistically controlled. It is also useful to get a feel for the size of the zero-order relation of these various factors to survival. Table 7.3 shows the relation of grades in high school, verbal scores, mathematics scores, and homework to survival. These relationships are all quite similar (the categories of the independent variables are chosen so as to make the distributions similar). They show that students with an *A* average in high school are only half as likely to drop out by the end of the first year as those with a *B* average and about a third as likely as a student with less than a *B* average. The verbal and mathematics cognitive test distributions are divided (approximately) between the lowest sixth, the next third, the next higher third, and the highest sixth of the population entering college. For both tests, those in the lowest sixth are about twice as likely not to survive the first year as those in the highest sixth. Somewhat surprisingly, leaving college is slightly more related to performance on the mathematics tests than to performance on the verbal tests. The relation of survival to homework shows that those who did more than five hours of homework a week in high school were less than half as likely to leave college as those who did less than an hour per week.

TABLE 7.4

Percentage Leaving by the End of the First Year Among All Those Who Enrolled in a Four-Year College by the Fall Following High School (Fall 1980), by Absences and Disciplinary Problems as High School Seniors

Days Absent in Fall Semester of Senior Year			
	5 or more	3 or 4	0–2
Percentage	35.9	24.7	23.4
Disciplinary Problems Reported by Student as a Senior			
	Yes	No	
Percentage	29.2	24.8	

In contrast, table 7.4 shows that disciplinary problems and absenteeism in high school have considerably lower relations to survival in college. Those who were absent five days or more in the first semester of their senior year in high school (about a sixth of the college-going population) were only about half again as likely to leave college during the first year as those who were absent two days or less. Those who reported disciplinary problems or probation in high school as seniors were not much more likely to drop out than those who did not.

None of these variables, or others mentioned, show much relation to survival in the second and third years of college.* Both high school experience and family background appear to have their principal effects on college survival by the end of the first year.

Returning to a four-year college after leaving the college first attended is related to grades in high school, verbal and mathematical cognitive skills, and homework, to just about the same degree that remaining in one's first college does. And just as discipline problems in high school show a much lower relation to leaving college than do academic preparation and work habits, they show a similarly lower relation to reentry into college.

A portion of the students who went to college left their first colleges and never returned to college during the first four years after high school (based on those who began college by fall of their first year out of high school). For convenience, we will call this the proportion dropping out: This does not include dropping out after entering a second college, but only dropping out after the first enrollment—and it is based only on those who entered college by the first fall after graduation from high school.

The results presented in table 7.5 indicate that this proportion is strongly related to all the measures of academic preparation and study habits discussed earlier. Among the one-quarter or one-fifth of those who enter college least well prepared academically, about 40 percent leave and do not return to college. Among the one-quarter or one-fifth who are best prepared academically, the dropout rate reduces to about 15 percent or below, as table 7.5 shows.

It appears, then, that the focus on coursework and on homework that

*The Catholic high schools, for which a considerably higher proportion of loss is in the second and third years, seem to show a different pattern. Losses in the second and third years show a stronger relation to the relevant variables—high school grades, cognitive skills, and homework in high school—than do losses in the first year. It seems possible that the same community that protects Catholic school students from dropout in high school also continues into college, especially in Catholic colleges. This may defer for these students the effects of the factors that lead to leaving college until the second and third years.

194

Success in College or Work

TABLE 7.5

Percentage Leaving First College Entered and Not Returning to College by Spring of Fourth Year Beyond High School, Among Those Who Entered College in Fall of First Year After High School[a]

	Grade Average in High School		
Below *B*	*B*	*A–B*	*A*
36.3	29.3	19.1	13.2
(886)	(791)	(1,111)	(879)
	Verbal Scores		
Lowest Sixth	Next Lower Third	Next Third	Highest Sixth
38.5	27.3	17.2	13.2
(680)	(1,190)	(1,140)	(326)
	Mathematics Scores		
Lowest Sixth	Next Lower Third	Next Third	Highest Sixth
39.9	28.5	17.1	12.7
(697)	(1,034)	(1,219)	(345)
	Hours of Homework per Week		
Less than 1	1–3 hours	3–5 hours	More than 5 hours
38.2	29.5	21.8	17.0
(393)	(813)	(880)	(1,581)

[a]Sample sizes in parentheses.

is much stronger in the private sector provides important assets for remaining in college rather than dropping out. In contrast, the strict discipline which is especially characteristic of Catholic schools does not in itself create habits that are strong assets for remaining in college—though the discipline may, of course, be important in helping to bring about the academic preparation that is important, especially in the large classrooms of most Catholic schools.

These results indicate that the popular conjectures expressed at the beginning of this chapter are in some considerable part true, but that the academic preparation and study habits parts of these conjectures are much more correct than are the discipline parts.

What remains to be seen is the question raised toward the beginning of the chapter about whether the high school performance in grades, test scores, or behavior by a private school student carries over to college as fully as does the equivalent performance by a public school student, once the private sector student has left the "hothouse" environment of the high school. Concretely, do high grades, high test scores,

TABLE 7.6

The Relation of Dropping Out of First College and Not Returning to a Four-Year College to Scores on Mathematics Achievement Test, for Those Students Who Entered College by Fall of First Year After Graduation, by Sector

	Mathematics Achievement			
	Highest Sixth (%)	Next Third (%)	Next Lowest Third (%)	Lowest Sixth (%)
Public	14.3 (268)	17.8 (944)	30.1 (816)	39.7 (596)
Catholic	5.9 (37)	10.5 (198)	19.1 (185)	42.4 (92)
Other Private	3.7 (16)	18.3 (50)	20.0 (30)	36.2 (9)

Sample sizes in parentheses.

good study habits in high school lead to equal success for private sector and public sector students? The question cannot be answered in fine detail, because the college environments that these students are in are not homogeneous, but differ widely. What we can ask is whether, given the college environment selected and accepted at, the academic and behavioral measures of high school performance lead to equal success in continuing in college. First, considering each sector as a whole, the dropout rate is about 6 percent higher for public sector students (24.4 percent) than it is for the Catholic and other private sectors (18.3 percent and 18.4 percent, respectively). This lesser college dropout is as one would expect if the measures of academic preparation and high school study habits, which are higher in the private sectors, are effective not only for public school graduates but also for private sector graduates in aiding college success.

Although there is some instability in the private sectors because of small numbers, the dropout rates tend to be comparable for those public and private sector students who performed at high levels in high school on these measures of academic preparation and study habits. Table 7.6 shows the relation in each sector of college dropout to the mathematics test score, which was the most highly related of these four measures to college dropout.

Success in College or Work

Grades in College

More of the variation of grades in college than of survival in college (about 20 percent) is accounted for by background, academic preparation in high school, and behavior in high school. However, nearly all of that is accounted for by a single factor, that is grades in high school. High school grades have in fact a zero-order correlation to college grades (a correlation of 0.45 with college grade average after one-and-a-half years, 0.42 with college grade average after three-and-a-half years) almost as great as the multiple correlation (0.45 and 0.45) of the nineteen variables with college grades. The relation of college grades to verbal and mathematical cognitive skills is also reasonably strong, and beyond these, there is a relation of homework to survival in college. Thus, much the same high school factors make a difference for survival in college and grades in college: high school grades, verbal and mathematical cognitive skills, and homework.

Of these school factors that make most differences for success in college, the strongest effects of sector are on homework, and, to a lesser extent, on cognitive skills. There is little overall effect on grades (though there may be on a given student's grades), because grades are a relative measure within school and, as seen earlier, show quite similar distributions in all sectors. Thus, the principal effect of sector on success in college is through the greater focus on academic preparation and perhaps through development of better study habits. It is not principally through the better discipline in the private sector schools, except as better discipline contributes to these academic factors.

Success in the Labor Force

For 45 percent of 1980 high school seniors, there was no college beyond high school, at least up to the spring of 1982, nearly two years out of high school. What about their success in the labor market?* As in other outcomes of education, there are several grounds on which predictions about differences between public, Catholic, and other pri-

*This examination is limited to those who responded that they had not attended college by March 1982.

vate school graduates would be made. Before examining the evidence, it is useful to spell out some bases for alternative predictions.

First, however, it is important to recognize that we cannot examine labor force success in general for graduates of these different high schools. The last data point is in the spring of 1984, a few months away from college graduation for those 1980 seniors who went directly from high school into college and continued through the four years. For those who entered college, the mixture of work and school (whether on an alternating full-time basis or simultaneously) would give little information about the work setting in which they will ultimately make their occupational career—for jobs that are mixed with college are often merely to provide financial aid for further schooling and are unrelated to ultimate work careers.

For this reason, we restrict attention to those who did not enter college but went directly to work. These are very different fractions of the senior class in each of these sectors, as table 7.7 indicates. The proportion of public school seniors who did not continue education in college is considerably greater among both men and women, than the proportion of Catholic or other private seniors—an outcome that is quite consistent with the college preparatory orientation of the private sector schools shown in earlier chapters. A result of this is that, while students from all sectors who did not go on to college are lower in cognitive skills and socioeconomic background than the student body as a whole, this disparity is especially great in the private sectors, making the noncollege students from the private and public sectors considerably closer together in cognitive skills and background than the senior cohorts as a whole. This is shown in table 7.8. The table shows also that the Catholic and other private students who do not go on to college

TABLE 7.7

The Percentage of 1980 Senior Classes of Public, Catholic, and Other Private Schools Who Did Not Enter College (Full or Part-Time) in the First Two Years After High School by Spring 1982

	Public	Catholic	Other Private
Men	46	18	17
	(4,489)	(390)	(109)
Women	41	21	16
	(5,162)	(553)	(125)

Numbers of cases in parentheses.

Success in College or Work

are below the average public school senior in both cognitive skills and background.

Bases for Predictions About Differential Labor Force Successes

The most evident and obvious basis for prediction of labor force success of high school graduates who do not go on to college lies in the design and purpose of the curriculum in each sector. Most Catholic and other private schools have no curriculum designed for direct labor force entrants, that is, no vocational curricular program. They are more narrowly focused on college preparation, as is evident in chapter 2 and elsewhere in this book. This has two consequences. First, students who do not go on to college have no training that provides specific occupational skills; and second, the noncollege-going population in these schools is almost purely negatively selected: In a school designed for college preparation, they are the ones who could not or would not make it to college. This second consequence is some-

TABLE 7.8

Verbal Achievement and Mathematics Achievement as Seniors, and Family Socioeconomic Status for Those Who Had No College by Spring 1982 Compared with Total Sample, by Sector

		Public	Catholic	Other Private
Verbal achievement	Noncollege	20.02 (3,214)	22.69 (119)	23.65 (34)
	Total cohort	23.69 (8,925)	26.87 (940)	29.25 (182)
Math achievement	Noncollege	16.25 (3,146)	17.97 (118)	17.75 (34)
	Total cohort	19.13 (8,748)	21.20 (940)	21.97 (181)
Socioeconomic status	Noncollege	−0.36 (3,541)	−0.15 (120)	−0.15 (46)
	Total cohort	−0.7 (9,854)	0.24 (978)	0.76 (241)

Sample sizes in parentheses.

what less true for Catholic school graduates than for graduates of other private schools, because a larger proportion of students in Catholic schools are there for religious rather than college preparatory reasons. In some of their families, there is not a college tradition; and in some cases, they will move directly into a family business. Nevertheless, the Catholic school's curriculum ordinarily remains an academic one, not a vocational one.

Public high schools, in contrast, more often contain some kind of vocational curriculum to prepare these noncollege-oriented students for success in the labor force. If this curriculum has value as training, it should lead to greater labor force success for these students. Even if it does not, the fact that noncollege-going constitutes less of a negative selection in public schools should lead to greater success.

These considerations lead to a prediction of greater success in the labor force for public school graduates who do not go on to college than for those private school graduates who do not go on.

There are also grounds for prediction that Catholic or other private students who do not go to college might have greater labor force success than public school students. Despite the negative selection, table 7.8 shows that private sector students who do not go to college have marginally higher cognitive skills and marginally higher socioeconomic backgrounds than do their public school counterparts. These slightly greater personal and family resources of private sector graduates, and the greater community resources of Catholic school graduates, combined with the fact that jobs directly out of high school are often obtained with the aid of friends and relatives, suggests that private sector students who enter the labor force directly would do so with an advantage. Because of the availability of the religious community as a resource for graduates of Catholic high schools, this advantage should be especially great for graduates of Catholic high schools.

We will use two measures of success in labor force activity for those who did not enter college. One is wages in 1982 and 1983, and the other is tenure in the first job held after high school. The latter is a somewhat dubious measure, less clearly valid than remaining in the same college is for those who entered college, for leaving the first job can be for a better job, just as it can also represent instability in the labor force. Duration of first job held does show a positive relation to wages in 1982 and 1983, which indicates that it does have some validity as a measure of job stability. We will use it in the absence of longer-term measures of occupational success.

Table 7.9 shows the percentages of men and of women who still held their first post-high school jobs approximately four years after high school.* About 30 percent of the men from each sector still held their first job, with the percentages slightly higher in the two private sectors. (In this comparison, as in all those involving the noncollege fraction of the sample, the numbers of cases on which the figures for private sector students are based is sufficiently small to make generalization to the population they represent risky. The reader should be aware that such inferences must be made cautiously in this section, and especially so for the other private sector. In the Catholic sector, the total number of noncollege respondents is 127, and in the other private sector, 47.)

For the women, there are substantial differences between public and private sectors, with Catholic sector women showing the greatest stability—greater also than that of Catholic men—and public-sector women showing the lowest stability of all groups, considerably lower stability than public-sector men.

These, however, are measures of stability only at the end point. Figures 7.6 and 7.7 show the survival curves in first job throughout the first forty months after taking the job.† As Figure 7.6 shows, over half the Catholic men left their first jobs within eight months, a much larger fraction than for either of the other sectors. The stability they exhibit at the end of forty months is due to the low rate of leaving by the 46

TABLE 7.9

In the Fourth Year After High School, the Percentage Still Working at the First Full-Time Job After High School, for Men and Women, by Sector

	Public (%)	Catholic (%)	Other Private (%)
Men	30.9	32.0	37.8
	(1,654)	(50)	(20)
Women	23.3	42.0	34.9
	(1,548)	(59)	(21)

Restricted to those who did not attend college within two years after high school, and held a full-time job within four years after high school.

*Interviewing began in February 1984, and data on about half the sample were obtained in February. Interviewing continued through July, with 13 percent of the cases occurring in July.

†For those who had a job before school ended and kept it, job tenure was counted from the end of school, with June 1980 as the first month. These curves do not end with percentages remaining that are equal to those still working at time of interview, for two reasons: First, the chart continues only through forty months, which is October 1984. Second, some first jobs began not immediately at the end of school, but later.

percent who remain in their jobs at the end of eight months. This same difference between an unstable set of workers and a set of workers with low rates of leaving appears true as well for the men from other private schools, though the sample is small.

Among the women (figure 7.7), the Catholic sector women show highest survival in first job throughout the forty-month period. As with men, in the later months (beginning about thirteen months after end of school), women from both private sectors show considerably higher survival (flatter curves) than the public sector women, giving a considerable gap at forty months.

Thus, although both private sectors show somewhat greater percentages continuing in the same job than does the public sector, there are quite different patterns of job leaving in the three sectors. Among both men and women, the leaving rates among private sector graduates are considerably lower after the first months on the job; but among Catholic sector men and, to a lesser extent, among men from the other private sector, the leaving rates in early months are higher than in the public sector.

When we turn to wages, the results are no more simple and straightforward than for stability in first jobs. Figure 7.8 shows the distribution of wages among men in the three sectors in 1982 for all those who earned more than $1,000 in 1982. Figure 7.9 shows the 1983 distribution for all those who earned more than $1,000 in 1983.

In 1982, nineteen to thirty months after graduation, the Catholic sector men show the lowest wages (except that the distributions are about alike for the lowest 15 percent of wage earners). The distribution for public and other private sector men are nearly alike.

In the next year, thirty-one to forty-three months after graduation, the Catholic sector men have shown the greatest increase in wages (from a median income of about $8,000 to a median income of about $10,000). The public sector men have shown an increase from about $9,000 to about $10,000, while the other private sector men have stayed at about the same level of income. Overall, taking the two years together, few generalizations seem possible, except that perhaps the Catholic sector men show lower initial income but greater growth than the others.

For women, Figures 7.10 and 7.11 show that the pattern is quite different. Catholic sector women show higher incomes in 1982, especially in the lower two-thirds of the distribution. But they show *less* income growth in the next year (the median income is even lower, dropping from about $8,500 to about $8,000 while that of public sector women increase from about $7,000 to about $8,000). The women

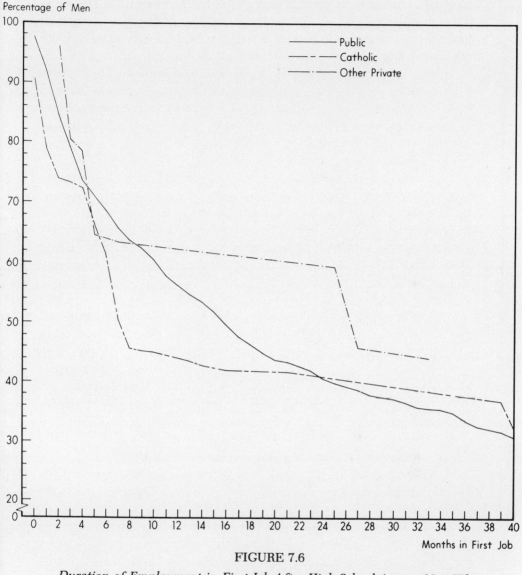

FIGURE 7.6

Duration of Employment in First Job After High School Among Men Who
Did Not Attend College After High School, by Type of High School
Attended

Percentage of Women

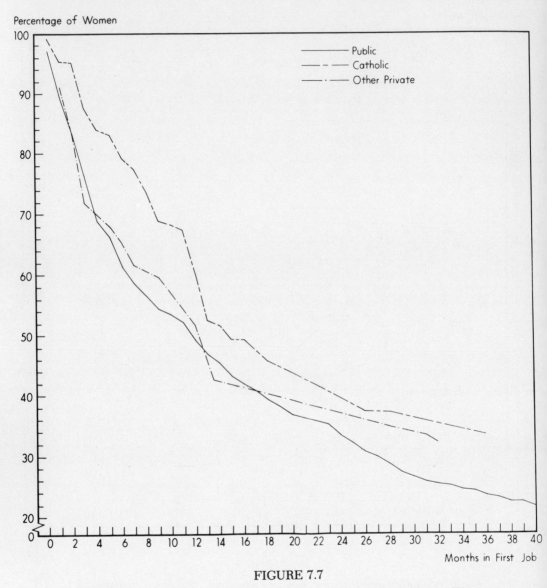

Months in First Job

FIGURE 7.7

*Duration of Employment in First Job After High School Among Women
Who Did Not Attend College After High School, by Type of High School
Attended*

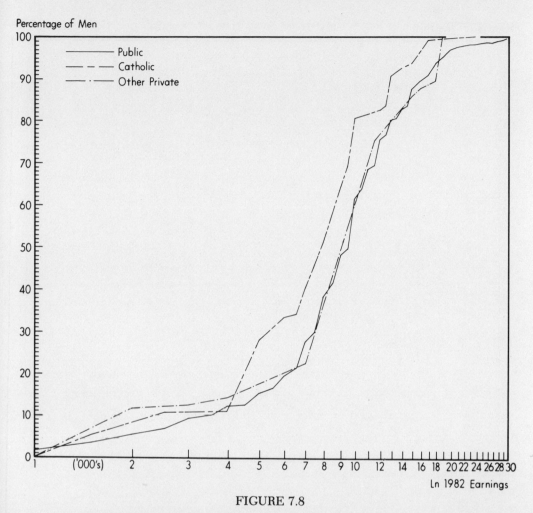

FIGURE 7.8

Cumulative Distribution of 1982 Earnings for Men Who Did Not Attend College After High School, by Type of High School Attended

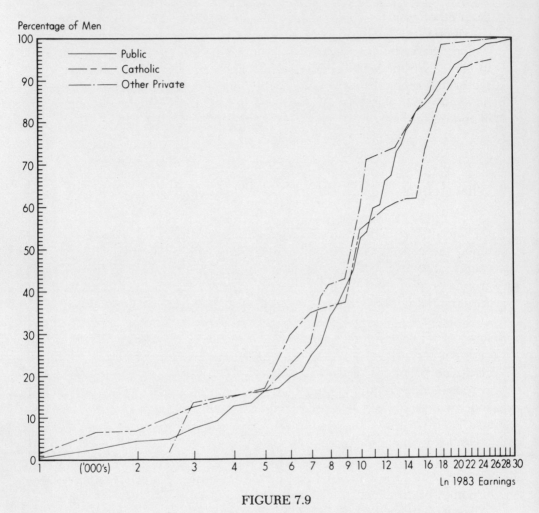

FIGURE 7.9

*Cumulative Distribution of 1983 Earnings for Men Who Did Not Attend
College After High School, by Type of High School Attended*

from other private schools show a general decline at all points in the distributions.

The differences between the sexes in each sector, both in levels and in changes from 1982 to 1983, inhibit any generalization about true sector differences in wages among the noncollege graduates. There is no evidence in these data of consistent wage differences of graduates of the three sectors.

What Actions in High School Affect Success at Work?

None of the measured background characteristics or measures of school performance showed much relation either to job duration or to wages in 1982 and 1983. In multiple regression equations with background and school factors included, the variance accounted for in job duration is less than 5 percent, and the variance accounted for in wages in either year is only about 5 percent. For job duration, only two measures of school performance approached statistical significance in a multiple regression including all three sectors: grades in school and discipline problems in school. A one point difference in grade point average is associated with one-and-a-half months' longer job duration, and having had disciplinary problems or having been on probation is associated with two months shorter job duration.

Grades in school and homework are associated with wages, with a one point difference in grade point average associated with a wage difference of $800 to $1,000 per year, and a two-hour per week difference in homework associated with about $500 difference in wages.

These relations indicate that behavior in school and academic preparation have some relation to early job success for high school graduates who go directly to work. However, the major determinants of early job success (as measured here) for those who enter the labor force directly are factors unmeasured in this study.

Conclusions

Success in college is measured here by remaining in the first college enrolled in after high school, by reentry into college among those who leave their first college, and by college grades. Success among those

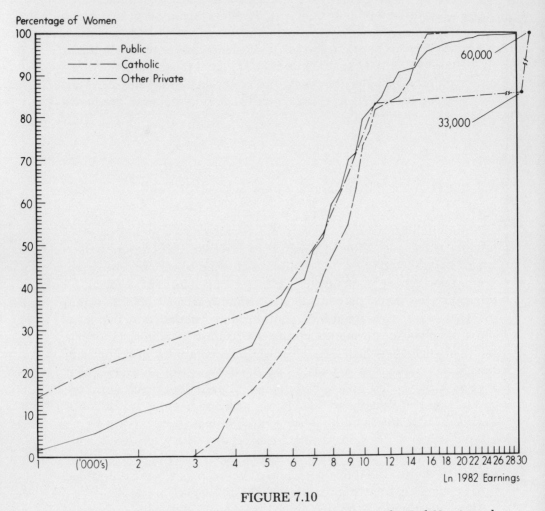

FIGURE 7.10

*Cumulative Distribution of 1982 Earnings for Women Who Did Not Attend
College After High School, by Type of High School Attended*

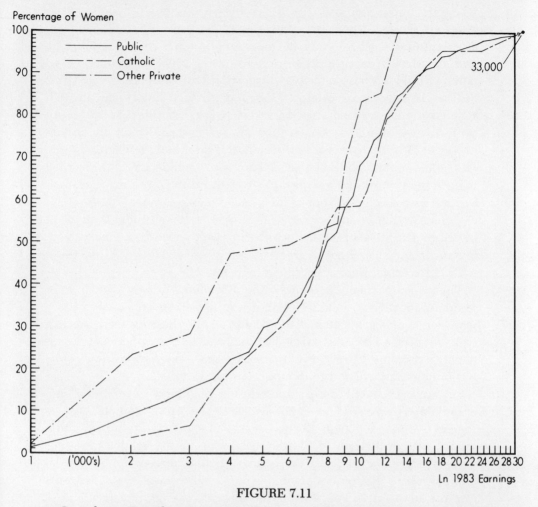

Percentage of Women

Public
Catholic
Other Private

33,000

('000's)

Ln 1983 Earnings

FIGURE 7.11

*Cumulative Distribution of 1983 Earnings for Women Who Did Not Attend
College After High School, by Type of High School Attended*

who enter a four-year college differs somewhat among graduates of the different sectors. There are slightly higher proportions of survivors among Catholic school graduates than among other private graduates, and slightly higher proportions among other private graduates than among public school graduates. A question that arises is whether this differential success is related to the performance differences in high school between sectors. The answer is yes: Success differs according to performance in high school on those dimensions on which the sectors produce differing levels of performance. These include cognitive test scores and amount of homework. They also include grades in school, which are quite similar among college entrants from the three sectors. Success in college does not differ greatly, however, according to the disciplinary dimensions in which the three sectors produce differing performance. Students with more absences and more disciplinary problems are slightly, though not greatly, less successful in college than those with better disciplinary records in high school.

Thus, success in college shows some differences among sectors, with graduates of the Catholic sector showing highest success among those who enter, and graduates of the public sector showing least success. College success is related to scholastic success in high school (a relation which is responsible for part of the relation of college success to sector) but only weakly related to discipline in high school.

Success in the labor force, among those who did not enroll in college, is only weakly related to sector. Neither the predictions of greater success of public school graduates because of vocational training in high school, nor predictions of greater success of private school graduates because of greater family resources are upheld. There are no substantial and consistent differences among sectors in success of direct entrants into the labor force. There are some relations, though not strong ones, between grades and discipline in school and stability in the first job.

8

Schools, Families, and Communities

$\mathbf{I}$N chapter 1, we characterized the three sectors of education—public schools, the religious private sector, and the independent private sector—as agents of the larger society and the state, agents of the religious community, and agents of the family. The body of this book has consisted of analyses of the effects of schools organized in these three ways on the young persons whom they are intended to serve. In this chapter, we will first take stock of what these analyses have shown and will then ask about some of the implications of these results.

First, however, it is useful to gain a perspective on the overall enterprise. Public schools are the schools attended by over 90 percent of children and youth in the United States. All private schools together enroll a very small minority of American children and youth. Catholic schools enroll about 6 percent, and non-Catholic private schools enroll less than 4 percent of the total of American children.

In many locales, and for many parents, there is no school other than the public school. The majority of children from every socioeconomic background are in public schools, including those from upper socioeconomic backgrounds. Because public schools are in such preponderance, the practical relevance of the results of this book lies much more in their implications for educational policy generally than for the choice between public and private school. And because the results involve more than the school itself, the implications for raising children go beyond schooling per se.

Chapters 3, 4, and 5 concentrated on differing effects of schools in the three sectors during the period of high school itself. Chapters 6 and 7 examined effects beyond high school. It is useful to summarize the results according to these broad classes.

Differential Effects During the High School Period

There are differences in achievement growth between sectors, and although some part of these can be accounted for by differences in the family backgrounds of students in the three sectors, a part is clearly due to differences in the schools themselves—a result that is evident not only in the differences that remain when background characteristics are statistically controlled, but is also evident in the correspondence between greater academic demands in particular areas and greater achievement growth, and evident as well in the differential achievement growth of dropouts, transfers, and those who remained.

Catholic schools bring about greater growth for the average student in both verbal and mathematical skills than do public schools, but not in science knowledge nor in civics, where the two sectors provide comparable levels of achievement growth for the average student. Other private schools bring about greater growth in verbal skills than do the public schools. They do not bring about greater growth in mathematical skills and may bring about less growth in science than do public schools. The results of achievement growth in verbal and mathematical skills generally correspond to those found for achievement levels using the 1980 data (Coleman, Hoffer, and Kilgore 1982a, 1982b; Coleman and Hoffer 1983) with the exception of mathematics achievement for other private schools, where the earlier research showed greater effects for other private schools than for public schools. The absence of any differential effect for other private schools in mathematics is consistent with the fact that when family background and academic program are statistically controlled, other private students are no more likely to take college preparatory mathematics classes than are public school students (and perhaps even slightly less likely), although Catholic school students are considerably more likely to do so (see table 6.14).

The achievement growth benefits of Catholic school attendance are especially strong for students who are in one way or another disadvantaged: lower socioeconomic status, black, or Hispanic. A corollary of this is that the benefits are least strong for those who are from advantaged family backgrounds. The result is a contraction between sophomore and senior years of the variation in achievement in Catholic schools (or less expansion of the variation than occurs in the other sectors).

None of this holds for other private schools, which show no stronger benefits in verbal skills, where the data show benefits for the average student, for those from disadvantaged backgrounds.

When the comparison is not for students from families that are disadvantaged by the usual socioeconomic criteria, but for students from families that have some kind of structural or functional deficiency, then the private sectors are especially divergent: Catholic schools show a considerably *less* depressive effect of these family deficiencies in achievement growth than do public schools; other private schools show a *greater* depressive effect of these family deficiencies on achievement growth than do public schools.

These differential achievement effects for students who are in one or another way disadvantaged are closely related in substance to the effect of school sector on another outcome of school: continuing in school or dropping out. The dropout rates from Catholic schools are strikingly lower than those from public schools or other private schools. This reduced dropout rate holds both for those who show no signs of problems as sophomores and for those who as sophomores are academically or disciplinarily at risk of dropping out.

What is perhaps equally as surprising as the low dropout rate from Catholic schools is the fact that the other private schools show no reduction whatever, when compared with the public schools, in the dropout rates of students who are at various levels of academic or disciplinary risk as sophomores. The percentages dropping out at each level of risk are quite similar to those in the public sector, and much higher than those in the Catholic sector. For students at different socioeconomic levels, the dropout rate at the higher socioeconomic levels is even higher in the other private sector than in the public sector. This indicates that the phenomenon of "middle-class dropout" from high school is more pronounced in the other private schools than in the public schools (while it is virtually absent in the Catholic schools). When we ask what protection against dropout a school affords to those children whose families have some kind of structural or functional deficiency (as examined in the case of achievement), the result in Catholic schools is like that found for achievement: Students from families with these deficiencies are hardly more likely to drop out than are those from families without the deficiencies, while these deficiencies make a strong difference among public school students, and an even stronger difference for students from other private schools.

The first prominent explanation for the difference is the functional community that exists around a religious body to which the families adhere and of which the school is an outgrowth. The independent private schools, in contrast, ordinarily lack such a community, consisting as they do of a collection of parents who have individually chosen a school but who do not constitute a community outside the school.

We attempted to find an alternative explanation for the exceedingly strong Catholic school effect on the dropout rate, still within the general hypothesis that some kind of social integration protected the student from becoming a middle-class dropout. One possible explanation concerned Catholic religion per se: It might simply be that Catholic students were less likely to drop out of school than others, whether in a Catholic school or not, because of greater social integration in the Catholic religious community itself. But this did not account for the difference, for while Catholics were slightly less likely to drop out of public school than were non-Catholics, they were no less likely to drop out of Catholic schools. Nor was it true that the degree of integration with the religious community, as measured by frequency of church attendance, was responsible for the special protection against middle-class dropout provided by Catholic schools. However, here too, there is an effect of social integration, with those who regularly attended church, whether Catholic or not, considerably less likely to drop out than those who never attended church.

These results are all consistent with a picture of middle-class dropout from high school as an act induced by a lack of social integration, either into a well-functioning and structurally intact family or into a close community, with the greatest protection provided by a school that is an outgrowth or agent of the community of which one is a member. Lesser degrees of protection, but still important, are provided by integration into a religious community, even if the school attended is not part of the community, that is, a public school, rather than a Catholic school.

Why does the religious community, rather than a community based on some other grounds, appear to be of such great importance in providing this integration? Part of the answer is that it is almost the only functional community (as distinct from a value community) around which private schools are organized. Private schools without a base in a religious community ordinarily draw children from a number of neighborhoods, and the parents have little or no occasion even to meet each other, except upon some school-related event. Only in rare circumstances, such as a university-affiliated laboratory school, in which the parents of most students are university staff, is a nonreligious-based private school grounded in a functional community.* Even some schools which do have a religious affiliation, such as Friends (Quaker) schools, lack a grounding in a functional community, for their student bodies are largely made up of students who are not of that religion. The lack of a functional community in these schools was shown in chapter 4 by the high dropout rates in religiously sponsored private schools with a religiously heterogeneous student body. (However, non-Catholics in Catholic schools are not more likely to drop out than are Catholics).

Part of the reason for the special importance of religious community for the effects of social integration found here is that we did not investigate the other principal basis of community in which a school may be grounded, that is residence. There are public high schools grounded in a residential community, in which parents know one another and know one another's children. But the study of which public high schools are grounded in a functional community and which are not, and of the effects of this basis of social integration on dropping out, goes beyond the scope of the present analysis. A third part of the reason for the special importance of the religious community for the effects of integration found here is that the religious community is one of the few remaining strong bases of functional community in modern society which includes both adults and children. Community based on residence has undergone a steady decline, as technology allows adults to scatter widely to their workplaces and allows communication media to enter the community and replace much of the face-to-face talk which was once the staple of neighborhood life. (See Nisbet [1953] and Stein [1960] for sociological discussions of the decline of community.) Only in areas where special circumstances, such as the low population density of rural areas, restrict the scattering of work for most adults, is a residential area constrained to close in on itself and continues to exist as a functional community including both adults and children.

The absence in the other private schools of a community base to provide the social integration which protects against middle-class drop-

---

*See Coleman (1985) for an account of the functional community in one such school.

outs and supports the educational demands of the school produced results just as unexpected as the very strong protective effect provided by the Catholic schools. Students are more likely to drop out from these schools than are students from comparable backgrounds in the public schools. While middle-class dropouts can be found in public schools as well as in other private schools, it is more pronounced in the other private schools than in the public sector. The most straightforward explanation of this result is an explanation that follows directly from the integration effect of the Catholic schools. The independent private schools constitute with few exceptions the extreme of individualism in education. The family acts individually, enrolling the child in a school that is not an outgrowth of a functional community, but one that collects children from a set of parents who have similar values and sufficient resources to implement these values. But this individual calculus on the part of the parent, attempting to maximize the fit of school to child, overlooks a set of social resources which are not provided by schools themselves, but are provided by these social relations that exist among the parents of students in the school. By placing the child in a school that is not embedded in such a set of relations—in some cases, removing the child from a public school which is embedded in such a set of relations provided by neighborhood association—the parent deprives the child of the social resources that can be provided by a community of adults. For certain children, particularly those with strong families containing a rich set of social relations, this deprivation of community may do no damage. For some, it may be beneficial, for it frees them from the compressive effects of community exhibited by the Catholic schools, and may allow them to race ahead intellectually. Of this we have no strong evidence in the present data. But for others, it is a serious loss, a loss which is evidenced in the analysis found in chapter 5. And the evidence is that it is more often a loss than a gain, when compared to the Catholic schools, where such integrative support exists.

Why the High Participation in Extracurricular Activities in Other Private Schools?

We noted in chapter 2 the higher level of participation in extracurricular activities in other private schools (but not in Catholic schools) without attempting to account for this fact. Part but not all of the difference is due to the fact that participation in extracurricular activities is higher in smaller schools. But then why do the Catholic schools which are smaller not show more participation than do the public schools?

A key to the answer may lie in an examination of extracurricular activities in boarding schools, for participation is higher in these schools than in any of the sectors examined in this study. The history of these activities is instructive, for it suggests an evolution through which institutions developed that had important functions for boarding schools. The most important point in that history was probably the headmastership of Rugby School in England, held by Thomas Arnold from 1828 to 1841. Arnold found life at the English public schools (that is, private boarding schools) to be a miserable affair, studded with conflicts, disputes, and general unhappiness. He was the originator of interscholastic sports among the boarding schools (and of the game of Rugby), in what was a conscious attempt to introduce some grounds for social cohesion and social integration at Rugby. Since that time, interscholastic and intramural athletic activities have come to be an important element in the social life of English Public Schools. In their American counterparts, the few boarding schools that exist in this country, there also exist vigorous programs of extracurricular physical activities, both intramural and interscholastic.

The independent private day school, consisting of students who are not part of the same neighborhoods, and who are from parents who are not in everyday contact, has many of the same problems of social integration as does the boarding school. It seems quite likely that the extensive participation in extracurricular activities in these schools is encouraged by the schools because of the integrative value it has in making the student body a functional community, and is engaged in by students because of the social integration it provides, when the student would otherwise experience the isolating conditions resulting from the individualistic educational path taken by the family.

Dropping out of high school by students whose counterparts in the Catholic sector are continuing in school is an indicator that suggests that the creation of community in these schools is far from wholly successful in providing the social integration that keeps a young person tied to friends and to the school. In a period of time in which family bonds were more intense, this would matter less for the psychic health of young persons than it does today. And, as indicated by the evidence which showed the greater dependence on structural and functional soundness of the family in other private schools than in public schools, and in public schools than in Catholic schools, the strength of a functional community, either in the school itself or surrounding it, matters more for some current families than for others.

Differential Effects Exhibited Beyond High School

When a cohort of students—say the cohort that would normally finish high school in 1980—leaves school, they are pointed in various directions. The high school they have attended affects the direction they are pointed as well as their success in pursuing that direction. One way it affects the direction is by its effect on their continuation in high school, that is, the school's effect in inducing or inhibiting dropout. Another way is by its effect on their enrollment or nonenrollment in college, if they do continue until graduation, and the kind of college they enter. Another way is by its effect on the choice of job or other activity if they do not enter college. But the high school young persons attend can affect not only the directions they are pointed when they leave school; it can affect their success in the path that is chosen.

We examined effects of the high school sector both on the path a young person takes at the end of high school and on success in following that path. The examination was selective: We examined only those who enrolled in a four-year college within the first four years after high school, and those who had no college whatsoever during the first two years out of high school. Left out of the examination of the path taken are those who attended a two-year college but not a four-year college (except for a cursory examination), students who dropped out of high school before completion, and those who graduated early. Furthermore, in examining choice of path taken at the end of high school, we studied only college enrollment, making no gradations beyond the four- versus two-year distinction.

Stronger effects of the high school sector were found on choice of path—that is, the probability of attending a four-year college—than on success in the path taken. This may be due to poorer measurement of success, or to insufficient analysis of success, or it may be that the impact of school sector is actually greater on the path initially embarked on than on success in following that path.

The overall differences between public and private sectors in rates of college enrollment are great, but about half of this difference is due to differences in backgrounds of students in public and private schools.

Between public and Catholic schools, these are primarily differences in orientations, but with differences in resources playing a greater role in explaining the public-other private difference in college enrollment. Of the public-private differences in enrollment that cannot be accounted for by differences in parental resources or orientations, about half can be accounted for by the much greater likelihood of Catholic and other private students than of public school students with comparable backgrounds and achievement test scores to be enrolled in an academic (that is, college preparatory) program in high school. This is a difference in school policy that derives directly from the fact that the private school is an agent of the family rather than an agent of the larger society—for parents have strong interests in seeing their children continue their education beyond high school, while authorities who design public schools see a greater role for vocational programs in high school.

Of the remaining differences in college enrollment that cannot be accounted for by background, nor by high school program taken by students from comparable backgrounds, a major portion can be accounted for by the fact that students in the private sector are more likely to take college preparatory courses and do more homework than students in the same program (academic versus general or vocational) and from comparable backgrounds in public schools. The proliferation of courses that occurred in the 1970s led to introduction of courses in public high schools that for many students took the place of traditional academic courses like foreign languages, European history, English composition, and college preparatory mathematics and science. Private sector schools were less likely to offer such a path of least resistance for their students when confronted by lack of interest in standard college preparatory courses. Very likely a considerable part of the difference in coursework is due to the lesser resources of Catholic schools and many other private schools, which constrain the flexibility and variability of courses. Another part of the difference in academic coursework arises directly from the role of the public schools as agent of the state. In the 1960s and 1970s, federal and state programs introduced a wide variety of programs, often with a portion of the school's budget contingent upon having such programs. Table 2.8 shows the differences in participation in these programs by public and private schools. In some cases these programs, as administered by state departments of public instruction, were not available to schools outside the public sector. In other cases, the private schools chose not to participate.

Besides the greater range of academic and nonacademic courses available in public schools, another coursework-related factor is responsible for some part of the additional college enrollment of Catholic school students, though not of other private school students. This is the taking of college preparatory mathematics (and to a lesser extent, science) courses by students in Catholic schools. This was not true for students in other private schools, where the lower level of taking courses like algebra 2, geometry, and calculus among students with comparable backgrounds and college plans indicates a more humanistic and less technical orientation of these schools. This less technical orientation is confirmed by the lower frequency of college students from other private schools majoring in technical subjects and the higher frequency of majoring in humanities or social science subjects.

Fewer sector differences were identified in investigating success in college (for those who went to a four-year college) or the labor force (for those who did not go to college). Because of the greater college-going propensity of private sector students than of public sector students from comparable backgrounds, the background differences within the college-going group and within the noncollege group are considerably smaller than for the overall student populations. This appears responsible in part for the small sector differences in survival rates in first college or work and the lack of substantial differences in wage distributions. There are, however, small differences in survival rates in first college among sectors, with slightly higher survival among students from both private sectors than from the public sector, for both sexes. There are greater differences in rates of returning to college, resulting in a substantially greater proportion of public sector students than of private sector students leaving by the end of the first year and not returning to college.

These survival rates in college are strongly related to academic performance in high school, as well as to the amount of homework done during high school. They are only weakly related to absenteeism and behavior problems in high school—indicating that if private sector policies have an impact on survival in college, it is more through the academic preparation they provide and study habits they inculcate than it is to shaping behavior patterns in more disciplined directions.

Success in work, as measured by survival in first job, is also related to grades in high school (controlling on other high school factors and on background), but it is more highly related to discipline-related behavior than is survival in college.

These are the overall results in brief of the analyses carried out in this book. The results have a number of implications for the functioning of schools, implications which are very much related to the social context of the school: the kinds of families whose children are in the school, and the kinds of social structures in which family and school are embedded. These relations constitute a set of resources that can be usefully described as "social capital." In the next section, we will discuss the ideas behind this term, as well as its relation to the well-known concept of "human capital."

Human Capital and Social Capital

Probably the most important and most original development in the economics of education in the past thirty years has been the idea that the concept of physical capital as embodied in tools, machines, and other productive equipment, can be extended to include human capital as well (see Schultz 1961; Becker 1964). Just as physical capital is created by working with materials to create tools that facilitate production, human capital is created by working with persons to produce in them skills and capabilities that make them more productive. Indeed, schools constitute a central institution for the creation of human capital. And just as decisions are made on investment in physical capital based on expected rates of return to these investments, it is useful to conceive of educational decisions as being made on the basis of expected rates of return to investments in human capital (see, for example, Mincer 1974).

There is, however, something quite different and distinct from human capital, yet no less important, which we have called social capital. If physical capital is wholly tangible, being embodied in observable material form, and human capital is less tangible, being embodied in the skills and knowledge acquired by an individual, social capital is less tangible yet, for it exists in the *relations* between persons. Just as physical capital and human capital facilitate productive activity, social capital does as well. For example, trust is a form of social capital. A group within which there is extensive trustworthiness and extensive trust is able to accomplish much more than a comparable group without that trustworthiness and trust. (For example, some economic activities depend greatly upon such trust relations for their very existence. Perhaps the example that shows this best is wholesale diamond markets, in which one merchant will give another possession of a valuable lot of diamonds for inspection, with no formal security whatsoever.)

The distinction between human capital and social capital can be exhibited by the diagrams sometimes used by analysts of social networks. In a diagram like that of figure 8.1, representing relations between four persons, *A, B, C,* and *D,* the human capital resides in the nodes, and the social capital resides in the lines connecting the nodes. Social capital and human capital are often complementary. For example, if *B* is a child and *A* is an adult parent of the child, then in order for *A* to be useful for the cognitive development of *B,* there must be capital in both the node and the link, human capital held by *A,* and social capital in the existence of the relation between *A* and *B.*

Furthermore, certain kinds of social capital arise only in networks with a high degree of *closure.* In a network like that of figure 8.1, the existence of relations between *A, B, C,* and *D* means that two can discuss a third's behavior and develop consensus about what is proper or appropriate behavior, that is, develop social norms. For example, if *A* and *D* are parents of *B* and *C,* they can develop norms about appropriate behavior for their children. If, in contrast, the network does not exhibit closure, so that *A* and *D,* who have parent-child links to *B* and *C,* respectively, do not have links to one another, then norms to govern and constrain *B*'s and *C*'s actions cannot develop.

Thus, if we are correct, the social capital that we have described earlier as existing in religious communities surrounding a religious school resides at least in part in the norms and sanctions that grow in such communities. These norms and sanctions in turn depend both on social relations and the closure of networks created by these relations.

Social Capital in the Family

Students' families differ in human capital, as, for example, measured in years of parental education. And this research shows, just as has much other research, that outcomes for children are strongly affected by the

FIGURE 8.1
A Network with Closure

human capital possessed by their parents. But this human capital can be irrelevant to outcomes for children if parents are not an important part of their children's lives, if their human capital is employed exclusively at work or elsewhere outside the home. The social capital of the family is the relations between children and parents (and when families include other members, relationships with them as well). That is, if the human capital possessed by parents is not complemented by social capital embodied in family relations, it is irrelevant to the child's educational growth that the parent has a great deal, or a small amount, of human capital.

There are striking examples in the biographies of particular persons that illustrate the importance of social capital in the family. For example, Bertrand Russell once remarked, in response to a comment on his brilliance, that he had no greater endowments than many others; that his grandmother, who engaged him in extensive discussions on intellectual matters when he was a child, is what made the difference. Assuming that his statement contained some truth, it is evident that the major difference between Bertrand Russell's childhood and that of others was not the intellectual resources his grandmother had, but the use of those resources in extended interaction with the boy. John Stuart Mill, who at the age of four had been taught Latin and Greek by his father, James Mill, and later in childhood would discuss critically with his father and with Jeremy Bentham drafts of the father's manuscripts, is another example. John Stuart Mill probably had no extraordinary genetic endowments, and his father's learning, while extensive, was no more so than that of some other men of the time. The central difference was the time and effort spent by the father with the child on intellectual matters.

A third example is from contemporary America. In one public school district where texts for school use were purchased by children's families, school authorities were puzzled to discover that a number of Asian immigrant families purchased two copies of each textbook needed by the child, rather than one. Investigation showed that the second copy was purchased for the mother to study in order to maximally help her child do well in school. Here is a case in which the human capital of the parents, at least as measured traditionally by years of schooling, is low, but the social capital in the family available for the child's education is extremely high.

These three examples contrast greatly with the situation in which many children of well-educated parents find themselves today. The human capital exists in the family, but the social capital does not.

It is the absence of social capital within the family that we have labeled "deficiencies" in the family. What we have labeled as *structural* deficiency is the physical absence of family members. The two elements of structural deficiency that we have used in the analysis are single parent families and families in which the mother worked before the child entered elementary school. However, the nuclear family itself can be seen as structurally deficient, lacking the social capital which comes with the presence of grandparents or aunts and uncles in or near the household.

What we have labeled *functional* deficiency in the family is the absence of strong relations between children and parents despite their physical presence in the household and opportunity for strong relations. This may result from the child's embeddedness in a youth community, from the parents' embeddedness in relationships with other adults which do not cross generations, or from other sources. Whatever the source, it means that whatever human capital exists in the parents, the child does not profit from it because the social capital is missing. The resources exist in node A of the diagram of figure 8.1, but the weakness of relation between the parent A and the child B makes them unavailable to the child.

It is, in fact, precisely the distinction between human capital existing in the family and social capital existing in the family that constitutes the differences between what we have called "traditional disadvantage" of background and what we have called "family deficiencies", in the analyses of chapters 3, 4, and 5. What is ordinarily meant by a disadvantaged background is the absence of resources embodied in the parents, primarily represented by parents' education but also represented by a low economic level or racial-ethnic minority status that stand as surrogates for low levels of human capital that is useful for economic success. What we have counterposed to that in identifying "deficient families" is the absence of social capital, the weakness of links between the adult members of the family and the children. If we consider a fourfold table as shown in figure 8.2, where the two dimensions are human capital and social capital, we can see immediately that there exist families in all four cells of the table. In cell 3 are families in which the parents are of low economic level and low education but with a strong and facilitating set of relations within the family. Poor and uneducated but strong families, such as those often found among immigrants from underdeveloped country to a developed country exemplify this cell. In cell 4 are families that are poor, uneducated, and disorganized, structurally broken or weakened by the personal disorganization of the parent or parents. In cell 1 is the family with both human and social capital: The adult mem-

		Social Capital (strong vs. deficient families) Yes	No
Human Capital (traditional advantage of background)	Yes	1	2
	No	3	4

FIGURE 8.2

Families Characterized by Presence or Absence of Human Capital and Social Capital

bers are capable and educated, and relations within the family are strong. The resources of the parents are available to the children to encourage and aid their educational and social development. In cell 2 is the family that is becoming more prevalent today: The adult members are well educated and individually capable, but for a variety of reasons—divorce, involvement with other adults in relations that do not cross generations (as is typical of most work settings), exclusive attention to self-development—the resources of the adults are not available to aid the psychological health and the social and educational development of the children.

By confounding these two dimensions of family resources those concerned with educational policy have targeted their efforts at children from families in cells 3 and 4, and it is those from families in cell 4 that are by far the most deprived. But there has been little attention altogether to children from families in cell 2. Yet, as chapter 5 showed, students from these families have considerably lower rates of achievement growth and considerably higher rates of dropout than do children from families in cell 1. Perhaps if we could identify sufficiently well children from these four types of families, the children from families in cell 3, that is, disadvantaged but strong families, might have fewer problems in school than those from cell 2, that is, advantaged but deficient families.

Social Capital Beyond the Family

Beyond the family is social capital of other kinds that is relevant to the child's development. The most striking instance of that shown in the present research is the social capital provided by the religious community surrounding a Catholic school. The social capital that has value for a young person's development does not reside merely in the set of common values held by parents who choose to send their children to the same private school. It resides in the functional community, the actual social relationships that exist among parents, in the closure exhibited by this structure of relations and in the parents' relations with the institutions of the community. Part of that social capital is the norms that develop in communities with a high degree of closure. If, for example, in figure 8.1, *B* and *C* represent students in school who see each other every day, and *A* and *D* are *B*'s and *C*'s parents, respectively, then there is closure if the parents A and D know each other and have some kind of ongoing relation. The importance of this closure for the young persons, *B* and *C,* lies in the fact that only if *A* and *D* are in some kind of ongoing relation can they establish norms that shape and constrain the actions of *B* and *C.* Indeed, in such a structure, there develop relations between one child and the parent of another, as exemplified in figure 8.1 by the links between *A* and *C,* and between *D* and *B.*

A social structure that does not exhibit closure is represented by Figure 8.3. If *B* and *C* are two students who know and see each other in school, and *A* and *D* are the parents of *B* and *C,* respectively, then if *A*'s friends and daily contacts are with others outside *(E),* and *D*'s are also with a different set of others outside *(F),* A and D are not in a position to discuss their children's activities, to develop common evaluations of these activities, and to exercise sanctions that guide and constrain these activities.

Figure 8.1 represents what we have described as a structure with *intergenerational closure,* while figure 8.3 represents what we have described as a structure without intergenerational closure. However much closure there may be in the youth community, among *B, C,* and other students in the school, it is the absence of intergenerational closure that prevents the human capital that exists among the adults from playing any role in the lives of the youth. This lack of intergenerational

FIGURE 8.3

A Network Without Closure

closure constitutes the missing social capital that we have identified earlier as resulting in tangible losses for young persons: lower achievement growth, greater likelihood of dropping out of school. The social capital does exist in some isolated small towns and rural areas where adults' social relations are restricted by geographic distance, and where residential mobility has not destroyed it. It exists in schools based on a religious community, such as the Catholic schools and the few other religious schools in our sample, though the social relations which make up the community are more narrowly focused around a single dimension of social life, a religious institution. In rare circumstances it may exist for private schools without a religious base.

This form of social capital once existed for many public schools, when they served a clientele in which mothers worked in the home, and everyday contacts were largely with neighbors. It may have once existed in elite private schools, when the social elite whose children attended the schools constituted a community with relatively dense interaction. But neither in most modern public schools nor in most nonreligiously based private schools does that intergenerational closure now exist. The evidence presented in this book indicates that the absence of this social capital represents a real resource loss for young persons growing up.

Social Capital as a Public Good

There is, however, a central fact about social capital that does not exist for physical capital and human capital—and it is this fact which most threatens the social, psychological, and cognitive growth of young persons in the United States and, indeed, throughout Western society. Physical capital is ordinarily a private good, and property rights make it possible for the person who invests in physical capital to capture the benefits it produces. Thus, the incentive to invest in physical capital is not depressed; there is, as an economist might say, not a suboptimal investment in physical capital because those who invest in it are able to capture the benefits of their investments. For human capital also— at least human capital of the sort that is produced in schools—the person who invests the time and resources in building up this capital reaps its benefits, in the form of a higher-paying job, more satisfying or higher work status, or even the pleasure of greater understanding of the surrounding world—in short, all the benefits that schooling brings to a person.

But social capital of the sort that is valuable in the ways we have shown for a young person's education is not like this. The kinds of social structures that make possible social norms and the sanctions that enforce them do not benefit primarily the person or persons whose efforts would be necessary to bring them about, but benefit all those who are part of such a structure. For example, in some schools where there exists a dense set of associations among parents, these are the result of a small number of persons, ordinarily mothers who do not hold a full-time job outside the home. Yet these mothers themselves experience only a subset of the benefits of this social capital surrounding the school. If one of them decides to abandon these activities, for example to take a full-time job, this may be an entirely reasonable action from a personal point of view, and even from the point of view of that household with its children. The benefits of the new activity may far outweigh the losses arising from the decline in associations with other parents whose children are in the school. But the withdrawal of these activities constitutes a loss to all those other parents whose associations and contacts were dependent on them.

Or there are the kinds of decisions of parents described in chapter 1: The decision to move from a community so that the father, for example, can take a better job, may be entirely correct from the point of view of that family. But because social capital consists of relations between persons, other persons may experience extensive losses by the severence of those relations, a severence over which they had no control. A part of those losses is the weakening of norms and sanctions that aid the school in its task. For each family, the total cost it experiences as a consequence of the decisions it and other families make may outweigh the benefits of those few decisions it has control over. Yet the beneficial consequences of those decisions made by the family itself may far outweigh the minor losses the family experiences from them alone.

Social Capital and the Future for Youth

There are further suggestive implications that this analysis holds for the future of youth and education in modern society. Two sets of facts taken together suggest a future with special problems. One set of facts is the results contained in this analysis (principally in chapters 4 and 5) that show the importance of social capital within the family and social capital outside the family in the religious community for supporting the involvement of youth in school and their achievement growth. The importance of the social capital outside the family was especially apparent in certain sections of chapter 5: the section that showed the importance of religious participation generally (not only among Catholics or among students in Catholic schools) in lowering the probability of dropping out of high school, and the section that showed that among the non-Catholic private schools, dropout was least in those which were grounded in a religious body and served a religiously homogeneous set of students.

All these results emphasize the importance of the embeddedness of young persons in the enclaves of adults most proximate to them, first and most prominently the family and second, a surrounding community of adults (exemplified in all these results by the religious community).

But there is a second set of facts as well, not from the data of this study, but observable from social trends. This is the declining embeddedness of youth in these enclaves, that is in families and in intergenerational functional communities. This decline comes from two directions. One is the decreased strength of the institutions themselves, the family and the local community (religiously based, neighborhood-based, or otherwise). We have discussed at length the "modern family deficiencies," and it is apparent that these deficiencies are growing rather rapidly. An example of one is the declining presence of father and mother in the household, through work in settings outside, and organizationally distant from, the household. Much attention has been directed to the recent rise in proportions of women working outside the household, but what is often forgotten is that this exodus from the household merely follows (by about a hundred years) that of the men. Figure 8.4 shows the proportion of the male labor force engaged in agriculture (used as a proxy for men working in the household, though some nonfarm occupations were, especially in early days, in the household as well) and the proportion of women not in the labor force (that is, in the household).* These curves show a nearly parallel pattern, with the men's complete and the women's following the same course. These curves show the household progressively denuded of its adult members.

Other statistics could show different aspects of the loss of social capital in the household. One would be, for example, the declining number of

*Data from U.S. Bureau of Census (1975) Table 182–282 for proportion of labor force on farms 1900–1970, and proportion of labor force in agriculture, 1800–1890; and Table D49–62 for proportion of females in labor force 1890–1970. U.S. Bureau of Census (1984) is used to bring series up to 1982.

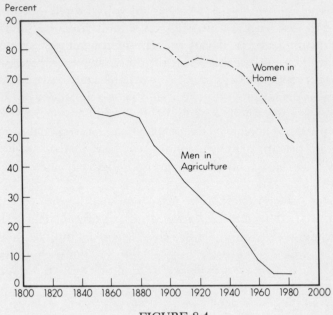

FIGURE 8.4

Percent of Male Labor Force in Agriculture, 1810–1982, and Percent of
Women Not Employed in Paid Labor Force, 1890–1982

adults in the household of the average American child—a decline that first saw members of the extended family vanish, and now sees one of the parents vanishing. And similar statistics could be presented for the decline of adult social capital available to children in the community outside the family.

But the decreased embeddedness of children and youth in family and community arises from a second source as well. This is the increasing psychic involvement of the youth with the mass media. This involvement is intense only for a fraction of youth; but the fraction may be increasing with the growth of the youth-oriented music industry from radio to television, with MTV (continuous rock video cable TV) its most extreme current expression.*

Thus, youth are pushed from psychic involvements in family and

*The question is often raised (ironically, often in the mass media itself) about "the effects of the mass media" (especially television, and the sex and violence on television) on children and youth. A frequent conclusion is that the "effects" are minimal or absent, and that children who have strong psycho-social foundations are impervious to any "undesirable" elements in media contents. But the discussion should make apparent that this misses the point in at least two ways. First, the very attention directed to these media is attention directed away from the adults who have traditionally constituted the social support for education and social development of the youth. Second, if it is the youth with strong psycho-social foundations who are unmoved by these elements, these are precisely the youth who, because of declines of family and community, are decreasing in numbers.

230

community by the reduced substance of those institutions and are pulled by the mass media toward involvements with "persona" of the media. The implications of this movement are many, but one is of special concern here: The former institutions, whatever their failings in specific cases, supported and strengthened the formal educational institution in which children and youth are placed. The latter do not. The implications are that the goals of schools become increasingly difficult to attain, as the social base that supports them comes to be less and less important in the lives of children and youth. The further implication is that something must give, and the most likely direction would appear to be a radical transformation of the institutions into which children are placed, from the schools we now know to something different.

The Inegalitarian Character of Functional Communities

The evidence presented in this book indicates that functional communities with intergenerational closure constitute social capital that is of widespread value for young persons in high school. Furthermore, the evidence indicates that this social capital is particularly valuable for young persons from families in which the social capital or the human capital of the parents is especially weak. Yet there is a body of research and theory that would predict just the opposite: Students from disadvantaged backgrounds, and perhaps those from deficient families, would do less well in schools surrounded by strong functional communities.

According to this theory and research, higher expectations and standards will be held by teachers for those students from families with high status, while those students from low-status families will be stigmatized with the reputations of their parents, low expectations for their achievement will be held by teachers, and adult members of the community outside the school will treat them differently.

This general thesis has a strong tradition in social psychology and sociology, both in research and in theory. "Expectation theory" or its close relative in sociology, "labeling theory," asserts that persons live up or down to others' expectations of them or to the labels attached to them by others. (See Merton [1968, pages 475–90], Becker [1973, pages 177–208], and Rosenthal and Jacobson [1968] for seminal treatments of the thesis.) This, in conjunction with the fact that it is only where there is a strong functional community that the expectations or labels attached to particular students will be widely held in common by teachers, parents, and other students strengthens the prediction that schools based on a strong functional community will be most effective for students from advantaged backgrounds and may depress performance of students from disadvantaged backgrounds. Where the community extends only to the student body of the school (and nearly all high schools have a community within the student body itself, whatever its attachments to the adult community), these expectations and labels will be shared only among the students and can be expected to be less powerful in their effects on behavior. But where the school is based on a strong adult functional community, it would be predicted to be powerful.

A tradition of research in educational sociology has also held the general thesis of labeling theory and furthermore has used strong functional communities as the site for demonstrating its importance. The best known of these is *Elmtown's Youth* (Hollingshead 1949), based on research in a small Illinois town in 1942. Hollingshead showed the intergenerational inheritance of status in Elmtown and the way this was reinforced through the high school. Although Hollingshead's evidence was suggestive and illustrative rather than conclusive, it provided a graphic portrayal of how a functional community can strengthen the advantages of the already-advantaged and block the opportunities of the disadvantaged.

These theoretical positions, expectation theory and labeling theory, lead to the general prediction that those private schools based on a functional community (Catholic schools in our sample) will confer more benefits on those students from advantaged backgrounds relative to those from disadvantaged backgrounds than is true for public schools, or for those private schools not based on a functional community. In short, they will be internally inegalitarian.

How then can we account for the different findings in this book, particularly those in chapter 5? The answer can be only conjectural, due to the lack of direct evidence. However, our conjecture is that a functional community based on the single dimension of religious association is different, in just those respects that relate to inegalitarianism, from a functional community that encompasses all arenas of social and economic life. In part, this is due to the egalitarian ethic of religion itself ("All God's children are equal in His eyes"). In part, it is due to the abstraction of a single arena of activity from the total fabric of social and economic life. This abstraction allows a child to escape a single encompassing evaluation of the family (including its children) based on the totality of its activities. This is an instance of the "role-segmentation" of modern social life, and according to our conjecture, the role-segmentation is important in inhibiting the inheritance by the child of the status of the parent.

Implications for Schooling Decisions and School Policies

The preceding sections have examined the implications of the social context surrounding a school and changes in the social context that have reduced the social capital available to children and have reduced the school's ability to educate its students. It is important to ask a further question as well: Given the changes that have reduced the social capital outside the school, what can be done to increase the social capital available to children? This question must be answered in different ways by different parties. Parents must ask what they can do for their own children. Principals must take the children in their school as given, and ask what they can do to increase the social capital available to these children, especially to those children whose families are deficient (whatever their socioeconomic status). District superintendents have a different set of questions, for they ordinarily have more than one school, with an important question being how children are to be distributed among schools. Finally, state and federal governments (education departments and legislatures) have still a different set of policies that they can initiate. In the following sections, we will examine this question as it presents itself to each of these parties.

WHAT EDUCATIONAL DECISIONS SHOULD A FAMILY MAKE?

Families of course can make decisions that can affect the human and social capital within the family or the social capital in the community. They can increase the social capital within the family by playing a stronger part in their children's lives. They can attempt to increase their human capital, like the Asian-American families cited earlier who buy two textbooks rather than one. They can attempt to find communities in which there is a high degree of intergenerational closure among parents of children in the school, that is, communities with a large amount of social capital available to their children.

Apart from these actions, however, there are educational decisions. Whatever the educational policies in force, a family must attempt to do what is best for its children, not what is best for the educational system as a whole, nor even for the other children in the immediate community.

There are a number of elements that a family should reasonably take into account in making a decision about what kind of school a particular child should attend. Some of these obviously involve the characteristics of the child. For example, some families will send one child who is not doing well in the local public school to a private school and leave another who is doing well in the public school. Powell, Farrar, and Cohen (1985, p. 197) quote staff members of a private school to this effect:

> We do well with the average college-prep child who would be swallowed up in a big school. . . . The one who doesn't need us is the bright well-motivated self starter who will do well anyway. . . . the public school can't be beat if the kids are really great, but when they are round about average, we can do a much better job of providing individual instruction. . . . If I had a child who was at the top of his class . . . I'm not sure I would put down the [money] to send him [here].

The design of independent private schools, with their very low pupil-teacher ratio (less than half that of the average public school) is suited to the child "who needs extra attention." It is also sometimes believed by parents, in disagreement with the private school staff members previously quoted, that if they have a child with special capabilities, who can progress more rapidly than most, the child will be well served by the extra attention that the low ratio of a private school allows. On the other hand, Catholic schools, which enroll the majority of private sector students, have even a higher pupil-teacher ratio than do public schools; they are hardly designed to cater to students with special needs.

However, the evidence in this book indicates that not only characteristics of the child, but also characteristics of the family and the local community are important in the choice of school. In addition to this evidence, there are everyday occurrences that indicate the same thing. For example, in a *New York Times* report of the current status of Erasmus High School in Brooklyn (a high school with a strong past but an uncertain present), the principal is reported as saying: "It's like two schools here. If you are really interested in school and have a stable family situation, you will do very well for yourself here." (*New York Times*, 7 December 1985, p. 29).

We suggest that a family's action in deciding among schools should take into account three elements that we have examined at some length in this book: the human capital in the family (as exemplified by the educational and cultural level of the parents), the social capital within the family (as exemplified by the presence of adults in the household and their degree of interest and involvement in their children's lives), and the social capital in the local community surrounding the household (as manifested by the degree of intergenerational closure in the community).

A given family in a given local neighborhood can be characterized according to these three dimensions, and if we take those as given, then we can ask just what kind of school choice would be reasonable for a family characterized according to these three dimensions. Table 8.1 shows the eight possible circumstances and the kind of school that would be especially effective for children from families in each of these circumstances. The types of schools considered, in addition to the religious private, independent private, and local public, are magnet public (more specialized and recruiting students from a larger area than local public) and boarding schools. Both of the latter are outside the local community and thus cannot make use of the social capital of the local community. As indicated in the table, the magnet public school and the independent private school are indicated for those children from families that are strong in both human capital and social capital; the local public schools are indicated when there is a high degree of social capital in the local community; and religious private and boarding schools are indicated when there is little social capital in the local community, and either human or social capital are missing in the family. For a child in a family with low human capital but high social capital or in a commu-

TABLE 8.1

Schools Optimal for Various Configurations of Human Capital and Social Capital in the Family, and Social Capital in the Local Community

In Family		In Local Community	Schools				
Human Capital	Social Capital	Social Capital	Local Public	Magnet Public	Independent Private	Religious Private	Boarding
+	+	+	X	X	X		
+	+	−		X	X		
+	−	+	X				
−	+	+	X				
+	−	−				X	X
−	+	−				X	X
−	−	+	X			X	X
−	−	−				X	X

nity with little social capital, the magnet public, religious private, and independent private appear best.

These are, of course, crude delineations, for each family and community configuration is unique. Nevertheless, they give some indication that certain kinds of schools are especially valuable in certain circumstances, and that choice of a school should take into account these three types of resources available in family and community.

WHAT POLICIES SHOULD A PRINCIPAL HAVE?

For parents, we asked what kind of school they should choose, given the human and social capital they are confronted with. Here we ask what a principal should do about social capital, given the school and the human capital in school and community. The answers of course must differ depending on the kind of school. First, however, it is important to recognize that several types of social capital are relevant and can be affected by school policies. One of these, the most important from the point of view of school policy, is based on the relations between students themselves. The importance of what is variously termed the youth culture, the adolescent society, peer culture, or the youth community, in the lives of high school students can be very great. The strengths of these relations and the pressures they can exert on a young person are exceedingly great, which implies that they constitute an extraordinarily powerful form of social capital.

This social capital varies among schools in two ways. First, it varies in strength. In some schools, nearly all of a student's social relations beyond the family are circumscribed by the community of youth in the school. In other schools, most of most students' social relations are outside the school, either with others the same age, or at work, or elsewhere. In the former schools, these social relations with a high degree of closure constitute extensive social capital for the formation of norms and sanctions that can shape behavior of students. The absence of this social capital in the latter schools reduces their power to affect their students.

In the 1960s and 1970s, there was a general decline in the strength of the youth communities in schools, a decline manifested in the decreased interest in such school events as interscholastic sports, and an increase in the proportion of students holding part-time jobs and an increase in attention to phenomena that cut across schools, in particular popular music. The reduced focus of students on others within the school reduced the social capital in the youth community of the school, and thus reduced the potential of schools to change students over this period. As a principal might put it, the principal "had less to work with."

A second dimension of variation in the social capital of the youth community is the direction of its content. In some schools where the norms of the youth community of the school are strong, they reward athletic prowess; in some, delinquent activities or drug use are extolled; in some social attractiveness; in others, academic achievement. The variations in direction, in what is rewarded and what is scorned, are great, and we make no attempt to describe these variations adequately. But the effect on educational goals of a difference in direction to which the social capital is employed is great when the social capital is strong. If it is employed toward educational goals, then the achievement is enhanced; if employed in other directions, it is reduced. The kinds of outcomes that can be expected are shown in figure 8.5, which shows variation in these two dimensions of social capital among students. In the four cells are four configurations of this social capital. In the cell labeled 2, educational goals should be best realized; in cell 4, they should be least well realized. Schools that fall into cells 1 and 3 should be intermediate between these two extremes.

We have gone into an extended description of the most important form of social capital to which a principal must attend, simply because of its importance. This description indicates two goals for the principal: to have a student body sufficiently integrated and cohesive that it constitutes social capital which can be a force in the lives of students; and to direct that force toward, rather than away from, education.

The most important ways of achieving the first goal are collective events, in which the school as a unit is involved, events which overcome the individualistic character of the educational process. Interschool competitions are most effective in building this social capital, because they replace the interpersonal competition of the classroom with a social cohesion that comes from a common goal. The most important

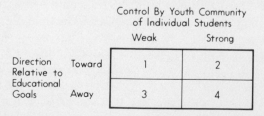

FIGURE 8.5

Hypothesized Effects of Youth Community in School on Attainment of Educational Goals

form this has taken for most schools is interscholastic sports, to which most educators have an ambivalent attitude. The ambivalence probably arises because the very power of interscholastic sports in creating the cohesive force also gives a direction to this force, with norms and goals around athletic achievement rather than academic achievement. Thus, a principal must be skillful employing this social capital toward educational ends, rather than letting it determine the direction of students' energies.*

For principals in certain settings, the first goal of creating social capital within the student body in order to establish norms to shape the lives of students is especially important. These are schools in which there is no natural community outside school among the members of the student body: boarding schools and, to a lesser extent, independent private day schools and central or magnet public schools which draw students from different neighborhoods. It is in these schools that the greatest danger exists of the school being in cell 1 or 3 of figure 8.5. A major task is to move the school from the left to the right hand side of this figure.

For principals in all kinds of schools, the second goal, of directing the social capital so that the youth community reinforces educational goals, is important. For this goal also, collective events, which shift the structure of competition from interpersonal to interschool, can be valuable. There are some such activities such as debate, or mathematics teams, or statewide drama or music competitions. In some cases, individual academic achievements that go beyond the confines of the school, can serve such a purpose, if acknowledged and rewarded by the school.

There is a second form of social capital within the school that is also potentially important for learning. This is the social capital that arises from close relations between students and teachers. Most teachers do not play a strong role in most students' lives, and thus whatever human capital the teacher has does not have a powerful impact on that teacher's students. Some extraordinary teachers do create social capital, often through a charismatic relation with their students, making possible a powerful educational impact. A principal can facilitate this, by organization and scheduling that make possible more extended and intensive contact of students with a smaller number of teachers, rather

---

*A remarkable New York City high school principal, Abraham Lass, once described in conversation how he managed to do this. Among his tactics was never to downgrade or denigrate athletic accomplishments; but he always used school assemblies to bestow honors both on those with high athletic achievements and those with high academic achievements. In so doing, he acknowledged the cohesion generated by interscholastic athletics and redirected it to encompass academic activities.

than shorter and less extensive contacts of students with a larger number of teachers.*

Finally, a principal can help bring into being or strengthen social capital among the parents, by strengthening their relations with one another and with the school. The principal can, in short, increase the intergenerational closure that was shown in figure 8.1, though the school is in a setting more like that of figure 8.3. This can come about through parents' meetings over problems that have arisen in the school (ranging from problems of drug or alcohol use among students to the financial problems that exist for private schools), as well as schoolwide events (though the latter ordinarily produce a more superficial form of contact than do problem-oriented foci). The most important point is the recognition on the part of the principal that the social capital that exists in the community, its power to make and enforce norms for the youth of the school, is not fixed and immutable but can be affected by actions of the school. A second important point is the recognition that parental involvement in the school is not an inconvenience to the "professional" management of the school but can constitute valuable social capital for the school to use in the joint school-family task of bringing youth toward adulthood.

WHAT SHOULD A SUPERINTENDENT DO?

The possible actions of a superintendent overlap with those of the principal, though there are some policies, such as those involving the student body itself, over which principals have more control, and others over which superintendents have more control. In a district with a number of schools, the creation of neighborhood schools, which maximize the potential for parents' establishing and enforcing norms for youth, has been a policy that superintendents could adopt. However, other goals, such as that of racial or socioeconomic integration, or allowing students' choice among specialized (or magnet) schools, are important as well, and these directly conflict with such a policy. Policies that encourage interscholastic competition in a variety of areas can aid greatly in the principal's task of creating social capital within the student body.

The superintendent can also affect the social capital in the adult community that is available to the schools. We will offer only an indica-

*As with any powerful forces, this also has its dangers. The most evident is the possibility of a teacher's sexual exploitation of the strong attachment that can arise on the part of a student. This probably most often arises in homosexual form, in single-sex boarding schools.

tion of how this may be done by describing briefly some activities initiated in the Atlanta school district by the superintendent, Alonzo Crim. Crim recognized that the adults in the community, both parents and others, constituted an important potential resource for the schools and based several policies on that recognition. One was the strengthening of PTAs, increasing greatly their activity and their membership. Another was to establish a program to find a "personal sponsor" in the business community for each of the students in the bottom 10 percent of the student bodies of high schools of the city, to help bring these students through to graduation and to productive activity after high school.

Other school systems have used some of these same policies, as well as others. Different policies are possible and potentially productive in different districts. The starting point for such policies is the recognition that the adults of the community constitute a resource for the schools, but only if they are involved with the school or involved with one another on matters concerning youth and the schools.

WHAT SHOULD STATE AND FEDERAL POLICY DO?

Here we will first ask a broad question about the social capital that exists in the community surrounding a school. Is there any way to re-create this social capital, where it has vanished, or to maintain it, where it still exists?

The fact that this social capital continues to exist for Catholic schools and apparently also for other schools based on a religious community gives a clue to the source of its survival there. Unlike a set of norm-generating relations that is based wholly on voluntary association—for example those on which neighbor relations are based—the relations that surround a religiously grounded school are based on a single formal institution, the religious body. That institution experiences serious losses when those relations die out, for its survival depends on them. It experiences gains when those relations are strengthened, quite apart from the benefits experienced by those involved in the relations. Those at the center of the institution (in the case of the Catholic church, the priest) have a strong interest in maintaining and developing the relations, for these relations benefit the church—and as a byproduct, they constitute social capital available to the school sponsored by the church.

An example of a similar pattern can be found in some nonreligious-based schools that have another institution at the center, such as a university laboratory school attended by faculty children. At University of Chicago, for example, the university's interest in survival led it to take a variety of actions involving housing in the immediate area, which had the consequence of creating a strong residence-and-work-based community that provides, as byproduct, social capital available both to the university's laboratory school and the other public and private schools in the area (see Rossi and Dentler 1961). The public school closest to the university is regarded as one of the very best in the city, despite the loss of most faculty children to the laboratory school, and one important source of its quality is the functional community that surrounds the university, and thus the school.

It is clear that only a relatively small fraction of American families would enroll their children in a religiously based school, even if there were no financial costs to doing so. The fraction of families in a setting dominated by an institution like that described for the University of Chicago is far smaller. The question then arises whether this "institutional solution" to the public-good problem of social capital can be generalized beyond religious institutions or the scattered other instances where a similar pattern can be found. That is, is it possible that there are other institutions around which functional communities with intergenerational closure can develop?

As a step toward an answer, one can look toward those institutions in which both men and women spend much of their time and develop many of their social relations, that is, work institutions. It is conceivable that appropriate social policy could provide support from tax revenues for schools located within work institutions, either solely or principally for the children of employees. This solution would remove the school from the neighborhood, just as the functional community that once existed in the neighborhood has vanished from it, and would relocate the school in the workplace of one or both parents. Unlike most neighborhoods, many workplaces are well integrated by race and socioeconomic status, thus overcoming some of the segregative properties of neighborhood-based schools. The workplace, outside the home and most often outside the neighborhood, is the single institution that has come to constitute the central locus of activities for most adults of both sexes in American society. To make it the central locus of activities for children and youth as well would seem to constitute the next step in a social evolution that has by degrees replaced the informal social relations and the social communities composed of these relations with formally defined relations and formal organizations.

Such an institutional solution may not be feasible. There may be other alternatives. But the evidence of this book suggests that as the social capital within the family comes to be eroded in various ways, the creation of social capital outside the family that is available to the young becomes increasingly important. It is often not in the interest of any individual to expend the effort necessary to bring such social capital into being. It is here that the problem lies.

State and federal policy could make possible the initiation of some experimental schools constructed around institutions in which parents are involved, such as workplaces. The precedent exists with day-care centers and nurseries that exist at a few workplaces. For schools to be possible, a voucher or capitation for each student would be necessary, for a firm in a competitive market, or another privately funded institution, cannot reasonably pay the costs of educating children of its employees or members. Obviously, policies to make this possible should be initiated only on a small scale, accompanied by research evaluating the schools.

Another related question may be raised about the potential value of vouchers in general, as well as other ways of increasing choice in education.

This book has found extensive benefits of certain private schools for children who attend them—and special benefits for children from families that have low levels of human capital or social capital. The latter result is certainly to be expected, because it is those families with low economic resources and families of racial and ethnic minorities, whose choice of school within the public sector, through moving residence, is most severely restricted.

Yet the evidence does not point unequivocally to widespread benefits of policies that would increase freedom of choice in education, such as vouchers that could be used in any public or private school. The private schools in our sample that are not based on a functional community with intergenerational closure, that is, the other private schools, appear not to provide special benefits beyond the public school, except possibly in verbal cognitive skills, a result that is offset by their relatively high dropout rates and their weakness in mathematics and science.

These results may well be due to deficiencies of the sample of non-Catholic private schools, so that no strong inferences are possible. However, the possibility must be entertained that the very individualism that is embodied in the choice of a private school (unless that school is surrounded by a functional community) may destroy some of the remaining social capital that can still be found in residential neighborhoods, and impose costs upon the student whose family makes such a choice. The evidence is not strong, because of the weakness of the sample of other private schools, and because the high-performance private schools did not show the same patterns of outcome.

However, the general results in this book that show the value of a functional community surrounding a school are consistent with the findings for the other private schools. In the light of this evidence, partial, indirect, and possibly mistaken though it may be, we raise the question of the benefits and costs of a wholly individualistic policy that would increase the opportunity of the individual family to exercise choice in education.

We do so with some hesitation, because there are many circumstances in which increased freedom of choice for all has a beneficial consequence for all. There is one circumstance, however, in which this need not be true, and that is a circumstance relevant to education: when the decisions made by one person have extensive consequences for others. As described earlier in this chapter, this is precisely the circumstance that holds for decisions that affect those social relationships that go to make up the social capital of a community on which a school depends: One person can take an action unilaterally that results in breaking those relations, with a resulting cost to others involved in them.

This is not to propose that choice in education should be restricted, nor even that it should not be expanded greatly, for two reasons. First, it is seldom the case that all, or even most, persons are made better off by restriction of choice. Second, the restriction of choice leads to differential choice opportunities by income (since choice of high-income families is not restricted), and thus increases inequality of opportunity. Rather, the implications of our analysis are that policies which would bring about expansion of choice should contain provisions that encourage the growth of social structures that can provide the social capital important to a school. Policies such as those described earlier that would facilitate the creation of schools by institutions in which parents of prospective students are already involved exemplify this. Another example is policies that would provide resources for schools (public or private) to build and strengthen relations among parents of children in the school, as well as relations between parents and the school. There are many other state and federal policies that offset the strength of the family and that of the community. We can only point to the importance of these policies in affecting the social capital available for the young. It is clear that this is an era in which the young are seriously at risk because of the decline in strength of the family and those institutions that spring from it. Therefore, it is important that government policy be made in full recognition of this risk and of potential ways of reducing it.

243

REFERENCES

Alexander, K. A.; and Pallas, A. M. "School Sector and Cognitive Performance." *Sociology of Education* (April 1985): 115–27.

Barker, R. G.; and Gump, P. V. *Big School, Small School.* Stanford: Stanford University Press, 1964.

Becker, G. S. *Human Capital.* Chicago: University of Chicago Press, 1964.

Becker, H. S. *The Outsiders.* New York: Free Press, 1973.

Butler, R. J.; and Monk, D. H. "The Cost of Public Schooling in New York State: The Role of Scale and Efficiency in 1978–1979." *Journal of Human Resources* 20 (Summer 1985): 361–81.

Coleman, J. S. *Longitudinal Data Analysis.* New York: Basic Books, 1981.

———. "Schools, Families, and Children." Ryerson Lecture, University of Chicago, 1985.

———; and Hoffer, T. "Response to Taueber-James, Cain-Goldberger, and Morgan." *Sociology of Education* (October 1983): 219–34.

Coleman, J. S.; Hoffer, T.; and Kilgore, S. *Public and Private High Schools.* Washington, D.C.: National Center for Education Statistics, 1981.

———. *High School Achievement.* New York: Basic Books, 1982a.

———. "A Further Look at Achievement and Segregation in Secondary Schools." *Sociology of Education* (April/July 1982b): 162–82.

Cox, D. R. "Regression Models and Life Tables." *Journal of the Royal Statistical Society,* series B, 34 (1972): 187–202.

Durkheim, E. *Suicide.* New York: Free Press, 1951.

Educational Researcher 10 (August 1981).

Fienberg, S. E. *The Analysis of Cross-Classified Categorical Data.* Cambridge, Mass.: MIT Press, 1977.

Greeley, A. M. *Catholic High Schools and Minority Students.* New Brunswick, N.J.: Transaction Books, 1982.

Harvard Educational Review 51, no. 4 (November 1981).

Heckman, J. J.; and Singer, B. S., eds. *Longitudinal Analysis of Labor Market Data.* New York: Cambridge University Press, 1986.

Hoffer, T.; Greeley, A. M.; and Coleman, J. S. "Achievement Growth in Public and Catholic Schools." *Sociology of Education* (April 1985): 74–97.

Hollingshead, A. B. *Elmtown's Youth.* New York: John Wiley, 1949.

Jencks, C. "How Much Do High School Students Learn?" *Sociology of Education* (April 1985): 128–35.

Jensen, G. F. "Explaining Differences in Academic Behavior Between Public-School and Catholic-School Students." *Sociology of Education* (January 1986): 32–41.

Kozol, J. *Death at an Early Age.* Boston: Houghton Mifflin, 1967.

Lewin-Epstein, N. "Systems of Education and the Social Recruitment of Youth in the United States." Ph.D. diss., University of Chicago, 1982.

Lynd, R. S.; and Lynd, H. M. *Middletown.* New York: Harcourt, Brace and Co., 1929.

Merton, R. K. "The Self-fulfilling Prophesy." Chap. 13 in Merton, R. K., *Social Theory and Social Structure.* New York: Free Press, 1968.

Mincer, J. *Schooling, Experience and Earnings.* New York: National Bureau of Economic Research, 1974.

Morgan, D. L.; and Alwin, D. E. "When Less Is More: School Size and Student Social Participation." *Social Psychological Quarterly* 43 (1980): 241–52.

New York Times. 7 December 1985, p. 29.

Nisbet, R. A. *The Quest for Community.* New York: Oxford University Press, 1953.

References

Phi Delta Kappan 63, no. 3 (November 1981).

Powell, A. G.; Farrar, E.; and Cohen, D. K. *The Shopping Mall High School.* Boston: Houghton Mifflin, 1985.

Rosenbaum, P.; and Rubin, D. "The Central Role of the Propensity Score in Observational Studies for Causal Effects." *Biometrika* 70 (1983): 41–55.

Rosenthal, R.; and Jacobson, L. *Pygmalion in the Classroom.* New York: Holt, Rinehart & Winston, 1968.

Rossi, P. H.; and Dentler, R. A. *The Politics of Urban Renewal.* New York: Free Press, 1961.

Schultz, T. W. "Investment in Human Capital." *American Economic Review* (March 1961): 1–17.

Silberman, C. E. *Crisis in the Classroom.* New York: Vintage Books, 1970.

Sociology of Education 55, no. 2/3 (April/July 1982).

———. 56, no. 4 (October 1983).

———. 58, no. 2 (April 1985).

Stein, M. R. *The Eclipse of Community.* New York: Harper & Row, 1960.

Tuma, N. B.; and Hannan, M. T. *Social Dynamics: Models and Methods.* New York: Academic Press, 1984.

U.S. Bureau of Census. *Historical Statistics of the United States: Colonial Times to 1970.* Washington, D.C.: Government Printing Office, 1975.

———. *Statistical Abstracts of the United States.* Washington, D.C.: Government Printing Office, 1984.

INDEX

Ability grouping, 44–45

Absences, 113; college attendance and, 155, 156, 159, 191, 193–94, 210; of dropouts, 100, 102–4, 114–16; and post-high school success, 178; of transfers, 109

Academic problems, *see* Scholastic problems

Academic programs, 41–50, 212; achievement in, 42, 76; college attendance and, 153, 158–59, 163–64, 176, 219; coursework in, 47–50; minority students and, 143–44, 146–48

Achievement outcomes, *xxiii, xxv,* 25, 57–95, 212–13; in academic programs, 42, 76; areas of differences in, 58–60; college attendance and, 155, 192–96; deficient and disadvantaged background and, 121–25; of dropouts, 83–92; evidence on, 63–79; functional community and, 135–37, 142–43, 146–47; in non-Catholic religious schools, 140, 142–43; and post–high-school success, *xxvi,* 179, 180; predictions about, 60–63; relative, 92–93; resources and, 93–95; selectivity bias and, 79–82; social capital and, 227, 229; variability of, 82–83; youth community norms and, 237, 238

Admission criteria, 29

Adolescent society, 236

Alexander, K. A., 121n

Algebra, 76

Alternative schools, 5; values and, 9

Amish schools, 58

Anomie, 133–35

Arnold, Thomas, 217

Asian immigrants, 222, 233

Aspirations, post–high-school, 151–52

Athletic activities, 217

Atlanta school district, 240

Baptist schools, 141

Barker, R. G., 51

Becker, G. S., 221

Becker, H. S., 231

Behavior problems, *see* Discipline problems

Bentham, Jeremy, 222

Bilingual programs, federally-funded, 40

Biology, 166, 176

Birth rates, 119

Blacks: academic programs and, 46; achievement outcomes of, 122, 213; birth rate of, 119; in Catholic schools, *xxiv,* 12–13; civil rights groups and, 12; college attendance of, 192n; as dropouts, 127, 131n; functional community and, 143–47; in private schools, 31–32; segregation of, *xxiii, xxiv*

Boarding schools, 235; extracurricular activities in, 217; sexual exploitation in, 239n; social capital in, 238

Boston Latin School, 23

Brown v. Board of Education (1954), 5

Busing, 22

Calculus, 76

Catholic schools, *xxiv, xxvii;* achievement in, *see* Achievement outcomes; college attendance and, 152–

Other (non-Catholic) *(continued)*
tiveness of, 26; size of, 37–39; social
capital in, 227, 238, 242; socioeconomic background of students in,
30, 31; transfers and, 108–13

Pallas, A. M., 121n
Parental education, 30–32, 120, 222;
dropping out and, 128
Parental involvement with school,
52–55
Peer culture, 236
Physical capital, 221, 227
Physics, 76, 166, 176
Policies, 13–18; of principals, 236–39;
state and federal, 240–43; of superintendents, 239–40
Post-high-school outcomes, 26; *see
also* College attendance; Labor
force success
Preparatory schools, 9
Presbyterian schools, 141n
Principals, policies of, 236–39
Private schools, *xxiii–xxviii;* choice of,
23; family decisions on, 234–36;
goals of, 39, 40; problem students in,
97; socioeconomic background of
students in, 29–32; and success beyond high school, 150–51; transfers
between public and, 25–26, 106–14;
value consistency and, 9–10; *see also*
Catholic schools; Other (non-Catholic) private schools
Problem students, 97–99; *see also* Absences; Discipline problems; Dropouts; Transfers
Protestantism, 58; nineteenth-century, 4, 14; suicide rates and,
134
Public schools, *xxiii–xxviii;* achievement in, *see* Achievement outcomes; alternative, 5; choice of, 23;
college attendance and, 152–56,
159–63, 166, 168, 170–78, 182–97, 210,
218–20; courses and programs in,
42–50; deficient and disadvantaged

background and, 120–39, 144–48; design of, 24, 28–29; dominant orientations and, 14; dropping out of,
100–106, 115–17, 125–35, 213–15;
educational aspirations in, 32–33;
expenditures in, 35–36; extracurricular activities in, 51–52, 217–18;
family decisions on, 233, 235; family
structure and, 33–34; goals of, 39–
40; immigrants in, 5; and labor force
success, 197–206, 208–10; parental
involvement with, 53–55; participation in federal programs by, 40–41;
percentage of students enrolled in,
211; problem students in, 97–99; relative effectiveness of, 26; residence-
based attendance in, 11–12, 14, 17;
size of, 37–39; social capital and,
222, 227, 241; social policy and, 19;
socioeconomic background of students in, 29–32; and success beyond
high school, 150–51, 179–81; transfers
between private and, 25–26, 106–14;
value communities of, 12; value consistency and, 9, 10

Quaker schools, 9, 215

Race, 31–32, 120; achievement outcomes and, 122; college attendance
and, 191; disadvantage and, 118; of
dropouts, 125–28, 131n; *see also*
Blacks; Whites
Racial segregation, *xxiii, xxiv;* in
South, 4–5
Reading comprehension: achievement in, *xxiii, xxiv,* 60, 63, 69, 76,
79; disadvantaged background and,
120; standardized tests of, 59
Religion: functional community and,
9; value community and, 13
Religious schools, non-Catholic, 134–
35, 140–43; social capital in, 227, 240;
see also specific denominations

Index